SKINFUL

SKINFUL

A memoir of addiction

Robyn Flemming

For my mother
And for my father

First published in 2022

ISBN 9781922598950 (print)
ISBN 9781922598806 (ebook)

Cover and text design: Christabella Designs
Cover image: Dee Dee Choy, *A Glass of Tear* (detail)
Cover photograph: Jules Boag
Author photograph: Carla Lidbury
Typeset: Polly Yu

Published by:

Brio Books, an imprint of Booktopia Group Ltd
Unit E1, 3-29 Birnie Avenue
Lidcombe, NSW 2141, Australia

The names and identifying characteristics of some people have been changed. This is my story, not theirs, but I am grateful to them for being a part of mine.

booktopia.com.au

Skinful: 'an amount of alcohol that is enough to
make a person drunk'
urbandictionary.com

'Addiction is just a little hiding place where sensitive people can
go so we don't have to be touched by love or pain.'
Glennon Doyle

'The future is not some place we are going, but one we are
creating. The paths are not to be found, but made.
And the activity of making them changes both
the maker and their destination.'
John Schaar

'Your life is the fruit of your own doing.'
Joseph Campbell

'You are so fucking ugly.'

The taunt is from the passenger in a sedan that has slowed alongside me. It skewers me like a spear.

I hear laughter as the car accelerates away, before the shock and the thumping pulse in my temple block all sounds of the night.

What has he seen? Is my shell cracking apart? Is my jitteriness in my own skin apparent now even to a passing stranger?

Charlie is pawing and sniffing at a patch of grass beside the path. Butch is motionless at my feet, gazing up at me intently. I look away; it's too much, all this scrutiny.

I turn back, aborting our walk. The serrated edge of my house key bites into my palm. At my door, it takes three stabs before I can insert the key in the lock.

I don't want to feel this.

'Sorry,' I text to Diane. 'Won't run tomorrow. Sore knee.'

My need for numbness is greater than the shame of lying to a friend.

I break the seal on a new bottle of wine and pour large dollops into the glass I'd used earlier. The first cold mouthful tastes like the answer to any question I could ask.

PART ONE

Can't find reverse

CHAPTER ONE

'I don't want to alarm you,' my boss said one day when we were having after-work drinks, 'but I need you to go up to Hong Kong for a week.'

Our boutique publishing company was producing a four-colour business guide that was being typeset and printed there. I was the production editor.

'There isn't time to courier the proofs. You can go up to do the final checks.'

I exhaled cigarette smoke and reached for my wine glass.

'I'm not alarmed.'

Ten days later, I was in a taxi headed to Quarry Bay, an area that was home to Hong Kong's big English-language publishers, one of them a sister company to ours. As the small red-and-white sedan wove in and out of traffic on overpasses, underpasses and in-between passes, I swivelled my head from side to side, wanting to see everything at once.

I'm definitely not in Woolloomooloo anymore.

'Here, missy,' the driver said, pulling up outside an unremarkable commercial building.

I stubbed my cigarette in the ashtray near the door handle and dug in my purse for enough of the unfamiliar coins to include a tip with the fare.

It was exciting to be in a new place. I hadn't travelled much: to New Zealand as a teenager in the 1960s, and to visit my parents after they moved there from Australia a decade later; to Bali and Java in my twenties; to England on a three-month work assignment at age thirty. The extensive travel that a psychic had predicted seemed unlikely, although I gave some credence to an astrologer's comment that I had a tendency to change my circumstances instead of myself.

On the flight up from Australia, I'd done some reading about the British-administered territory's status as a gateway to China. The motherland had reversed its former economic policy and was now receptive to foreign direct investment in all its forms. Like a puppet master, China's silk-clad arms were pulling all of Hong Kong's strings and making it dance.

It seemed that everyone wanted to jump on board, and within days I wanted to do the same. The entire city hustled and bustled around the clock. It was exhilarating to walk the streets, or to perch upstairs on the front seat of a double-decker tram or to ride the Star Ferry across Victoria Harbour to Kowloon. The energy of the place suited me.

At the office where I would be based for the week, I went in search of a coffee. In the kitchen, an Englishwoman introduced herself as Linda. 'I heard we had a visitor from the Sydney office,' she said. 'Welcome!'

That evening, I took the funicular tram from Central up to The Peak and walked around Lugard Road. The city lay at my feet, the noise of traffic muted. Across the harbour, beyond Kowloon Peninsula and the New Territories, lay the border with China. It was a stunning looking city; vibrant, like Sydney's Chinatown on steroids, yet familiar, perhaps because of Britain's colonial imprint.

'With your experience, you could probably find a job here, if you wanted one,' Linda said. We were having drinks at a hotel in Central a few days later. I'd mentioned that I'd hopped from job to job during my ten years in publishing, seeking variety and new challenges. 'There's a lot going on here. And it's a good place to be an expat.'

'I *have* been thinking about it,' I said, and reached for my cigarettes and lighter. 'I can picture myself living here, but it's a big decision. I like my job in Sydney and my life there. I wasn't planning to make any changes.'

'It could be your destiny. This trip might be a turning point in your life.'

A curl of smoke wafted in the air between us.

'Maybe ...'

A HOTEL DOORMAN pocketed my small tip as he opened the taxi's rear passenger door. Soon, the cab was caught up in the stream of traffic winding up Cotton Tree Drive towards the towering apartment blocks of Mid-Levels. Just past a white, colonial-style building, we turned off and headed to Lan Kwai Fong, a narrow, sloping, cobblestoned street lined with bars, cafés and restaurants. My destination was 1997. The name of the restaurant referred to the date, still twelve years away, when British rule would come to an end and Hong Kong would again become part of China.

I drank Australian chardonnay with my meal and thought about Linda's comment. Was I at a turning point? Did my future lie in Asia? It was an unexpected notion. Sydney had been my home since 1971, when I moved from Albury, in regional New South Wales, to start my university studies. It hadn't occurred to me to live anywhere else. Would I find a job if I moved to Hong Kong? Or could I find enough work as a freelance editor? I liked the security and salary that came with a full-time position. I didn't have any savings to fall back on. Would my lack of Cantonese be a problem? I had a busy social life with friends in Sydney, mostly seeing live music in pubs and wine bars, and eating in cheap ethnic restaurants. I ran a couple of mornings a week with a bunch of guys along Bondi Beach and in Centennial Park. Would I want to leave that life behind and start again from scratch in a foreign city?

And what about Tom? I sighed and reached for my glass. *If only he were different, we'd be perfect together.*

We had met in our mid-twenties, seven or eight years before. I'd just started working in publishing; Tom was finishing a degree. From the moment I met him, I wanted to be with him. He was intelligent, creative, handsome, funny. But the pull was almost biochemical: the water in every cell in my body sloshed towards him. As I came to know him over the years, I continued to want him, but I couldn't figure out if he wanted me. Although he sought me out, he could be remote, critical, and dismissive of emotions. Sex was the only way to connect with him, and I became addicted to breaking through his barriers by bringing him to orgasm. For that brief time, he was mine.

Tom's closest relationship was with his dog. Whenever I slept over at his house, I had to compete with Rufus for his attention and affection. When Tom turned on his side, ready for sleep, Rufus would leap on to the bed and stretch out alongside him. Tom would wrap an arm around the dog's chest and nestle against his back. Soon, I'd hear the sound of man and beast gently snoring. If Tom later moved over to my side of the bed, Rufus would be lying flat on his back, his head on Tom's pillow, limbs splayed.

I wanted not just physical closeness – for him to touch me more and to welcome my touches – but also a close emotional connection. Instead, each time we got together was like starting over. Every disappointment was a reminder to hold back, to protect my heart, to expect little.

I finished the last of the wine and gathered my things. No, it would be a mistake to put my life on hold for Tom.

CHAPTER TWO

The following Monday, back in Sydney, I gave four months' notice at work. 'I'm going to try my luck in Hong Kong,' I said to my boss. 'I can stay for ninety days on a tourist visa. I'll see what happens in that time.'

At the last major turning point in my life, at eighteen, I'd become independent of my family. In March 1986, at thirty-three, I was again embarking on an uncertain future.

Tom drove me to the airport and sent me on my way with just a brush of his lips across my cheek. If he regretted my leaving, he gave no sign. Even as I was about to reinvent myself, I wanted to know that he wanted me.

In Hong Kong, a serviced apartment next to a massage parlour in the red-light district of Wanchai would be my base for the first month until I found somewhere more affordable to live.

For the past few months on Sunday mornings in Sydney's Chinatown, I'd pored over the classified job ads in the English-language *South China Morning Post*. That exercise hadn't borne any fruit beyond noting the names of a few people to contact again on my arrival. I would have to wing it. With limited funds, I needed to find, complete and be paid for some kind of work within a month. I had an open return ticket to Australia, but I didn't want to have to use it just because I hadn't tried hard enough to make something happen.

When my reference books and stationery supplies were arranged neatly on the desk by the window that overlooked a grimy tenement building, I took a deep breath, gave myself a pep talk, then picked up the phone and called an editor at the *Post*.

'Send me samples of your work,' he said.

'Um, I don't have any. I'm not a journalist. But if you'll give me a chance, I'll give it a shot.'

'The China Sea Yacht Race is coming up. Put together something on that and we'll consider it. Give such-and-such a call. He can give you the names of some people to talk to.'

Enthusiasm counted for little against my inexperience, and I made a hash of the short piece on the famous ocean race from Hong Kong to Manila.

'Thanks, but no thanks,' the editor said. 'You could try *The Standard*.'

The alternative English-language paper wasn't interested either, but someone I had talked with about the race invited me out for a drink. At the main bar of the Foreign Correspondents' Club, home to reporters and photographers who were covering events unfolding in Asia, I met someone who knew someone at a publisher of textbooks for the local secondary-school market. When I followed up the next day, I was invited to an interview. The publisher offered me a month-long contract to work in-house with another editor, Sue, on an illustrated geography textbook. The first payday would be the last day of the month, just before I ran out of cash.

My life as a freelancer had begun.

With guidance from Sue, I learnt how to shape raw text from specialist writers to suit the English reading level of Chinese-speaking teenagers. The book was also a perfect introduction for me to Hong Kong's development from a largely barren rock, when it became a British Crown colony in 1842, into a densely populated city.

Sue, too, was a smoker, and we worked companionably and productively in our cubbyhole of an office blanketed by a fog of cigarette smoke.

'We're having a party at our place tonight,' she said one day. 'Come along.'

A few hours later, my back was against a wall and a guy was chatting me up. I had a cigarette in one hand and a glass of wine in the other. The scenario was familiar, but the guy was American and I was on a small island off the coast of China. I was still getting used to the fact that my life had changed so dramatically.

Sue introduced me to a woman with a room for rent in an apartment in Mid-Levels.

'It's available now,' she said. 'A month's rent in advance and two months' security deposit.'

It was beyond my means, but she mentioned a members' club, the Helena May, that rented out rooms. 'It's a bit more affordable than a flat. There are lots of rules, but it might suit you until you find your feet.'

'I'll check it out. It could be just the thing.'

The next week, my work contract was extended for another month and I was accepted as a resident at the Helena May from the start of April. The 'HM', the white colonial-era building I'd spotted from the taxi during my first visit, offered a respite for its members from the noise and smells of the city just outside its doors. It also provided affordable accommodation for single women with a foreign passport who were in Hong Kong on a work contract. As a self-employed freelancer I didn't meet the last criterion, but the manager made an exception for me.

My large furnished room was on the second floor, with a

shared bathroom at the end of the hall. Downstairs, the lounge had wicker furniture, English and Australian women's magazines, and slowly turning ceiling fans. Filipino and Chinese staff served lunch and morning and afternoon teas to members and residents. The basement housed a lending library and a ballet school for tots. When Japanese forces had occupied Hong Kong during the Second World War, horses were stabled there.

Double doors from my room opened on to a concrete balcony that extended along the back of the building and overlooked a leafy, paved garden, the Peak Tram tracks and, just beyond, the feeder road to the upper slopes. To my right, apartment blocks were stacked one upon another up the hillside.

I smoked a cigarette and surveyed my new home with a happy heart. The shouts of children at play in a nearby schoolyard were audible over the sounds of the city: car horns and the constant swoosh of traffic, the distant clanging of a pile driver from a construction site, the rumble of the funicular tram. I'd given up my life in Australia to follow an impulse to move to an unfamiliar city in a different hemisphere. With no financial resources to fall back on, I'd known that I would have to swim hard, or sink. One month after my arrival, it seemed I might stay afloat for the time being.

WHEN THE WORK on the geography textbook wound up, a university press offered me a job editing a book about planned towns in the New Territories, the area between Kowloon Peninsula and the Chinese border. I loved that I was being paid to learn more about my new home.

I became pals with a group of Brits who lived at the HM. We would start each day at our regular table in the small breakfast room for residents. We knew how we each liked our toast and our eggs, and who didn't like papaya. If it was someone's birthday, we might add champagne to our orange juice for a mimosa.

After breakfast, my new friends headed down the hill to their places of work in town. My editing project was to be done out-of-house, so I would set myself up at a table in the lounge with my papers, pens and correction fluid, and a second cup of coffee, and sign on to my time sheet. The job was straightforward: mostly smoothing out the language, applying the publisher's house style consistently, and fixing the spelling, grammar and punctuation. Residents weren't permitted to run a business from the HM, but as a freelancer I was in a grey area that the manager had decided to tolerate.

The lounge had a regular rhythm. Mid-morning, members trickled in to meet a friend, return a library book, or play a game of bridge or mahjong. At lunchtime, there was a flurry of activity. Located on the edge of frenetic Central, the HM was a civilised oasis that offered familiar comfort foods: pumpkin soup, toasted sandwiches, baked cheesecake. The place then largely emptied until mid-afternoon, when there was a surge of after-school comings and goings. All the while, the ceiling fans revolved languorously, occasionally rustling the manuscript pages on which I was working.

By late afternoon, my friends would start to straggle in and we would settle in the generously sized upholstered armchairs for a chat about our day.

'Glass of wine?' someone would suggest.

'Don't mind if I do.'

Work on the urban planning book was scheduled to wind up just before my tourist visa expired at the end of May. I was planning to take a jetfoil to the Portuguese-administered territory of Macau for a night or two and then get a new visa when I re-entered Hong Kong.

'Missy, telephone.'

'Hi, Rob,' said my old boss. 'Any chance you could come back to Sydney for ten weeks and manage a big project for us?'

'I'm on my way ...'

A paid interlude in Australia would top up my coffers, and the tourist visa stamped in my passport on my return would permit me to stay for a further ninety days. I would have to do something about my immigration status soon, though, if I wanted to make Hong Kong my permanent home and work there legally.

CHAPTER THREE

In Sydney, I stayed in a private hotel in Potts Point, the more salubrious neighbour of the formerly bohemian but now seedy Kings Cross. Most nights, I ate dinner alone in a small restaurant on a leafy side street: pepper steak with a salad, and a couple of glasses of wine. Back at the hotel, I'd read in bed for an hour or two. Tom was out of the country. I saw a few friends for an occasional meal or film, but otherwise I didn't try to re-engage with the city. I'd been away only three months, but the umbilical cord that had bound me to Sydney for a decade and a half had been cut. Perhaps I didn't want to be tempted to make it my home again. In any case, the book project was challenging, with contributing writers, researchers, photographers and advertisers to coordinate. It was satisfying to pull it all together, and to return to Hong Kong with a nice wad of cash for my efforts.

MY NEW ROOM at the Helena May looked across to the flower shop on the corner of Garden Road that faced the US Consulate General building. On a chest of drawers beside a small, rented TV, I placed a drinks tray with two squat glasses, a bowl for ice, a pair of tongs, and a bottle of Johnny Walker Black Label whisky I'd bought duty-free. I'd always thought of myself as a social drinker with a busy social life. I'd never considered not drinking, even on those mornings when death seemed preferable to the latest hangover. All my friends drank. It's what one did. And I did all my drinking in company. I never kept alcohol in any of the many homes I'd lived in between leaving the on-campus residential college that was my first Sydney address and moving to Asia in 1986. Now, the prospect of having a nightcap in my room whenever I wanted one seemed sophisticated. The girl who had lived and worked in Sydney for the past fifteen years, studying, learning about men and starting her career, was now a woman. I was independent, self-employed and energetic, and I'd embarked on an exciting adventure in a rapidly changing part of the world.

Soon after my return from Australia, a runner's guide to Sydney was published that had been my idea and mostly my work. Seeing it in print reminded me that I always felt a sense of wellbeing when I was physically fit. When I'd first arrived in Hong Kong, I'd joined a local offshoot of the international Hash House Harriers. It was a way to meet people, and the weekly runs through coastal villages and country parks, following a trail of torches in the dark, were fun and took me to places I wouldn't otherwise have seen. But I'd somehow let it slide. The start of my second stint in the territory seemed an appropriate time to get back into an exercise routine of some kind and try to cut back on the ciggies.

I'd taken up smoking at twenty-seven, when a boyfriend and I started sharing a packet of cigarettes on the nights we hung out in inner-city bars listening to bands. It seemed a way of co-habiting a headspace, creating intimacy, in the same way that a shared marijuana or hash joint did. Cigarettes also helped to keep in check the addiction to sweets and fried foods I'd acquired as a teenager. Within three years of starting smoking, I had made my first unsuccessful attempt to quit.

I'll look at doing something about it when I'm more settled, I promised myself in Hong Kong.

The Helena May was close to Bowen Road, a flat and picturesque bitumen path that hugged the wooded lower slopes of the hilly north side of Hong Kong Island. I set my alarm for an early start for my first run in many months.

A steep flight of steps followed the tramline to the stone bridge that was my starting point. The new Norman Foster–designed Hong Kong & Shanghai Bank building in Central loomed in the pale morning light. Other runners and walkers were about. Two Filipino domestic helpers exercised their employers' dogs. A lone Chinese man at a viewpoint overlooking the luxury hotels clustered in Admiralty did vigorous arm and vocal exercises. In a small garden with concrete seating and paving, a group of elderly men and women performed a gentle, fluid tai chi routine accompanied by tinny, discordant music from a portable tape player. I could see, across on Kowloon side, Kai Tak Airport's runway jutting into the harbour. The city was literally at my feet, the start-of-day sounds muffled by altitude and foliage.

A wave of contentment washed over me as I found a steady rhythm. Near the Adventist Hospital on Stubbs Road, high above the racecourse at Happy Valley, I turned for home.

MY WORK AS a freelance editor was picking up. A travel-guide publisher offered me a job working in-house a couple of days a week. And Linda recommended me to Yin, a publisher newly arrived from England, who was developing a list of books about doing business with China.

When I heard I'd got the China books job, I knocked on Sarah's door, just along the corridor from my room. In the months that we'd been neighbours at the HM, I'd grown less intimidated by her proper British accent and manner. She was always up for some fun.

'Fancy a drink? I'm celebrating. I got a big new client today.'

'Sure. Downstairs?'

'No, let's go to the Hilton.'

Later, at a bar called Joe Bananas, we flirted with expat lads and danced to Wham!, Simply Red and The Pet Shop Boys. JBs had become our go-to place whenever we wanted to make a night out of an evening.

A taxi deposited us back at the HM, where a buzzer by the side gate raised the night watchman, who had been asleep on a camp bed in the kitchen. 'Sorry, John,' I said, as we stumbled inside. 'Can you spare a ciggie? Promise I'll pay you back tomorrow.'

I had found my feet in my adopted home, no longer a stranger in a strange land. It was easy to meet people. The Australian Association of Hong Kong hosted regular cocktail parties and other events. There were trips to the outlying islands on pleasure junks for seafood lunches with my HM chums. Sue introduced me to the budget-priced Mariners' Club, which had a decent swimming pool.

It was exhilarating just to walk the city's streets and be caught up in the constant activity. Chinese men, their singlets rolled high above their stomach paunches, trundled trolleys piled with slabs of Tsing Tao beer, or shallow polystyrene boxes of flopping fish, or woven baskets spilling out bok choy and other vegetables. Cooking smells wafted from *dai pai dongs*, which served as neighbourhood kitchens for locals whose minuscule flats were piled one upon another in the decayed looking buildings that lined the roadside. Older women, dressed in mauve or grey or green loose cotton tunic tops worn over wide black trousers, perched like white-crowned birds on the concrete benches in tiny community gardens, chattering loudly together in the Cantonese or Hokkien or Hakka dialect of their ancestral villages. Smartly dressed young office workers crowded The Lanes in Central, or the outlet stores in the back streets of Wanchai and Causeway Bay, or Temple Street night market on Kowloon side, in search of bargain-priced fashions.

I now had steady freelance work editing travel guides, China business books and technical trade manuals for a polytechnic. I also became the assistant editor of the *Hong Kong Law Journal*. Occasionally, fascinated by the lives they revealed, I sat in on murder trials at the Supreme Court, where the accused was usually a local Chinese and the proceedings were conducted in English.

My stars seemed all to be aligned, except for the imminent expiry of my latest tourist visa. I'd applied to the Immigration Department for a work permit as a freelancer but was turned down. In the government's eyes, freelancing for half a dozen steady clients didn't measure up to being employed by a single company that would act as my sponsor. I was going to have to take things up a notch.

I rolled a sheet of paper into my typewriter and wrote to a senior official in the Hong Kong Government. My former boss in Australia had given me his old friend's name in case I ever needed high-calibre help. Now was such a time, and I had nothing to lose by asking for it.

Later that week, an assistant to the official phoned to set up a meeting. On the appointed afternoon, I arrived at a private club in Central for a chat with one of the most important people in the colonial government. We settled in plush armchairs and a waiter took our drinks order. I wanted a gin and tonic, to take the edge off my nerves, but a soda water with fresh lime seemed prudent.

'What do you hope to achieve here in Hong Kong?' the official asked.

'I want to work across many areas of publishing – education, travel, business, the law,' I said. 'And I can only do that if I freelance. I don't want to be restricted to just one area, as I would be if a single company vouched for me. I've been trying to get the Department to consider my case on its merits.'

'There's certainly a need for your skills here.'

When we later emerged on to the street and shook hands, I thanked him for his time. A Chinese man opened the rear passenger door of a black limousine that was parked by the curb and stood aside, waiting. 'My driver will drop you back at the Helena May. Good luck.'

If John's on duty, he's going to be so impressed, I thought, as I stepped into the car's plush interior. The HM doorman was more used to seeing me fall from a taxi after a big night out than alighting from a limo with an impressive number plate.

The following week, I was again called to the phone. The Immigration Department wanted a word with me. I should bring along my passport. I hadn't heard anything more from the posh official.

Have I been busted for working illegally? Am I going to be escorted to Kai Tak and put on the first plane back to Oz?

'Please, take a seat,' the officer said. 'Would you like tea?'

'Thank you.'

His manner was unexpectedly friendly.

'Cigarette?' He held out a gold pack of State Express 555s and offered a light.

Is this normal?

'May I have your passport, please?'

My breath caught in my throat as I handed it across.

'Your situation has been reviewed. You can work in Hong Kong as a sole business operator.'

'Really?'

'An exception has been made for you. We will review your situation at a later time.'

That night, I wrote a letter of thanks to the government official. It seemed that his endorsement had given my application the green light.

My new status as a legal self-employed alien called for another celebration. Sarah was in her pyjamas when I knocked on her door. 'Fancy going to JBs?'

'Give me five minutes.'

AT LA BELLA DONNA, where we ate two or three times a week, Sarah announced one day that she wanted to run 5 kilometres. 'I'll never be a real runner, Jim. But I'd like to run that far just once.' (We had taken to calling each other 'Jim' after the catchphrase, 'It's life, Jim, but not as we know it.')

'That's easy,' I said. 'Start with walking the distance, then gradually add in more running until you can go the whole way.'

Over the following weeks, I helped her build up the running component of her 5K walks until she ran the whole distance non-stop.

Yet another celebration was called for.

'Whisky soda?' the waiter asked as he led us to our usual table beneath a poster of Napoleon with his hand down the bodice of Josephine's empire-line gown. When he returned with two hefty tumblers tinkling with ice, I clinked Sarah's glass with mine.

Many hours later, we were perched at the bar in a Wanchai pub known to regulars as The House of Doom, cigarettes in hand. When I tipped back my head to drink a B-52 shot, the stool overbalanced and I fell to the floor.

'You okay, Jim?'

I could see Sarah's face, framed by the legs of our stools, peering down at me.

'Ah, yep.'

But *was* I okay? That afternoon, I'd easily run the few kilometres that were my friend's goal. Now, in the lost hours of the night, I was lying on the sticky floor of a dingy bar. Was I a fit and focused woman who'd just had a teensy bit too much to drink, or was I simply a drunk?

CHAPTER FOUR

Suzie, another regular at our breakfast table, had decided that her destiny lay back in England. She resigned from her job and planned a three-week visit to Rajasthan, in northwest India, on her way home from Asia. Her itinerary would take in the most popular attractions: Delhi, the Taj Mahal in Agra, Jaipur, Jodhpur, the desert city of Jaisalmer, Udaipur, Pushkar.

'Would you like company?' I asked. The timing was good. I could squeeze a holiday into my work schedule. It was wedding season in northern India – an auspicious time of year.

I was intrigued by my friend's decision to change the course of her life based on a gut feeling. I'd done the same thing in moving to Hong Kong and had no doubt that I'd made the right choice. My new life was beyond anything I might have thought was on the horizon even two years before. I couldn't imagine going back to my old one, or what might make me even consider doing so.

AT THE GRAND, colonial-style hotel in New Delhi that Suzie had booked for the first night of our otherwise budget tour, we sat cross-legged on the massive bed we were to share and toasted each other in duty-free whisky.

As we were travelling with backpacks, the soapstone Buddha head I purchased in Agra on day three wasn't the most sensible of souvenirs. 'Don't you think it will be a bit heavy, Rob?'

I wrapped it in a sarong and stuffed it into the bottom of my pack. 'I'll manage.'

In Jaipur, we checked into a backpackers' hostel, then set off to see the pink city's sights. The piles of fresh manure and the free-roaming cattle, the limbless beggars, and the unbroken stream of motor scooters, three-wheeled autos and buses coming from every direction made navigating the streets on foot hazardous and stressful. Instead, we hailed an auto to take us the short distance to the historic centre with its terracotta-coloured sandstone Palace of the Winds.

Next was a visit to a bank. The Buddha head had depleted my supply of rupees and I needed to cash some traveller's cheques. After we'd lined up to get a token, we then had to queue again for a teller. The second line was long and slow moving.

'What a stupid system,' I whined.

'Try to see it as it's giving someone a job,' Suzie said.

Just as we reached the head of the line, the teller pulled down the metal security grille. 'Closed,' he said. 'Teatime.'

'You're joking!' I said. 'How long is this going to take? We've been queuing for *hours*.'

He was now at the rear of the cubicle.

'Don't just walk away!'

'Madam, I will reopen after tea. Wait.'

'Don't call me "madam". I want to see the manager. Where is the manager?'

The teller walked back to the grille and pointed further down the banking hall. I could see two hinged wooden doors of the kind one sees in a Western movie, where a figure wearing a hat and backlit by the sun strides into a saloon and fills the frame.

'Rob ...,' Suzie cautioned.

I crossed the room, approached the doors and surprised myself by giving one of them a hefty shove. It shot forward, then swung back towards me. I'd gone too far to back down now, so I pushed it open again and stepped inside. Two men seated at a small metal desk were looking startled. One held a pen poised, ready to sign a document that lay on the desktop.

'My friend and I want to cash our traveller's cheques,' I said. In my imagination, I coolly raised a thumb and forefinger and made a slight adjustment to the angle at which I wore my hat. In reality, I was trembling. 'We've waited long enough.'

The manager assessed my mood, then turned to his customer and said something in the local dialect. It was possibly: 'A thousand apologies, good sir, but I will have to attend to this very rude Westerner.'

He rose from his seat. 'Follow me, madam.'

I was about to call him on the 'madam' but thought better of it and followed him out into the main hall. Suzie was still waiting by the teller's shuttered cubicle and rolled her eyes when I gave her a discreet thumbs-up.

Five minutes later, our rupee cash reserves replenished, we flagged down an auto, agreed a price with the driver to take us to our hostel, and clambered aboard. 'I need a drink,' I said, and collapsed against the plastic-covered seat. 'My back is killing me.'

Karmic retribution for my appalling behaviour kicked in overnight, and for two days I was confined to my bunk with a urinary tract infection. When I began to feel somewhat human again, I ventured out in search of Suzie and found her chatting with a couple of American backpackers in the courtyard. Din, dark of hair and skin, tall and broad, was a college instructor. Mike, blond and sporting a mature moustache, was travelling in Asia before starting postgraduate studies somewhere in the Midwest.

Plans were made to eat a *thali* meal together at a nearby home-style eatery, but I was still wobbly on my feet from the infection.

'Hop up on to my shoulders,' Din said, and crouched at my feet. When he stood, my legs dangling down his chest, Suzie and Mike seemed to have shrunk to half-size. I held on to Din's forehead and we set off, my body swaying rhythmically, comfortingly, from side to side.

From Jaipur, we four travelled together by train across the Thar Desert towards the border with Pakistan. I spent much of the journey lying on the bench seat in our rattling compartment, my head in Din's lap, feigning sleep. I wanted only to remain in this cocoon, lulled by the movement of the train, by this lovely, gentle giant whose aura seemed to merge seamlessly with mine, and by the sound of Suzie's laughter as she and Mike played word games.

I fell in love with Jaisalmer. The terracotta-coloured walled city rose from the parched earth like a mirage. It seemed like it might all just dissolve in a downpour. In the narrow laneways beside the fort, hand-stitched cotton bedcovers and tie-dyed lengths of cloth were displayed for sale, their deep maroons, turquoise blues, golden yellows and splashes of silver vibrant against the earthen ramparts.

We trekked out into the desert on camels. After night had fallen and we had eaten, our small party spread out among the tussock grasses in our sleeping bags. The camels, tethered near their handlers, were black shapes against the glow of the campfire. The sounds of their occasional loud farts, and of the men talking softly together, carried on the still evening air. I gazed up at the immense star-studded sky, aware that all the choices I had ever made had brought me to this perfect moment.

Suzie's gut was troubling her when we boarded the train to Udaipur, and she spent most of the long journey in the filthy squat toilet at the rear of the carriage. She declared the experience so horrid that only a four-star hotel – a former maharajah's palace that overlooked the lake – would ensure her complete recovery.

At the end of our final week of travelling, we arrived by taxi at a gated community for expatriates in a suburb of New Delhi. Suzie had arranged for us to stay with friends of friends from Hong Kong.

I'd been tetchy the last few days, becoming irritated by the small discomforts of travelling even with an easygoing companion, and was in need of alcohol.

A tall British man dressed in a mauve satin frock, and wearing a blonde wig and black stilettos, answered our knock. 'Come in, girls! We've been expecting you.'

Suzie and I exchanged glances.

'Do you like my outfit?' He did a little twirl. 'I'm an ugly sister. The pantomime, you know. Jolly good fun. Now, what can I get you both to drink?'

IN DECEMBER, I flew to Australia and stayed for a few days with Tom. In the letters we had been writing back and forth, I looked for signs that he loved me, missed me, wanted me, but I only ever found casual affection. His career was about to take him to the other side of the world, and I fretted that the change might remove him completely from my orbit, though I was the one who had initially moved away.

I plonked myself on his lap and decided to ask for what I thought I wanted. The shape of his mouth was mesmerising. I wanted to attach my lips to his, to nibble away at them – at his reserve – like a doctor fish nibbling at dead skin in a Cambodian foot spa. Tom looked adoringly at Rufus, who was curled up beside the chair. He scratched the back of the dog's neck; his other hand dangled by his side, though my waist was within easy reach. I ignored his body language and tried to pin him down to some form of committed relationship.

'It wouldn't work, Rob.' He shifted in the seat.

'Why not?'

'Well, for a start, we'll be on opposite sides of the planet!'

'That needn't be a problem. It would just take some imagination.' I pressed on. 'It would be fun.'

Rufus yawned loudly.

'Good boy.' Tom's chuckle pierced my heart.

'What sort of feelings do you have for me?'

There … It was on the table.

His lips had formed a hard line. Did he love me but couldn't show it? He had always seemed to want us to be lovers. I was confused. I had come back to the question that had baffled me all the years I'd known him.

'Are you like this with everyone? Or just with me?'

'Just with you.'

I looked at him for a long moment. I could so easily picture us together. But I was dreaming. He sought me out, but then didn't know what to do with me. I kept responding, but then didn't know what to do with the man he actually was.

CHAPTER FIVE

It seemed time to venture out into the real world beyond the Helena May and rent an apartment. I found a flat beside the forbidding looking Victoria Prison. The lounge room, where I set up my desk, had a view across the laneway to grey stone walls topped with broken glass and tangled barbed wire. The saxophonist in the next-door apartment practised his instrument for hours at a time, perfecting a run of notes before moving on to another. An upstairs neighbour was my contact at the law journal. A few minutes' walk down the hill, towards the antique stores and art galleries of Hollywood Road, were the offices of my travel-guide client.

When I'd followed my instincts and moved to a foreign country, I'd had no idea of what lay ahead. Two years later, space for me had opened up in this crowded, mysterious metropolis. Most nights, I ate in cheap restaurants and drank in pubs with new mates. Sarah and I still met often for dinner. The cares we'd brought with us from our workplaces would have dissolved by the time we drained our complimentary after-dinner Irish coffees, fell out into the night air and headed for Joe Bananas to continue drinking, to dance, and possibly to connect with an enticing stranger. I felt I was in the right place at the right time in my life. If I was no longer running and was drinking more than I had been, I wasn't overly concerned. These were exciting times.

When things had settled a bit, I'd start exercising again and go a little easier on the ciggies and booze.

One morning in early August, I was driving with a client to her office. Emma would soon be leaving Hong Kong and we were to go over what work remained to be done on her projects. Although she was confident and capable behind the wheel, I kept a firm hold on the grab-strap.

'I've found there's really only one essential Cantonese sentence,' I said.

'What's that?'

'*Mm ho jar gum fai, mgoi.* Don't drive so fast, please.'

She snorted, then diverted suddenly from our lane into another that fed on to a curved overpass.

'It's very useful in taxis,' I said, wiping the film of sweat that had sprung up on my free palm on to the leg of my new black silk trousers.

'I'm going to have some free time,' Emma said, and swung the car off the overpass. 'I might be able to find some offshore clients for you. Have you thought about starting an editorial services agency?'

'Do you mean subcontracting my work out to other editors?'

'I could possibly send some extra business your way, if you wanted to expand.'

I was flattered. Emma and I worked well together. It might be fun to try something different, and it could mean more money.

'Let me have a think about it.'

That weekend, friends Peter and Amanda were married in St John's Cathedral. Being a part of the marriage celebration of people I'd come to know in Hong Kong seemed confirmation that the city was now my home. It felt unlikely that my life would follow a similar path to theirs. (*'It's life, Jim, but not as we know it.*') Although Tom wrote regularly, he signed his letters 'xx'. I wanted 'xxxx' – or at least 'xxx'.

It was the Year of the Dragon, my sign in the Chinese zodiac. The four eights in August 8, 1988, were also auspicious, signifying prosperity and good luck. Based partly on these signs from the cosmos, and a smidgeon of boredom now that my business was doing reasonably well and my back wasn't against a wall, I decided to leap again into the unknown and form an editorial services company to replace the sole proprietorship structure I'd been operating under since I was legal. Emma and two other investors came on board as directors. Hopefully, they would bring in new business and offer moral and other support. I would be the managing director.

I envisaged having a team of editors working for me on jobs for rates lower than those I charged the clients. The startup money the directors invested went on a fax machine, a Macintosh computer, some office furniture, and two months' rent for space that I sublet from a corporate video production company. The offices we shared in a bland commercial suburb near the harbour included a sizeable studio for filming. Frances, a Canadian scriptwriter, diluted the testosterone at their end of the office suite. For some reason, I had employed a secretary. It was probably obvious to everyone but me that I had no idea what I was doing. I would have done well to reread the book I'd edited for Linda on Hong Kong employment law, which her new publishing venture had just launched.

My advertisement in *The South China Morning Post* for experienced freelance editors who were native English speakers produced, first, a Cantonese-speaking engineer with minimal English. The second applicant was Monica, a quiet-mannered English expat wife with some publishing experience. She had time on her hands now that her kids were in school. I was happy to give her a trial, along with Jody, another expat mum. We planned a schedule of part-time hours to be spent working in-house at the office under my direction.

While we waited for my new partners to introduce some business, the team focused on a China-related business directory I had already taken on. With a lot of detailed work to be done and a tight schedule, it was a perfect trial project. The client wasn't concerned that I was subcontracting some of the work, so long as it was done to a high standard and within budget.

In the evenings, I was too tired to cook at home in my small flat by the prison. In any case, the kitchen cubicle had only a cold-water tap, a single hotplate, a bar fridge and one tiny cupboard. Instead, I ate out every night, either alone or with friends. Always, I would have two or three glasses of wine to mark the transition from my work day to 'me time'.

At Christmas, we threw a combined work party in the studio. The floor was suitable for dancing, and the space had a good sound system and a flashing disco ball. We had the party catered and invited our clients and contacts. Someone photographed me with a new client who had liked my work for a competitor and approached me to work on his publications. Another photograph showed me cradled in the arms of one of my authors, an English corporate lawyer, just before he flung me into the air.

BY THE LUNAR New Year of 1989, my investors still hadn't brought in any new clients. I was generating enough work for myself and to fill the hours that Monica and Jody wanted to work; but with their invoices to pay fortnightly, and office rental and a secretary's salary to cover each month, in addition to my personal expenses, I was feeling only the financial burden of my new business structure and none of the anticipated benefits.

As the edges of my day got sharper, I began to hang out for that first sip of a whisky and soda, or vodka and tonic, or glass of wine. From being a well-earned refreshment that signalled the start of evening down time, it became a necessity. Without it, I couldn't switch off the looming sense that I had dug myself an unnecessary hole at work. If I had a few drinks in me, I could muffle the voice that complained: 'Why did you go and complicate things?' I didn't want to get drunk. No more falling off bar stools, if I could help it. I just wanted to relieve the stress. But I had somehow lost sight of how to do that without numbing myself with cigarettes, fried noodles and other comfort foods, sex with enticing passing ships, and alcohol.

It didn't occur to me that I might care better for my wellbeing by hopping on a tram after work to explore unfamiliar parts of the city, by riding a ferry to an island, taking a walk around The Peak, seeing a film, or even by thinking of someone other than myself for a change and volunteering for an hour or two at an animal shelter. I'd lost interest in the world around me. My coping behaviours were starting to cause me more stress than they were intended to relieve.

ONE SUNDAY IN April, I was with Peter and Amanda on the way to lunch with the authors of a political dictionary of Hong Kong that Peter was publishing and I was editing. News came over the car radio of nearly a hundred fatalities at a soccer match in England, where fans were crushed up against the wire fences at Hillsborough Stadium in Sheffield. I could easily imagine the mounting claustrophobia and panic.

Six weeks later, in June, another shock went around the world, along with the image of a lone white-shirted young man holding shopping bags and standing in the path of a convoy of Chinese armoured tanks. Within days, there was talk in Hong Kong that troops of the People's Liberation Army were massing on the border just to the north of us. What had happened – what was still happening – in China was appalling. And suddenly it all seemed too close, too personally threatening.

How would I leave Hong Kong if the PLA crossed the border and attempted to take control of the New Territories, the Kowloon Peninsula and – the jewel in the crown – Hong Kong Island? I had enough free-floating anxiety from work stress as it was; I didn't need the additional worry that one small airport on the other side of the harbour might be the only means of escape for millions of people rushing to flee the territory in a panic.

When the rumours of an imminent invasion proved to be unfounded, the threat that a crush of humanity might descend on Kai Tak's departure gates receded. Normal life resumed for the expatriate population, who could return to their home countries any time they chose. But many Hong Kong Chinese without a foreign passport that entitled them to live elsewhere after the regime change in 1997, now only eight years away, stepped up their plans to gain citizenship in Canada or another country, just in case.

The two events rattled me. Aware that my regular evening drinking wasn't helping my nerves, I made an appointment for a check-up at the Adventist Hospital, just above where I had used to turn around on my morning runs. The results indicated I was in reasonably good health for my thirty-seven years, though my cholesterol was a bit high. Embarrassed to admit to drinking as regularly as I was, I'd understated the amount of alcohol I consumed. Even so, the doctor who reviewed my test results was concerned. 'You should cut back. You'd feel better for it. And you really need to stop smoking.'

'I know, I know. It's just hard to think about giving up while I've got so much on my plate at work.'

'We have a Quit Smoking program here.'

'I'll keep it in mind.'

AFTER I'D DONE a lot of work on two books for the new client who had attended our Christmas party, he refused to settle my invoice. 'There's no reason for him not to pay,' I said to Brian, the video producer whose office I was sharing. 'They needed a lot of work. I told him that. He's just being a dick.'

Although it wasn't a huge sum, I couldn't afford to write it off. Besides, there was a principle at stake.

'For that amount, you can take him to the Small Claims Tribunal,' Brian said.

The tactical aspects of preparing the case took a lot of time that I begrudged having to spend on defending myself. Brian coached me on what to say and came along to the hearing. The magistrate found that both parties had failed in our dealings with each other and instructed the publisher to pay only half the amount he owed me. I disagreed that I had been less than professional in all my dealings with the client and was angered by the injustice of the decision. When the publisher left the courtroom without once having looked me in the eye, resentment curdled in my gut.

CHAPTER SIX

Emma learnt that a Chinese property company in Hong Kong was looking to retain a Western public relations agency. 'We should pitch for the account,' she said in a phone call.

'But I don't know anything about PR!'

'I'll be in Hong Kong later in the week. It could be the opportunity we've been waiting for.'

I was dubious, but my other partners also thought we should go for it. 'What have we got to lose?' Brian said.

I agreed to at least approach the property company and see what happened. If we got the gig, we could figure out later how to do it, like a language teacher learning just enough grammar and vocabulary before the next class to stay one step ahead of her students. We pulled together a team, with Emma as account director, a designer we knew as art director, and Brian as media director. I was the managing director.

Linda's production manager in her new business, a Chinese woman named Polly, organised for our business cards to be designed and printed overnight. If necessary, she could double as our production director. It was an early model of a virtual work team.

The ink on our name cards was still damp when Emma and I arrived at an office tower in Admiralty and were shown into the serious boardroom of an important property company located on a dizzily high floor. I was so far out of my comfort zone, I couldn't have sneezed without embarrassing myself.

The Chinese boss got straight to the point. 'How can you help us increase our business?' He was looking at me.

'Um ... er ...'

'What is your strategy for us?'

'Ah ... er ...'

My eyes sought Emma's.

'What Robyn means is ...' She picked up the ball and carried us through the ten minutes we had been allotted for our pitch.

'Shit, that was *awful!*' We were in the lift on our way back to planet Earth.

'It wasn't great,' Emma agreed.

'It was the most humiliating experience of my life,' I moaned to Sarah that evening at Bella Donna. I was on a second whisky before our baked avocado with escargots had even arrived. The pitch had been a disaster because I hadn't given it any thought beforehand, believing I could just wing it. But I couldn't admit this and focused instead on the blow the meeting had dealt to my self-esteem.

'I'm never going to misrepresent myself like that again, Jim. I shouldn't have to.'

Some weeks later, Emma was in Hong Kong again and called into the office. We hadn't heard anything from the property company.

'We're thinking of bringing in someone new,' she said.

'What do you mean? As what?'

'As managing director. We think there's real potential in the PR area.'

'You want me to hand management of my company to someone else?'

'It's not actually your company. You don't have a majority of the shares.'

She was right.

'Who are you thinking of?' I said, stalling for time to allow my head to catch up. She mentioned a freelancer I knew.

'You're joking! Look, I've got no problem if you want to set up a public relations side of the business. *My* business – the editorial business – could service it. I'd be fine with that. But you're not seriously suggesting that *she* could do my job?'

'We don't need her to do what you do. We think we may want to move in a new direction. And we don't need to set up a whole new company. We've already got one. But if you're not able or willing to manage it in the way we – the majority shareholders – want, then you may not be the best person for your job.'

She had a legitimate case from a business point of view, but I was too emotionally involved to see it. Monica was proofreading case notes for the law journal in the glass-walled office next to mine and I could see that her cheeks had flushed red.

'You know what?' I turned back to Emma. 'You can do whatever you want. I'm going, and I'm taking the company with me. I'll pay you all back double what you put in. It's over. I don't want to have to deal with all this crap. It was stupid of me to complicate things. I was doing fine on my own.'

On the most auspicious day of the previous year, 8/8/88, I'd thought it a brilliant idea to employ other people to help me do my work. Monica and Jody were reliable, but no one would ever care as much as I did about my clients or about the quality of the work I produced for them. I had also handed over control of the business I had been building over the past nearly four years to partners whose vision for it differed from mine. And I'd done it out of greed and because of my ego. My partners were thinking like businesspeople; I wasn't. The past twelve months had been the most difficult period of my life, and I was now committed to paying a large sum of money to get myself out of a situation of my own making.

AFTER THE RELATIONSHIP with my investors ended, I set up business again back in the flat beside the prison. My lease still had a year to run. Nick, a translator and interpreter, and Mary, a writer, joined me there in what was now a co-working space. I cashed their rent cheques, but had no involvement in their businesses, nor they in mine. In the evenings, I hunkered down in a small room back at the Helena May and salved my wounds with whisky.

Once I'd dismantled and then reassembled my business life, I went to Scotland and the Outer Hebrides for a break. It was as far from Hong Kong as I could get. The Berlin Wall had come down, signalling, along with other events in Europe, the end of the Cold War. I'd hardly noticed there had been a tipping point in world history.

One early morning, before it was light, I took a taxi from Inverness to Loch Ness. The driver stayed with the car while I walked down to the ruins of Urquhart Castle on the lakeshore and watched the new day start. There were no crowds, no tourist buses, no ice-cream vendors; it was just me and, perhaps, a monster. It was easy to believe in its existence when everything around me was still and silent, the loch shrouded in mist.

On the west coast of the mainland, ferries ran from Ullapool to the Isle of Lewis. In Stornoway, I spent an evening in a back room of the local pub. A white sheet had been pinned to the wall to create a makeshift cinema screen. Occupying an assortment of ill-matched chairs were a couple of dozen of the town's teenagers, who had all paired off. I took a seat in the back row and hugged myself.

From Stornoway, I cadged a lift with the local postman to Tarbert. From there, a ferry went to Uig, on the Isle of Skye.

'It's so beautiful,' I said, looking out at the bleak landscape.

'Aye, lass. If you want, I can stop for a minute.'

From the top of a hillock by the roadside, I could see, across the peat moor, the coastline in the grey distance. The clammy air clung to my face. For much of the year, conditions here would be harsh and unwelcoming. The people who called it home needed to be strong and resilient.

It had been a horrible year. I'd gone into it feeling confident and excited by the potential and challenges it held. But the energy I had put out hadn't given me any of the returns I'd imagined. Now, battered and bruised by the blows to my self-confidence and by the breakdown of relationships with people I respected and liked, I would have to dig deep and rediscover my own strength and resilience.

I blew my nose and took a deep breath. I'd make the new year – the new decade – a new start.

CHAPTER SEVEN

Nineteen-ninety was the Chinese Year of the Horse. Nothing in Hong Kong ever happened at a slow trot, but the galloping pace of the past year had taken a toll.

Depressed by my tiny room at the Helena May, where I chain-smoked, drank and stared at the television late into the evenings, I moved to a share flat above Central. ('It smells bad in here,' the manager had commented when I gave notice. 'We'll have to repaint it.') For half the rent on the new place, I had the large master bedroom. Nick, my office mate in the apartment by the prison, and Andy, a copywriter, took the two tiny bedrooms.

My room became my sanctuary. Two black-lacquered bases placed side by side and topped with Japanese tatami mats and futon mattresses formed a king-size lounging/sleeping platform. The hand-stitched mirrored cushion covers and brightly coloured cotton bedcover were souvenirs from Kathmandu and Rajasthan. I'd bought the Buddha statues in India, Thailand and Nepal. A bookshelf held travel guides, some of which I had edited, biographies and memoirs, photography books, and histories of Hong Kong and other places I had visited in the past four years. A reading lamp stood beside the bed.

On a heavy rosewood side table sat a tape player and a woven basket I'd bought in the Philippines that held favourite cassette tapes. I listened compulsively to Sade, Chris Rea, Fine Young

Cannibals and Bronski Beat's Jimmy Somerville, whose songs made me yearn for something I couldn't articulate. Music always evoked emotions for me. When I was a child and my mother was younger than I was now, the songs I heard playing on the radio had often been about wanting, seeking and sometimes finding love.

The voices of Doris Day, Mario Lanza, Harry Belafonte and Rosemary Clooney could still transport me back into that childhood home, where I had early realised I was essentially on my own and would have to nurture myself. Perhaps my mother, too, had yearned for a love that was big enough to fill her own void from childhood. My puberty had coincided with the start of the new music of the 1960s – The Beatles, The Kinks, The Easybeats, Georgie Fame. At the pop concerts I'd attended as a twelve- and thirteen-year-old, I had literally screamed to be seen, to be heard, to be loved.

THE FOUNDATIONS OF my life in Hong Kong continued to change. Friends moved away: Sarah to Canada, Yin to New York, Peter and Amanda to Botswana. When Din, the gentle giant I'd met in India, passed through town, we spent the night together as friends, listening to music in my room and talking quietly of the dreams we had for our lives. Just before dawn, I took him up to The Peak. Fog blanketed the city; only the tips of the tallest towers were visible above the clouds at our feet. It was as if the world had turned upside-down.

Then Tom wrote to say that he would be making a visit to Australia from Europe. 'Should I come and see you on the way?' It was three years since I had sat on his lap in his Sydney flat.

'Absolutely!'

Maybe he's missed me. Maybe he's realised how good we could be together.

I met his flight and whisked him home. After a shower, he stretched out on top of the bed. The towel he had tucked loosely around his hips had come undone. His thick black hair, long around the ears and neck and now flecked with grey, looked mussed and sexy. His body was still lean and fit, with shallow, neat folds across his tanned stomach and a smattering of hair in the dip of his chest. Two glasses of wine on the bedside table glowed red in the candlelight.

The attraction between us was still strong. Our lives had taken unexpected, intriguing turns, and we were still interested in each other. But however much I wanted it to be, it wasn't intimacy, it wasn't love. We weren't even very kind to each other when, inevitably, my excitement and hopes turned to frustration. Along with the sexual play, I wanted physical affection and emotional closeness. I wanted Tom to hold my hand, to enjoy my stroking his arm, to want me to hug him, and to want to hug me back. The more I asked for, the more he retreated into himself.

In bed on his last night, I tried to bridge the chasm that yawned between us, but he brushed away my kiss. Giving up hope that he might relent and allow me in, I reached for a cigarette from the pack on the bedside table, flicked the lighter and sucked the smoke into my lungs. After I'd puffed on it a couple of times, he took it from between my fingers and dragged on it. I loved his lips, the shape of his mouth, and resented that a cigarette could go where I couldn't.

'You *always* do this,' he said. The smoke he exhaled curled in the candlelight. 'Everything is fine, then you go all weird.'

I bristled. His idea of *fine* was very different from mine. And why was he making me responsible for everything? Unlike in my claim against the publisher, who had out-and-out cheated me, I knew that I was half the problem in my relationship with Tom, but I wasn't going to accept *all* the blame. I was spoiling our remaining time together by not accepting him for how he was. I was crazy about him, and crazy around him. I craved him, but I wanted him to be different. I held back because he wasn't giving me what I wanted – and he was doing the same.

When he didn't return the cigarette, I reached for another.

'What are you *doing*?' he said, thrusting the now half-smoked stick at me. I pulled on it, dragging my feelings deep into my chest where they might not hurt so much. I'd been feeling this same pain since I was a child.

I don't want to feel this. Something is wrong. This shouldn't be happening to me. I keep my eyes closed tight and try not to breathe. I lie motionless and pretend I am dead.

When Tom left the next morning, it was as if I could breathe again.

I STARTED TO stay out later in the evenings after work. At the Furama Hotel in Central or the Excelsior in Causeway Bay, I would order fried noodles and glass after glass of wine, read a book, smoke. Hotel coffee shops and lounges were generic and anonymous – I could imagine I was in Manila or Bangkok – and offered the possibility of a conversation, a fleeting connection, with a stranger. I was of an age now, approaching my forties, where in that world of expatriate privilege and entitlement, I was fast becoming invisible to men of my age. *I exist. I'm here,* I wanted to say. *See me, hear me, love me.*

When I let myself into the apartment, my flatmates might still be up, watching a video in the living room with their girlfriends, who seemed to have moved in. Their wholesomeness made me irritable, and I resented that I was paying half the rent for an apartment that now accommodated five people.

'Hi,' I'd say, annoyed that I had to engage with them. 'Anyone want a drink?'

'No,' they would chorus.

I'd pour a large glass of something strong from the array of liquor bottles Andy had inherited from his parents when they left Hong Kong, and would then retreat to my room. Later, if I could face running the gauntlet a second, or even a third, time, I'd venture out again and pour another drink. *Fuck it.*

One day, I passed two Western women in the street. 'She's the sort of person who …,' I heard one of them say before they were out of earshot. The snippet of overheard conversation lodged in my mind. *What sort of person am I?* I could no longer see myself clearly. Who did people who knew me see? Was I that person? What sort of person did I want to be? Did normal people hide themselves away each night, wanting to be alone in order to wallow in loneliness? Surely, normal people were like my flatmates and their girlfriends, watching a movie together, laughing and drinking cups of tea? At the end of my workday, I just wanted a drink. If an activity didn't include alcohol, I wasn't interested. That was *my* new normal.

Where once I was caught up in the excitement and fun of starting a new life in Asia, there was now stress, disappointment and mounting anxiety. I'd fallen into a rut of medicating myself in order to feel differently, or to not feel at all.

CHAPTER EIGHT

To shake myself out of my funk and focus on someone else for a change, I flew to Australia in December to pick up my niece Kellie for a three-week holiday in Asia. I was closely involved with my family, despite living far from them. Their kids were still young, and I wanted to know them and for them to know me.

I also needed a daily routine that would force me to limit my drinking. There could be no passing out after too many whiskies, no hangovers that would keep me pinned to the bedsheets long after a child's breakfast time, no hook-ups with enticing but inappropriate strangers. If I couldn't keep myself in check, perhaps an eight-year-old might do it for me.

'We'll be back for *LA Law* on Sunday,' I told Nick on the Friday when I left for the airport. With only a small carry-on case in hand and a return ticket for the day following my arrival, I was obviously a drug mule of some kind. Customs officials in Melbourne pulled me aside and questioned me closely.

At the resort in Kota Kinabalu, in Malaysia, where we flew after a few days back in Hong Kong, the other guests were mostly young couples who spent a lot of time in the pool, their legs, arms and lips entwined. Wearing a two-piece bathing suit, and equipped with a pair of blue rubber flippers, a diving mask and a snorkel, Kellie would patrol the pool's irregularly shaped perimeter, appearing unexpectedly alongside the startled couples like a predatory shark.

One morning, she emerged from the bathroom wearing an oversized cotton bathrobe. A shower cap from the amenities kit covered her hair. Tissues tucked under the sides of the cap suggested a surgical mask.

'I'm Doctor Dork,' she announced, and placed the doll she had brought from home on its back on her bed. 'I'm going to do an operation.'

'What's the matter with her?'

'I don't know yet. That's why I'm doing the operation.'

'That makes sense,' I said.

She held out her hand. 'Scissors.'

'Scissors …? Oh, just a second, doctor.'

'Hurry up. She might be dying.'

In the bathroom I found a pair of nail scissors in my travel kit.

'This is all I could find, doctor.'

'I suppose they'll have to do.'

She fussed over the doll for a few minutes.

'Just in time. She'll live.'

'What a brilliant surgeon you are!'

'I know. I'm Doctor Dork.'

She attached to the doll some lengths of coloured tinsel that I had brought along to decorate our room for Christmas and draped the other ends over the mirror. To all appearances, the patient was now on an intravenous drip and resting comfortably. The crisis had been averted.

When we returned from spending the morning harassing honeymooners in the pool, we found that the cleaners had straightened everything in the room except for the rather bizarre nativity scene laid out on Kellie's bed.

On Christmas morning, she unwrapped the gifts from Santa that my sister had given me. She felt unwell, she said, and I placed a wet flannel on her forehead. I put it down to homesickness and gave her my present of a purple plastic heart, mounted on a stick. Battery-powered, it glowed in the dark. On the flight to Nepal for the second half of our holiday, we held it aloft when the cabin lights were turned off to guide each other back to our seats after using the bathroom.

On the way to our room at the hotel in Kathmandu, I looked across to the bar where I'd spent time on a previous visit and suddenly craved a whisky. I'd succeeded in limiting myself to just a couple of glasses of wine with dinner each night, but the end of our time together was approaching and I was champing a little at the bit. While Kellie ate a room-service supper, I cracked the seal of a small bottle of scotch from the minibar. *I've been good. I deserve this.*

Kathmandu was a fascinating place to share with a curious child. We explored the streets of Thamel and ate lunch at the Rum Doodle, a home base for serious mountain climbers. We took day trips deeper into the valley and wandered around the ornate temples and palace buildings of Bhaktapur. I was happy I could provide such experiences to a child I loved, and felt grateful that I'd been able to fulfil the role of designated responsible adult.

In a photograph I took on our last afternoon, Kellie is facing a young Nepalese girl of about her own age standing in a carved wooden doorway. The two are regarding each other intently. Kellie is dressed in pants and a fleece sweatshirt; her blonde hair hangs in a plait between her shoulder blades. The local girl is wearing a traditional outfit trimmed with embroidery. Her black hair is pulled into a bun; her eyes are outlined heavily with kohl.

Their lives couldn't have been more different, and yet they were so similar. Each saw themself as 'normal' and 'ordinary', and the other as 'exotic' and 'extraordinary'. Looking from one to the other, I thought about what lay ahead for them in life. What sorts of choices would they have? What paths would they make for themselves? Would they do a better job of it than I seemed to be doing?

CHAPTER NINE

'Do you drink a lot of alcohol?'

The dental hygienist had stopped probing at my teeth. Her eyebrows were raised.

Blood surged to my cheeks. 'Um, some.' I swallowed hard.

'I can smell it on your breath. I noticed it the last time you were here, too. I made a note.' Her latex-covered finger rested on my patient record card.

I closed my eyes, too embarrassed to speak.

I'm going to have to find a new hygienist.

It was unbearable that anyone should know that I was having trouble managing my drinking – managing my *life*. I felt exposed and vulnerable in the way I had as a child when faced with my father's disapproval. Dad had pounced readily on my weaknesses, but rarely commended my strengths. If I was so flawed, how could he love me? If he didn't love me, how would I survive? The wounds hadn't healed, even after thirty years.

I WAS ABOUT to leave on another trip, to Botswana. When I'd collected stamps as a child, fascinated by the world they hinted at beyond my suburban confines, the country had still been known as Bechuanaland. I couldn't have imagined then that I would ever visit Africa. Peter was publishing textbooks for the secondary-school market there and Amanda was writing a novel. We planned a driving tour from the capital, Gaborone, to Victoria Falls, on the Zambezi River, and to game parks in the area formed by the borders with Zimbabwe and Zambia.

When I arrived at Kai Tak for my flight to Johannesburg via Taipei, I was refused permission to board. 'You don't have a visa for South Africa stamped in your passport,' the airline representative said at check-in.

'I was told I didn't need one!'

'You can fly to South Africa without a visa, but you won't be able to leave the airport. You can only transit there. You'll need an onward ticket before I can issue a boarding pass.'

'My friends are already on their way to meet my flight!'

We'd planned to spend a few days in Jo'burg before driving back to neighbouring Botswana.

I was thrust into an hour of frenzied activity. By the time I'd sent word to Peter and Amanda of the change of plan, purchased a ticket for an onward flight to Botswana, and booked temporary hotel accommodation in Gaborone, my original flight had closed.

'You'll have to go standby for another flight to Taipei. With luck, you'll arrive in time to join your original connecting flight from there.'

'What do I need to do?'

'Just wait here.'

The minutes ticked away, and nothing happened. I couldn't even go to the loo in case a seat became available. Suddenly, there was action. 'We can get you on a flight, but you'll have to run!'

I was processed and spat out within seconds, pointed towards the 'Flight Departures' sign, and given a virtual shove in my back to speed me on my way. The cabin was sealed moments after I fell through the doorway.

In Taipei, in the mirror of the ladies' loo in the transit lounge, I noticed a white hair near my temple that I was sure hadn't been there earlier in the evening when I'd set out for the airport.

I was cheered to find that the plane transporting me to the bottom of the world was almost empty. The past hours had been stressful, but the problems were now resolved. My in-flight reading was a biography of Nora Joyce, wife and muse of the Irish writer James Joyce. When the flight attendant plonked a full-size bottle of cold white wine on my seat-back tray, any tension I was still carrying drained straight down my body and out through my toes.

ONE AUGUST AFTERNOON, not long after my return from Africa, I picked up the ringing phone in my Chancery Lane office. A guy whose family I'd known since high school was visiting Hong Kong. Would I like to meet for a drink?

'Absolutely. Do you have a swimming costume with you?'

We swam and had drinks at the Mariners' Club, on Kowloon side. Liam was funny, sexy and a bit of a lad. He was just the tonic I needed.

'I haven't finished with you yet,' he said, when he flew out a fortnight later.

THE MID-LEVELS apartment wasn't working for me. I never used the kitchen, and I'd grown tired of sharing the one bathroom/toilet in the morning with four other people, one of whom had irritable bowel syndrome. 'I strongly advise you not to go in there for a while' wasn't what I wanted to hear after I'd already been waiting 30 minutes during rush hour to take a shower.

But the truth was that, apart from occasional stretches of time when I functioned something like the normal person I suspected I wasn't, I didn't want witnesses. I didn't like my flatmates knowing that I drank every night alone in my room; that I played, over and over, tapes of songs that seemed to speak to my yearning; that my skin reeked of stale alcohol as I waited impatiently for the bathroom to be free. Even in my own eyes, I was turning into a lonely, passionate spinster like the character Judith Hearne in the movie I had seen somewhere in recent years. God knows what I looked like to Nick and Andy and their girlfriends; certainly not a well-adjusted, happy career woman in the prime of life.

It suited everyone, then, when I moved out and took a lease on a renovated bedsit apartment just across from the office by the prison. It was small but comfortable, conveniently located, and I wouldn't feel scrutinised there. Now that I was free to drink the way I wished when at home, I could switch to white wine. In the share apartment, where I hadn't wanted to deal with empty wine bottles every morning, I'd nipped at Andy's inherited stash of Wild Turkey and other spirits.

The astrologer had been right about me all those years before: I did have a tendency to change my circumstances instead of myself. But a change of place could also kickstart a change in my routines, which might give me some breathing space. Switching to wine would be a move in a healthier direction. And the possibility of Liam's return put a bounce in my step.

POLLY, LINDA'S PRODUCTION assistant, decided to go into business for herself as a desktop publisher, and I invited her to join Mary, Nick and me in our freelancers' co-op. One Wednesday evening, she and I were at the China Tee Club with some friends from an informal professional network I'd cobbled together in the past year that had started to gain some traction. Two women approached our table. 'Is this the publishing group?' one asked.

'Yep,' I said. 'Pull up a seat.'

They were newly arrived from Europe and were looking to make contacts in the industry. One was a copywriter, the other a graphic designer. Somehow, word of our nascent network had reached them.

'I think we might be on to something,' I said to Polly the next day. 'Let's take things up a notch.'

As a newly minted freelancer, Polly was looking to find clients for her layout, typesetting and print-broking services, and I was keen to promote my editing business. We decided to give our loose association a proper name, expand our membership, and compile a directory in which members could advertise their skills and services.

Women in Publishing groups had been formed in the UK and Sydney, and as 'Hong Kong Women in Publishing' best described our current and potential members, we adopted that name. I asked every woman I knew who worked in any aspect of publishing, whether in-house or freelance, to contribute a listing for the new directory. Within a few months, our numbers had grown to include publishers, managing editors, freelance editors, travel writers, copywriters, photographers, illustrators, translators, and more. Linda recommended her accountant, Millie, to be the group's financial secretary. *The South China Morning Post* heard about us and sent a reporter and a photographer to do a story.

We moved our monthly get-togethers to the Foreign Correspondents' Club. The directory became a monthly newsletter, with a featured member ('Woman at Work'), news and announcements of interest or relevance to our members, and updated directory listings.

WIPS was an outlet for my energy and initiative, and the newsletter helped Polly and me to showcase our services to potential clients. My role as initiator and coordinator of the group meant I had a growing public profile in the field where I earned my living. But more than that, the group felt like a comfort zone – a safe place I was creating around myself.

Liam arrived back in Hong Kong towards the end of 1991 on a ninety-day tourist visa. I was excited to have him move in with me. My workload was heavy, and I was still paying off my former partners, so time and money were tight. But he and I settled into a domestic routine that seemed to suit us both. He wasn't seriously looking for a job, though he scanned the classifieds.

'What about this one?' he would say. 'Managing director. Car and driver. Megabucks.'

'I don't think so …'

He showed me how to use the computer that had sat on my desk like a paperweight for the past two years. I finally figured out how the stove worked and made dinner for us. We smoked a little hash, shared a bottle of wine, watched TV and had sex. The hash and the hugs smoothed out the remaining edges that two glasses of wine on their own couldn't reach. I felt happy with Liam in my little inner-city bedsit. He was witty and fun. Although he wasn't in love with me, he was loving. Neither of us could picture a future together beyond these three months, but it was lovely to share with him simple daily routines, physical affection and laughter.

CHAPTER TEN

Though I'd not expected to have a long-term relationship with Liam, when he returned to Australia I missed the comfort of living with an easygoing man who was fun in and out of bed. To help fill the gap in my life that he left behind, I drank his share of our nightly bottle of wine as well as my own. *I'm not going back to the way I was,* I assured myself. *It's just until I get over my disappointment.* Besides, I was becoming very visible in my professional community and networks, and I needed to appear credible.

Polly and I had signed a lease on an office in a building on nearby Wyndham Street. An escalator was being built from Central up through the decayed residential areas on the southern fringe of Hollywood Road to the high-rise apartment blocks of Mid-Levels. New bars and restaurants were opening every week in the neighbourhood to cater for the overspill from the nightclub district of Lan Kwai Fong, just down the hill.

Our new office had access to an outdoor terrace. We furnished the unattractive expanse of concrete and exposed drainage pipes with beach chairs and a large, colourful umbrella. Polly had a *feng shui* expert come in to check the space's auspicious and inauspicious aspects, and performed rituals involving oranges and coins that were intended to ensure our good luck. I was amused that she believed in such things, but I wasn't going to tempt fate by scoffing at them. Lunchtimes, she would sunbathe on the terrace in a swimsuit. Soon, we were providing our combined editing and typesetting/layout services to other boutique publishing businesses that were springing up in our rapidly gentrifying neighbourhood.

Our business model was a co-working office with space for one or two extra freelancers whose skills complemented ours. We could offer our clients the extra services that were on hand without having any financial involvement. It was a much simpler and less stressful way to work than the editorial services company structure I'd had in 1989.

We kept a fully stocked bar and on Fridays invited our clients for drinks. The vicar from the cathedral (Polly's client) chatted with my client from the law journal. The flamboyant art-book publishers from our building (a joint client of mine with Frances, who had moved from corporate videos to freelance writing) talked with the editor of *HK* magazine (Polly's and my client), the new weekly what's-on tabloid put out by a WIPS member. Mary, who had joined us from Chancery Lane, invited people from the world of ESL (English as a Second Language) teaching. The latest publisher of the China and Hong Kong business books talked with Linda about her employment law journal, or with the crew from up the road who published books on the securities and hedge fund markets, or with one of his own authors, an academic from Hong Kong University I'd worked with. The crazy people from a new action sports magazine were in a huddle with the proprietor of Wanderlust, a nearby travel bookstore. An Australian photographer we knew through WIPS took pictures.

WIPS was also expanding, and we registered it as a society. Our membership had grown, and the newsletter was attracting attention. Committee meetings – I was the president and Polly the treasurer – were held on our terrace. I loved the new office, our innovative work set-up, and the swirl of energy around us.

'I think we're in the right place at the right time, Pol.'

It seemed I was okay, that I had survived, that I could justly hold my head high. I'd been given a reprieve in the past half-year and could now enjoy the changes that were happening in my professional life. The experience of living intimately with Liam had been healing. It had helped to pull me out of a steep dive and to level off. Perhaps the problem *didn't* lie in me if changes to my circumstances could have such a dramatic effect. I just needed to manage my drinking better whenever I started to feel stressed. No more than one bottle a night.

When an opportunity for a short break arose, I booked a berth on a slow boat to China. The small, mainland Chinese-run ship chugged north through the Taiwan Strait to where the Huangpu River that flowed through Shanghai entered the sea. My first-class cabin was tiny, the food in the dining room unappetising. There was nothing to see during the voyage, no one to talk with, and no on-board activities other than card games played for money in a noisy lounge. Not wanting to draw attention to myself as one of the few Western passengers, I stayed in my cabin and read a new book about Australia's notorious 'dingo baby' case.

On the last morning at sea, on what would be my third day without a drink, I woke to my alarm well before dawn and went on deck. As the sky gradually lightened, the squawking of sea birds filled the air. I could taste salt spray on my lips and feel the strong breeze whipping at my hair. I stood holding the railing, feeling fully alive. There was nowhere else I would rather be. I hadn't known that I would find this peace here, just as I hadn't known I would find it under a star-studded sky in an Indian desert, or by the shore of a Scottish loch, or on a peat moor on a Hebridean island.

There was something to be said for travelling. Somehow, I seemed to find myself in the places I needed to be.

After our vessel turned inland from the coast, the river was lined all the way to Shanghai with huge *go-downs* (warehouses) and container shipping terminals. The books I was editing on how to do business with mainland Chinese companies were about exactly this: manufacturing products in China for shipment to the world for sale.

I'm a part of all this, I thought. *I'm a cog in this huge machine.*

MY SISTER JOINED me on a ten-day holiday in Sri Lanka to mark my fortieth birthday. A civil war between the government and Tamil Tigers had been going on for nearly a decade, but we hardly gave it a thought. We'd never travelled together as adults. Our lives had diverged when we were teenagers.

We rendezvoused in Bangkok and flew the next day to Colombo, where we stayed at the colonial-era Galle Face Hotel. On an overpass across a busy stretch of road, we came across a family – a couple and a small child – who had made a home there from pieces of cardboard and other discarded items. The sight was distressing and I averted my eyes, embarrassed at the privilege of my life and everything I took for granted.

A car and driver ferried us around Sri Lanka's main sites. Each morning, we stopped at every denomination of shrine – Christian, Hindu, Buddhist – for the driver to offer prayers for a safe journey. He would then drive like a madman. In the back, we were too frightened to look at the island we had flown thousands of miles to see, sure that we were about to die in a head-on collision with an overcrowded bus. At the end of each day, we staggered from the car in search of alcohol.

LATE ONE AFTERNOON, I was editing an article for *Action Asia* magazine about hang-gliding in Thailand, or perhaps it was scuba diving in Borneo, when my phone rang.

'Fancy a drink?'

Bella operated a small publishing company from an office nearby. We'd become friends and often met for a drink after work.

'Give me 20 minutes.'

Relief coursed through me. Despite my best intentions not to drink more than one bottle of wine at night, I'd made inroads into a second one the night before. I'd had to drag myself through the day, feeling seedy, remorseful and anxious. I'd vowed to have some alcohol-free time, but Bella's invitation let me off the hook. It didn't cross my mind that I might visit a bar after work with a friend and order a non-alcoholic drink.

The problem with having one drink was that I then wanted to have a second one, followed by a third and then a fourth. A couple of hours later, after seeing Bella into a taxi, I called into a 7-Eleven store near my apartment. From a small selection of chilled wines, I chose a Portuguese *vino verde*.

'*Wah*, you drink so much,' said the proprietor as he rang up the sale. He recognised me as a regular customer.

Blood rushed to my face. 'We like to have wine with our dinner,' I said.

There *was* no 'we'. There *was* no 'dinner'.

I'm going to have to find a new convenience store.

CHAPTER ELEVEN

By the end of 1992, I'd built a career in Hong Kong that was a perfect fit. The projects I worked on were interesting and challenging. I was my own boss, working in a vibrant office environment. Polly and I felt in tune with the pulse of the city. I had everything I wanted, but I was falling apart on the inside. I was too embarrassed to confide in anyone my fears about the way I was drinking. Despite all my resolutions and self-imposed rules, my psychological dependence on alcohol had grown even when, for short periods, I could physically go without it. Whenever I'd managed either to string together a few wine-free days or not to exceed a set number of glasses, it had required all my willpower. Although it couldn't have been clearer that I'd crossed a line and was in trouble, I fought against admitting that alcohol was no longer a balm to soothe any problem but had itself become my main problem.

One Sunday morning, working alone in the office, I was marooned by a severe storm. The wind howled. Papers, vegetation and other flying debris buffeted the expanse of windows, and the sky turned a deep pink. I huddled under my desk, my arms around my knees, and prayed for the tempest that seemed a manifestation of my own inner turmoil to pass.

On New Year's Eve, home alone and determined to make a fresh start, I sipped slowly at what remained from a second bottle

I'd opened the night before. The small amount only made me feel jittery and anxious about going to bed under-medicated. Somehow, I fell asleep before the year turned to 1993.

Very few people were about when I walked to the office the next morning. The window-lined corridor on our floor overlooked Lan Kwai Fong, where I could see a huddle of white-robed monks. Later, on the evening television news, I saw that twenty partygoers had died in that crowded, narrow street at midnight. The stones were slippery from rain and spilled beer. People fell, couldn't get to their feet and were crushed by others. On the same night the year before, Liam and I had been caught up among the revellers there and I'd felt claustrophobic and anxious until we were clear of the crowds. The world around me seemed to be spinning out of control.

One night, I attended a work function with clients at a local university. My determination not to drink had lasted only a day or two. Wine was served and I drank two glasses. Once I'd had those, I wanted more. I planned to pick up a bottle on my way home in a taxi, but someone offered a lift to my door. I'd now either have to brave the knowing looks of the proprietor of the 7-Eleven near my home after I'd been dropped off, or go straight to bed without having a nightcap.

I made the excruciating choice to go upstairs, brush my teeth and call it a night. For the next hour, I tossed nervously, restlessly, unable to relax my breathing or my body. When I lay on my back, I panicked; sitting up, I began to hyperventilate. My breath came in shallow pants; my heart rhythms bounced all over the place. I thought I might have a heart attack. My mind was racing: *If I don't stay vigilant, I'll stop breathing and die.*

For the first time, I understood just how much fear and panic lay beneath the lid I was keeping precariously in place by anaesthetising myself every night. The two glasses of wine I'd had at dinner weren't up to the job that I required alcohol to do.

Frightened that either my heart or my mind would give out, I dressed, went downstairs to the street and hailed a passing taxi. 'Adventist Hospital, *m'goi.*'

I slid into the rear seat and clutched at the grab-strap. The attending doctor at Accident & Emergency asked a few questions, then knocked me out with an intravenous sedative. I left the next day with a prescription for the anti-anxiety medication Xanax.

For the next few months, I tried to numb myself with both alcohol and prescription meds. As my anxiety levels seemed to increase in parallel with my alcohol consumption, using alcohol to treat the anxiety only worsened the problem. The uncomfortable feelings that had fed my early addictions to sugar and fried food, then to sex, cigarettes and alcohol, lay somewhere deep beneath the anxiety that was now the most obvious manifestation of my discomfort in my own skin. I was in a vicious circle. It seemed like years since I'd associated alcohol with having fun. My drinking rituals were now so entrenched I rarely ever drank anything but white wine. Throwing a whisky and soda, vodka and tonic, or a beer into the mix would screw up my finely calibrated calculations about exactly how much I could have. To get the effect I needed, I had to keep myself nudged against a fine line. The temptation to go over the line was ever present and I couldn't always resist it.

I know that Polly sensed I was unhappy, but as I hadn't confided in her she was hesitant to pry. She didn't have the same restraint, though, when it came to my smoking in the office.

'It's very selfish, Robyn. Can't you go outside?'

The terrace was just metres from my desk, but I needed to smoke to tamp down my fears and didn't want to have to keep getting up. 'I'm a smoker, Pol. Smokers smoke.'

I huddled inside my skin, on edge. Unsure of the ground beneath my feet and fearing that I would topple over if I walked at a relaxed pace, I propelled myself forward when on the streets. Where Hong Kong's busyness had once enthralled me, it now seemed to be chaotic, out of control, verging on mayhem.

In an attempt to distract myself from my whirling headspace, I flew to Kuala Lumpur for a few days. The city's sights were a blur. My return flight was early in the morning, limiting how much I could drink the night before. But I feared that if I didn't numb myself enough to fall sleep, I would have another panic attack. I'd then need to take a Xanax and might sleep through my wake-up call.

Confused about how to medicate myself precisely, I spent the hours before dawn chain-smoking in the hotel's ground-floor public areas and trying to hold myself together. If I broke down, I didn't know what might come out. The dead-of-night quietness was broken only by the insistent whine of a floor polisher being pushed back and forth through the space.

At the airport departure gate, where there was no longer a risk that I might miss my plane, I took a full Xanax. It knocked me out for the duration of the flight, and on disembarking I stumbled like a drunk.

Not long after that trip, I had a dream. I was on the ground floor of a terrace house of a type I'd lived in in Sydney. A presence of some kind led me up a flight of stairs to a closed door. It seemed that I should open it and enter the room. I was initially hesitant. What would I find there? When I turned the door handle and stepped over the threshold, I had the sensation of the floorboards giving way beneath me in slow motion, and of being enveloped and supported in a blissful embrace, the safest of loving hugs. The brittle edges of me dissolved. The feeling that I was holding myself together by an effort of will fell away. I didn't have to try to control *anything*. It was how I imagined heaven might be.

After some time, I opened my eyes. The sun was bathing my small apartment in warmth. The dream lingered as a state of calm mixed with awe, a sense of acceptance, a promise of hope.

During the day, I thought about the experience and what it might mean. It had been so powerful. Was it simply a dream, or had it been a visitation of some kind? I decided that it meant I needed to take a step in my life that I feared and the outcome of which was unclear. It promised that I would find the support I needed; that I would be safe. I could see only one course of action that fit this interpretation.

'Robyn!'

Polly was shocked when I told her I was returning to Australia, abandoning our co-working office, our mutual clients, WIPS, and possibly even our friendship.

'We've just set everything up! Why do you want to leave? I thought Hong Kong is your home now!'

I had no explanation that made sense, that didn't disappoint and frustrate her. It was crazy just to walk away, but I believed I must. Hong Kong had been my home for seven years. In that time, everything in my life had changed; every cell in my body had been replaced. A habit of social drinking had become a dependency that was affecting my physical, mental and emotional health, but I was too ashamed to admit it to people who cared for me and to seek help. I'd always relied on myself, but I was no longer sure of who I was, of what was normal. I wanted to be in Australia, closer to my family, in case I split even further apart.

I had no idea what lay ahead. I knew only that it would take all my strength to start over again in Sydney. I was embarking on a new life from the lowest of ebbs. As I had done when I moved to Hong Kong, I would have to hit the ground running, making things up as I blindly sought a new path.

Removalists arrived to pack up my corner of the office and my flat: the rosewood bookcase I'd had made by a carpenter in 'Coffin Street', the Buddha statues and kilim rugs, the bed that I'd shared with Tom and with Liam, the hand-painted, black-lacquered furniture, the computer and hundreds of books.

Frances moved in and took over those of my clients who were a good fit with her business and that I couldn't continue to work with from Sydney.

The South China Morning Post again sent a reporter and a photographer. It seemed that my departure from Hong Kong, and from the society of women working in publishing that I had created with Polly, was news. I was proud that I would be leaving something behind, that my time there had made some sort of difference.

Friends and clients gathered for one last party on our office terrace. Perhaps the noise that rose into the autumn night was too loud for the disgruntled neighbour who threw a raw egg into our midst from an upper floor. The missile splattered on the concrete near my feet, a mess of yoke, slimy albumen and broken shell.

PART TWO

Mind the gap

CHAPTER TWELVE

The chequered pattern of the linoleum looked distorted from where I lay, my cheek pressed against the floor. An old friend had come for dinner the previous evening. We'd shared two bottles of wine. When he left, I'd made deep inroads into a third. I couldn't recall going to bed. Coffee grains, sugar granules and ceramic shards littered the lino. I'd been trying to spoon sugar into a mug, when my vision faded to black. The pulse in my head pounded.

What's happening to me?

The move to Hong Kong in 1986 had been a turning point in my life. I hadn't felt I was running away from anything, least of all from myself. The prods and nudges from the universe, the change of location in response to doors opening and opportunities presenting, seemed to be steering me towards my destiny.

Eight years later, the adventurous thirty-something who had landed on the coast of China with a suitcase and a typewriter was now forty-one, back in Sydney and filled with fear. I'd achieved everything I'd hoped for when I moved to Asia. I had much to be proud of. But something in me was cracking apart and threatening to put my shame – my self-sabotaging use of alcohol – on public view. I would have to find a way to put myself back together. The return to Australia had been intended to kickstart the change process, but I hadn't yet found the courage to take the first step.

At a client's Christmas party soon after my return, I drank a lot of champagne. Later, there were whisky nightcaps in a bar with a book designer. I'd broken my rule about sticking to wine. My speech began to slur.

'Time to call it a night.'

'Really?' My mouth turned down. It was a wrench to have to stop drinking.

The next day, I couldn't remember parts of the evening. What sort of impression had I made on people in my industry? Had I embarrassed myself?

Since then, I'd kept my head low. It was more prudent to drink alone at home. But I wasn't safe even there. From where I lay on the kitchen floor, I saw that I had fallen another rung down the ladder that led to hell.

I can't do this anymore.

I said the words again, aloud: 'I can't do this anymore.'

By my desk were two volumes of the Sydney phone directory. I found the number I was looking for. The phone rang just twice before someone answered.

'I have a problem,' I said.

'There's a solution,' I heard.

That evening, I walked to a church in my neighbourhood. In a meeting room, people were talking and laughing together, arranging chairs and exchanging hugs. I sat in the back and listened as men and women of all ages and backgrounds told their stories of what life had been like for them when they drank, what happened, and what it was like now. A businesswoman in her fifties spoke of the years she had spent getting up before dawn to groom herself so carefully that no one might suspect she ended each evening drunk and alone. She spoke not of a broken life, but of a broken spirit; not of disaster, but of despair.

My shoulders slowly relaxed. I uncrossed my arms. The people in this room had once been where I was now. They knew my remorse, my shame, my fear. And they told me that I didn't have to feel that way anymore.

'Come back,' they said.

Walking home, I understood that I couldn't continue to live the way I had been, trying and failing to manage how much I drank. I was willing to believe that there was a solution to my problem and that I'd taken an initial step in seeking it. I would need to delve deep, to try to understand the nature of my discomfort and dis-ease and why I was the way I was. But for now, I would just try not to drink.

I followed the advice I was given and went to a meeting every day. The routine helped to break time into chunks that I could grasp on to and that would keep me afloat. The reprieve felt both precarious and hopeful. I needed only to take each day as it came and not get ahead of myself. As one day followed another and I still didn't drink, my anxiety gradually diminished. I awoke clear-headed and free of regret. Mornings were no longer a black sludge that I had to force myself through. A week became a fortnight; one month turned to three.

I gave myself over to the fellowship I found in the rooms filled with people in all stages of addressing addictions such as mine. Sometimes, in a restaurant, my heart beat a little faster when I saw someone sip from a glass of wine, but the compulsion that had ruled my daily life in Hong Kong in recent years and during the first months back in Sydney had lifted.

The solution, I'd found, lay in attaching myself to a group of people who knew exactly how I felt, and in not trying to manage the third, fourth, fifth or sixth drink, but instead not having the first one.

JOBS HAD STARTED to come in from publishers. Those clients in Asia who weren't inconvenienced by my new location continued to send me work. Socially, I kept a low profile. I was no longer the woman I had been when I moved to Hong Kong, and my old friends had moved on, too. Where once we hung out in pubs watching bands, they were now married and raising children, or were deep into their careers, and I was spending my evenings with recovering alcoholics at twelve-step meetings.

After six months, I moved to an apartment on a clifftop at North Bondi, on the edge of the continent. I felt I deserved a treat, and while the rent was high, it was less than I'd been paying in Hong Kong for a renovated shoebox. Waves pounded the base of the cliff, shaking the building and speckling my picture windows with salt spray. There were views straight out to sea. It was beautiful. One morning, from my bed, I saw the plumes of migrating whales.

In August, on the weekend of the City to Surf fun run from the city centre to Bondi Beach, a close friend came for a visit. Janet and I had met in our first year of high school, when we were on the cusp of turning thirteen, and had looked out for each other ever since. We were standing on the corner of my street, watching the runners pass by on their final approach to the beach and the finish line. I'd run the event a couple of times in the early 1980s and knew how exhilarating it felt to reach this part of the course. Suddenly, I envied the people now jogging past me. I hadn't run since before the dark days descended in Hong Kong, but I recalled the sense of wellbeing – even, sometimes, of joy – it gave me.

'I'm going to start running again,' I said to Jan, and flicked my cigarette into the gutter.

Not today, but soon.

IN NOVEMBER, I flew to Queensland. An educational publisher at an industry event in Sydney had mentioned there might be part-time work available in their Brisbane office. A full-time in-house position didn't interest me, but this sort of arrangement would provide a financial cushion while allowing some time for freelance work. I'd returned to live in Sydney because it had once been my home, but I wasn't committed to remaining there. The meeting with the publisher went well. There would be work if I wanted it.

I'd been given the name of another contact in Brisbane and made a date with her for coffee. While we were chatting at a pavement café in the city, an acquaintance of hers stopped to say hello and she introduced me. I liked the look of him: salt of the earth, a bit rough around the edges, quiet.

The next afternoon, our paths crossed again. 'It's a small town,' he said. 'So, you're up from down south?'

'Just for a couple more days.'

We stood looking at each other. *Definitely fanciable.* After seven months without a drink, I knew I was looking better than I had in a while, without the furtive shiftiness of eye that meant I didn't want to be scrutinised too closely, and I held his gaze.

'What are you doing now?' he said.

'Nothing much.'

'I'm going over to Kangaroo Point. Wanna come?'

'Sure!'

We spent the afternoon together and a tug developed between us. 'There's a Jacuzzi at my hotel,' I said. 'Want to try it?'

'I won't say no to that.'

We drove to his house to pick up his swimming shorts. By the time we sank into the tub on the hotel rooftop, the sun was setting. I leaned back against the edge of the pool and stretched my legs out towards him. With his eyes on mine, he reached for my foot, raised it to his mouth and closed his lips around my big toe.

The next morning, he called in sick to work and we spent the day together. It had been a long time since a man had made me feel so desirable. Tom wasn't on the same planet as me; and though Liam had reappeared on the radar in recent months, our affair was casual. I suspected he was on the lookout for a mother for his future children, and that wasn't me. There was space in my heart for someone new.

When I returned to my clifftop perch in Sydney, the Brisbane guy phoned every day. Our conversations were awkward. We didn't know what to say to each other, except that we wanted to spend more time together. 'My lease is up next month,' I said. 'I could move to Brisbane. There's work I can do there.'

'Come to my home town for Christmas and meet my family,' he said.

I knew he had a young daughter living there. In that moment, I decided to relocate to Queensland. To mark yet another fresh start, I tore up the diaries I'd been keeping since the early 1980s. They revealed too much about me that I didn't want him to know.

In mid-December, removalists packed my belongings into boxes for the third time in just over a year, for the journey north. I would follow them after the holiday.

Within days of my arrival at his mother's house, it was apparent that he and I were ill suited in every way. We had nothing to talk about, no shared interests, differing views on just about everything. Why had I imagined that physical attraction alone might hold together a relationship between two people who had nothing in common? I hadn't had a drink in nine months, but I wasn't thinking like a sober person.

We'd been snapping at each other all morning at a local

scenic attraction, and by late afternoon things had gone further downhill.

'I'm going for a walk,' I said, bailing out.

He didn't respond.

In the town centre I found a beautiful art deco cinema.

'A ticket for whatever film is starting next, please.'

The opening minutes of *Pulp Fiction* pinned me to the back of my seat, and for the next two hours I forgot about my own predicament.

'You have to see the film I just saw,' I said, back at the house. 'It's incredible.'

He wasn't interested.

On New Year's Eve, he went out and I spent the evening with his mother, stroking her hand awkwardly while she talked about her daughter who had died of a drug overdose on this night some years before.

The next day, the mother was still grieving, the son was still angry with me, I was depressed, and the daughter was picking up the vibes from everyone and feeling anxious. It was an inauspicious start to 1995.

'I'm leaving,' I said. He was working on his car and didn't respond. I packed my bag, phoned for a cab, and said goodbye to his womenfolk. He didn't look up as the taxi pulled away.

At the airport, I was waiting to board my rebooked flight when I heard a small voice call my name.

'Dad's sorry.'

I picked her up and hugged her. He hung back. I was sorry, too. We weren't each other's *one*, but we could have been kinder to each other.

CHAPTER THIRTEEN

Everything I owned was now in storage in Queensland, awaiting a new home. I had no choice but to follow. What had I expected: that someone would come along out of the blue and be the perfect man for me? I would just have to brush myself off, get myself a good sunhat for the tropics, and start over again.

Brisbane was more affordable than Sydney, and the two-storey townhouse I rented in an inner-city suburb was spacious and comfortable. There were no views of whales, but the lushly landscaped gardens included a swimming pool. The local publisher gave me regular part-time hours. Couriers meant I could continue to work for my new Sydney clients and my remaining offshore ones. But instead of establishing routines that would help me to make the best of my new life, I fell into a rut.

I still wasn't drinking, but my mood was flat. I wasn't running – or even taking brisk walks – along the nearby riverside path, so there were no feel-good endorphins from exercise. I didn't seek out recovery meetings, where I might have made friends and experienced some sense of community. At the office, I made no attempt to get to know my colleagues and, inevitably, remained an outsider. Yet, walking to work, I resented the groups of people having breakfast together at pavement cafés. When I wasn't in the office, I isolated myself at home. Days would pass without my making any meaningful connection with another person. I went into the city only rarely: on Friday evenings for a meal or to see a film. Again, I wanted to be alone in order to wallow in loneliness. I stared at the television, hardly taking in what I was watching, and sipped at mugs of peppermint tea.

Even the woman who cleaned for me knew that I was adrift. 'Have you talked to anyone since last week?' Anna would ask, as she unwound the vacuum cleaner cord or ran a polishing cloth over the rosewood bookcase and the Buddha statues.

'Maybe. A courier?'

'You should get out more.'

IN FEBRUARY, LIAM phoned. 'I thought I'd come up for a visit. Should I?'

'Absolutely!'

And then, out of nowhere, I wanted to drink again; to have wine with dinner, to smoke a joint, to experience again the simple domestic and sexual pleasures we had shared in my bedsit in Hong Kong, to not feel my loneliness so acutely. Once I had the idea, I couldn't dislodge it.

After eleven alcohol-free months, I chose to forget that in the last couple of years of my drinking I'd had to hold myself together with gritted teeth. Again, I found myself playing the same mental tapes I'd played then: *If I can just drink moderately, I can have it both ways: I can have a couple of glasses of wine and not feel bad about it.* I didn't want drinking to be such a problem. It seemed so unfair that my preferred substance for lifting my mood or giving me relief from my feelings had become tempestuous, demanding and unpredictable. Why should alcohol be the boss of me? I would just try even harder to manage my drinking better.

Liam looked surprised when I opened a bottle of wine and poured glasses for us both to toast his arrival. He'd been just as surprised the year before when I'd quit.

'When did you start drinking again?'

'Now,' I said, and raised the glass to my lips.

For the four days of his visit, I was happy to be with him and to drink wine with him at dinner. We weren't in love, but we knew how to enjoy each other. I found him sexy and amusing. He cared for me and was an ally, and that was enough.

Soon, I was again opening a bottle of wine every evening to drink on my own. As before, I awoke feeling seedy and regretful; and then, within hours, I'd be planning to do it again. The anxiety that had once been a constant companion returned.

Unable to see my way forward, I asked my childhood friend Janet to visit and help me decide what to do.

'I think you should come back to Albury, Rob,' she said. We were walking into town along the riverside path. 'You're not very strong at the moment. You need your family and old friends around you.'

Was my fragility so apparent? The air seemed oppressive with the threat of rain.

'Shit.'

CHAPTER FOURTEEN

Albury was the last place I had imagined calling home again. My life was meant to be going forward, not backward. I hadn't given up Hong Kong just to move back to the town I couldn't wait to leave as a teenager. It held too many complicated memories. Every night, the Sydney-bound train had passed by the end of our street. As it gathered speed for the journey north, its whistle had called to me. Sydney was where I imagined my real life would begin.

While in high school, I'd studied every morning and evening to give myself the best chance of winning a scholarship that would give me freedom and independence. I found at school the affirmation that was lacking at home. My father rarely offered encouragement or praise. Success at something meant only that the bar had been set too low. His approval and love seemed always out of reach. My mother's love felt distracted and was tinged with bewilderment. Where had I come from? We were so different.

I had resented that my father's authority over me was absolute – that his discipline was physical, harsh and unpredictable – and that my mother couldn't intercede. Dad had only to suspect that one of us children had misbehaved or been disobedient and he would grab the cane-handled duster from beside the fridge, pursue us into the confined hallway of our small suburban house, and repeatedly whack with the cane at our legs and bodies until he had vented rage that had nothing to do with us. It took many years for me to understand that he was a man of his time, a victim of his own upbringing, perpetuating what he had known.

Some version of 'love' lay beneath my dad's actions, but I missed feeling it. I was always vigilant. Even when he was in a jovial mood and all seemed calm, he could tip into a rage without warning. I learnt early to try to assess situations and defuse threats. The absolute nature of my father's authority over all of us, my mother included, not only created fear, but also offended my sense of what was fair and just. *When I grow up, I won't let anyone control me.* Until then, I would have to get by in whatever way I could: by trying to fill the empty space inside with approval and affirmation at school, and with the thick milkshakes and greasy potato cakes I stuffed myself with on my way home afterwards.

Mum, too, wasn't without a psychic load to bear. She had grown up with a war-damaged father and a long-suffering mother. She was a typical housewife of the 1950s and 1960s, supported by a husband who felt entitled, by his status as breadwinner, to be the boss of everyone under his roof. She must have tried to intercede for us in private, but she had little power in her marriage. Mum found her agency and her strongest sense of self in sport. She excelled at any physical activity she took up: football and running as a child; squash, golf, waterskiing, canoeing, hiking and bowls as an adult. She was fearless physically, but otherwise lacked self-confidence.

Even before I was five, just after my youngest brother, Col, was born, I knew my role in our family: I was the 'peacemaker', Mum's 'helper', the 'self-reliant one'. My mother's hands were full with looking after two toddlers and a baby, and with managing our house to my father's critical standards. She had no hand available for me to hold, and my father's hands were for punishing or working or driving. Mum did what she could for me in many practical ways. She made me my favourite meals, sewed clothes for me, picked me up in the dark and rain on winter Mondays from after-school ballroom dancing classes. But she needed me to be low maintenance. She didn't have anything spare to give. In the evenings, she sought relief from her own feelings by staring at the television and crunching on ice cubes.

Our family may have been no different from any other in our working-class street: young, poorly educated parents with their own emotional baggage trying to figure out how to raise their kids, pay their bills and have a bit of fun occasionally. You just got on with things and found enjoyment where you could. Mum's two sisters lived locally with their families, and we all grew up together. We all learnt to waterski out at the lake not far from town, went camping together during the long summer holidays, and partied at the drop of a hat.

The year I turned fourteen, we lived in New Zealand for twelve months, crowded into a tent during the warmer seasons and into a small tourist cabin in the winter. I went to a girls' high school, where I was streamed into a general, non-academic class and came first in all my subjects. Success felt good. Donovan's song 'Mellow Yellow' and the Beach Boys' 'Good Vibrations' were all over the radio, and a boy called Butch taught me how to kiss.

The many happy times in my childhood and teenage years moderated the effects of the difficult ones. But damaged people damage people, and I, too, emerged from childhood a damaged person, if a resourceful one. My character was formed in part by the perception that love was elusive and life somehow unsafe.

Those years spent growing up in Albury taught me that, if I wanted more than my mother's life, a different future from hers, I would have to create it for myself. I learnt that I was bright enough to achieve some success if I worked hard. I learnt to make my own fun, to comfort myself, to hold my own hand. Books were places I could disappear into and imagine other ways to live. When I formed a neighbourhood group with eight local kids that I called The Rainbow Club, I was creating a community around me in the same way I would do many years later in Hong Kong with women who worked in the publishing industry.

It had been a turning point in my life when I could finally venture out on my own into a larger world. Now I was facing the prospect of returning to my home town in my middle years, still alone, because I hadn't been able to find a way to live happily with myself in Hong Kong or Sydney or Brisbane. And yet, something in me perked up at the prospect of another move – *any* move. Brisbane had shown me that I didn't need to be in the same city as my clients, and Albury would be no different. Plus, it would be cheaper to rent there. And Janet was right: maybe I did need my family and old friends around me at this time. My sister, Deb, and brothers Geoff and Col were there with their families. My mother had returned there from New Zealand after her marriage to my father had finally broken down. And I counted Jan's family as mine.

'Maybe just for a year,' I said to my oldest friend. 'Until I get back on my feet.'

I knew that my problems would accompany me, but for the moment there seemed no better solution.

CHAPTER FIFTEEN

Albury had grown up since I'd moved away, but I felt that I had grown more. I wasn't seriously considering making it my long-term home; I'd just catch my breath there.

A twin city with Wodonga on the Murray River, it had a pretty downtown area and an expanse of leafy suburbs. A major regional hub between Sydney, Canberra and Melbourne, with a population now double what it had been when I left at eighteen, it serviced the farming communities of the Riverina district. People mostly made their own fun with friends they'd known for a lifetime. Many of my extended family still lived locally and I had memories embedded all over the place.

'I've found a flat that might suit you,' my sister said in a phone conversation as I was packing up my Brisbane life. 'It's out near us. But wouldn't you rather be closer to town?'

'It'll be fine.' I wanted to wrap my family around me like a security blanket. 'I'll get a bike.'

My new home was in a complex of eight single-storey townhouses arranged around a common area with a swimming pool, pergola and barbecue facilities. I set up an office in the second bedroom facing the pool, signed on with a local internet provider (the internet was the latest thing), and got to work on creating yet another new life.

It was a world away from Hong Kong's grimy streets, rattling trams, neon restaurant signs and congested road systems. It bore no resemblance to any place I'd lived since I'd left suburbia for bohemia in 1971. There were no Asian grocery stores, no antiquarian bookstores presided over by ponytailed, greying poets, no basement art-house cinemas or poky coffee houses. The wide suburban streets I cycled on my way to the supermarket were lined with single-family brick or fibro homes of the type I'd been raised in, or with low-rise blocks of flats. Two or three cars would be parked in the driveway, under a carport or angled across a scratchy patch of front lawn. Flowering shrubs added dabs of colour, gum trees a touch of magnificence. The light traffic noise was punctuated with the rhythmic sputtering of garden sprinklers, the whine of lawnmowers, the ascending calls and chattering of magpies, the barking of dogs.

Near an ugly shopping mall was a strip of small businesses – accountants, banks, dental surgeries, fast food franchises, medical practices. A family-style pub offered poker machines, Sunday roasts and meat raffles. Town – with its shops, cinema, art gallery, library, and a museum on the river foreshore – was about 5 kilometres away.

Family and a few old friends were bemused by my return to the fold. None of them expected I'd want to stay, but they were welcoming in their laconic way. A card for my forty-third birthday from my cousin Dianne predicted a possible outcome: 'She came. She criticised. She left.' I thought it was hilarious. And despite my initial reluctance, the move back to the country proved to be a tonic. I felt invigorated – even excited – by the new challenge.

When summer arrived, my brother Col, sister-in-law Tracey, and nieces Cassie and Chloe often hung out by the pool at my place. In my garage were floaties and my new bicycle. I arranged for a fitness instructor I'd met at the nearby gym to hold water aerobics sessions at home and roped in Mum, her sister Audrey, Tracey and the girls, and some of the neighbours. We followed Julie's instructions and tried to synchronise our underwater leg kicks to Donna Summer singing 'I Will Survive' while spluttering with laughter.

There were barbecues in the pergola and a sit-down Christmas lunch. I drank at every social get-together with my family, but that was to be expected and there were no embarrassing incidents. I began to believe that I had turned a corner; that maybe I could drink and yet still be at peace with myself. The recovery group in Sydney had kept me sober for eleven months, but I'd been alone then and had come off a low bottom. Now that I was back in the family fold, enjoying my small routines in the suburbs, busy working on interesting jobs – now that I was *happier* – perhaps I could manage things better.

I tried not to recall too clearly my long relationship with alcohol. But if I were honest with myself, I would have seen that I'd behaved alcoholically from my teenage years. My first drinks, at around thirteen, were a Pimms with lemonade at the apartment of an older friend's art teacher, and brandy in a sugar-crusted glass at a coffee lounge to celebrate the same friend's sixteenth birthday. There was no responsible service of alcohol in those days. Once, on a school excursion to Canberra, Janet and I shoplifted miniatures of vodka and whisky. The next morning, the empty bottles lay scattered on the lawn outside our motel room where we had thrown them, thinking we'd lobbed them over a hedge. At teenage parties I drank port and lemonade and petted heavily with cute boys a year or two older.

At university, I was a scholarship student, with goals that kept me mostly on track with my classes, assignments and preparations for exams. The dollars I earned by typing up essays for my college mates and fixing their spelling, grammar and punctuation covered my bill for Saturday afternoon drinks in a nearby hotel beer garden. On long solitary walks around the suburbs on Sundays, I binged on sugary snacks. When I drank at college balls, I got drunk; when I was with friends who were smoking marijuana, I never passed up a joint; and after I finally had sex for the first time, I had sex every time.

In the mid-seventies, when I had graduated and was starting my career in publishing, weekends revolved around drinking, seeing bands, and getting stoned at parties in the share houses of people I didn't know. I'd sit on the floor, my back against a wall, listening to concept albums by Pink Floyd and Genesis and feeling too paranoid from the hash to move. One hot summer afternoon, I passed out on someone's lawn after drinking a bottle of Cointreau. When I was well into my career, I didn't return to the office one day when lunch with a friend turned into a drinking session. The next morning, nauseous from a sangria hangover, I dragged myself into work for a meeting I couldn't reschedule. The author and I were at my desk when bile rose into my throat. I made it to the loo in time to spill my guts into the toilet bowl and not over him and his manuscript.

I used whatever drugs the man I was with at the time was using: marijuana, hash, speed, acid, mandies and, in the early 1980s, cocaine. I didn't want to be left on my own, outside of the headspace the drugs took *him* to.

If my drinking and drugging past was any gauge, my problem with using an addictive substance to cope with living in my own skin hadn't started with the stresses I experienced in Hong Kong. I had just reverted to type. The problem started with *me* and had always done so.

ONE MORNING EARLY in the new year, a few months after I returned to live in Albury, I saw that I'd drunk another bottle of wine by myself after an evening of steady drinking at a family barbecue. I couldn't remember getting home. I'd been managing things well, I thought, but the beast had only been biding its time. If I couldn't remember the last part of an evening, couldn't remember what I had said or done, what must I have looked like to my family, whose love and good opinion were important to me? No one had mentioned my drinking, but I felt guilty and ashamed.

I found a recovery group in town, but I couldn't stick with it. I would go to a few meetings and not drink, and then relapse. It was embarrassing to keep fronting up and having to admit I was on day one again.

What I needed was a plan B.

CHAPTER SIXTEEN

I put on my trainers and started to jog again. Being able to run for an hour at a comfortable pace had always given me much more than just the benefits of being physically fit: my moods were more even, and I felt less agitated. A fitness regimen required self-discipline, but it offered tangible rewards (measurable progress towards achieving meaningful personal goals) in exchange for forgoing something else I wanted (wine). I loved the social aspects of running, too. I was simply happier when I was running regularly than when I wasn't. Now that I felt part of a community again, I was ready to make healthier choices that would help me to moderate those parts of my life where I lacked discipline.

My townhouse became the starting point for an occasional group jog through the nearby streets in the early evening with my brother-in-law, Steve, his mate Robert, fitness instructor Julie and a neighbour, Giulio.

Soon, I was running four mornings a week around the local streets with Giulio or Robert. The prospect of a dawn date with an attractive man who made me laugh saw me in bed at a reasonable hour with a book and up again in time for a quick shower and a squirt of Chanel before our rendezvous. The new routine did the trick. Despite the hiccup at the start of the year, I was up off my knees and on my feet within six months of moving back to Albury, instead of the year I'd predicted to Janet.

IN A RUNNING magazine, I read about an online community called the Dead Runners Society. I found their website, joined as 'Robyn from Oz', and was instantly addicted to the daily digests of postings from other DRS members. In the evening, I read updates from my new online friends while drinking just a couple of light beers. It was sufficient alcohol to signal I could now relax, but it didn't send me down a rabbit hole, like wine did. A vet from the American Midwest wrote about the difficulties of training during the frozen winter months. John 'The Penguin' Bingham described in his posts and in his book *The Courage to Start: A Guide to Running for Your Life* what it meant to him to call himself a runner. Jo, from Auckland, made me laugh with a post about sloppy punctuation: 'It's its, not it's.' Karl in California, Vida in Canada, Jim in Arizona, Chris in Texas who started the group in 1992, became my online running family.

By May, when Albury's signature race, Nail Can Hill, came around, I was obsessed with running. I was eating healthy meals, staying clear of rabbit holes, and mostly bludging the few cigarettes I allowed myself. Sometimes, late at night, I buckled and phoned for a taxi to home-deliver a packet of Benson & Hedges Extra Mild from the pub a kilometre away. The small pool of local taxi drivers soon knew me.

Nail Can was a difficult course that went straight up to the top of the spine of hills on the western side of town, along an undulating fire trail, and then down to the Murray River. It had been over a decade since I'd last taken part in a running event, and I was surprised when I placed fourth among the veteran women in the race.

A week later, I set up a meeting with John, a personal trainer with sculpted arms and thighs. I didn't doubt he had serious abs.

'What are your goals?' he said.

'I want to see what I could do if I trained properly. Run a half marathon. Maybe even a full one ...' I was surprised to hear the words come out of my mouth.

'Do you have a marathon in mind?'

'Honolulu?' I'd seen some of the Deads on the DRS list talking about it.

John pursed his lips. 'That's in December, right?'

'Yep.'

'And your longest run up to now has been ...?'

'Fifteen kilometres.'

He thought for a moment. 'It's possible – *if* you do the work. We'd need to add weights and include some swimming and cycling for cross training. If you're serious, you could be ready in time.'

'I'll be forty-four this year. I want to set some big goals.' I didn't mention that I was trying to use a positive addiction to keep a negative one in check. 'So, you'll take me on?'

Soon, I was swimming lengths or lifting weights at the gym and running intervals at a local track to improve my speed. My long runs around the suburban streets grew steadily longer. Giulio or Robert or Julie, or Col on my bike, would join in for part of the way to keep me company. I started to see more of my town as I ventured further from home base, and to notice how it had changed – or not – since I'd moved away a quarter-century before.

To sharpen up, I entered 10K races around the region and placed high among women in my age group. I shared my marathon preparation with the Dead Runners in frequent posts to the mailing list, and in private chats off-list with a growing number of new friends in America. I added a weekly massage to my routine. I was sleeping like a log, and getting up before dawn to head out for another run that I could tick off my training program.

The move back to Albury had helped me to manage *me*. I still sometimes drank too much at a family party, or at a barbecue at Janet and her husband Peter's house, but I was usually able to back away from the edge of the precipice. Something had shifted since I'd resumed running and had started to set goals and visualise outcomes.

By October, I was set to attempt my first official half marathon – 21.1 kilometres. Julie and I ran together at a relaxed pace until about the halfway point. 'Go on,' she said. 'I'll see you at the finish.'

My body took over, pumping out the final 10K seemingly effortlessly, carrying me so lightly it felt like I was just along for the ride. With a few hundred metres to go, I took back the reins, lengthened my stride, pumped my arms and crossed the finish line in a time of 1 hour and 47 minutes.

The following month, I was invited to make up a team of two runners in the Brindabella Classic, a race held just outside of Canberra. The course was 53.8 kilometres from Mt Ginini down to a reserve at its foot. My teammate ran the first 26.5 kilometres, and I ran the rest. We placed first in our category and broke the course record for a two-woman team. *Yay, us!*

I was proud of my achievements as a runner. Running with friends was fun, and goal setting had itself become addictive. The payoff for my persistence and determination was discovering that I had an unexpected ability as a veteran competitor. I'd found a way to pat my own back.

ON THE SUNDAY of the marathon in Hawaii, I was up by around 4 am for a shower and breakfast. It was still dark when

I joined the thousands of runners streaming through the streets towards the assembly point. We each had our own reasons for being there. We'd set ourselves a goal that had challenged us to do things differently, to be a different person, to be our best selves. Not too long before, I was so ill at ease in my skin, so ungrounded, I literally couldn't feel the earth beneath my feet.

At the start of the race, I jiggled my legs to loosen them and tried to ignore a tinge of claustrophobia as runners pressed against me from all sides. The horn sounded and we were away. Fireworks exploded overhead. I was too busy watching where I put my feet to see much of the display. There were 24,000 runners and, mindful of the New Year's Eve crush in Hong Kong of a few years before, I didn't want to fall and be trampled by half of them.

At the turnaround point at Diamond Head, I felt focused and strong. In the final part of the course, after a rain shower cleared and the sun came out, a rainbow formed over Kapiolani Park, the end of the race. I knew then that I would make it. Tears were mixed with sweat and raindrops on my cheeks as I made the final turn, reached for my last reserves of energy and surged across the finish line.

After a champagne brunch with the other Dead Runners who had gathered from the US, Japan, Canada and Western Australia, I bought a packet of cigarettes. At dinner, which I ate alone in a restaurant near my hotel, I drank white wine and smoked.

As I'd been vigilant and mostly 'good' for the past six months, I decided I deserved to let my hair down for one night to celebrate my achievement. I ordered a fourth glass of chardonnay. But dehydration, nicotine and alcohol proved a toxic mix. By the time I stumbled into bed, I'd lost confidence that I knew who I was in my core. How could I be both a disciplined and goal-focused athlete and someone who was seemingly powerless over a compulsion to numb myself with alcohol and cigarettes? Were all my addictions just different manifestations of the same thing – an attempt to fill the empty space inside of me?

CHAPTER SEVENTEEN

Perhaps I still thought that a man might fix me. I had sought my whole life, in all sorts of inappropriate places, a loving male who might fill the vacuum created by a father whose love and approval always felt precarious and conditional. The internet seemed as good a place to find him as any other.

For some months I'd been exchanging emails with a runner I 'met' through an online chat group. He was an expatriate living in Asia, intelligent and well read, and unattached. The photos he sent were unclear; there was the suggestion of a strong profile – like a Renaissance nobleman. We had agreed to meet in New Zealand for a road trip at the start of 1997. He would pay for the hire of a car, we would share the cost of food and fuel, and I would pay for accommodation if we weren't camping.

I had a fantasy that he might turn out to be someone I could sink into and trust with my heart, my body and my soul. Should it prove to be so, I would happily uproot myself and live wherever in the world he wanted to be.

When my taxi from Christchurch Airport pulled up at the hotel, my palms were itchy from nerves.

'I'm in the lobby,' I said, when he picked up the room phone.

'Hurry. I have a surprise for you.'

The door of our room was ajar. The lights were low. I walked into the small hallway. There was no sign of him in the bedroom.

'Where are you?'

I retraced my steps and saw, in the recess between the hallway and the bathroom, a tall, naked man with an erection.

'Welcome to New Zealand,' he said, and lunged at me.

I'd hoped for lots of sex, but I hadn't expected quite so much flesh to be on display at our first meeting and so few preliminaries. *I haven't even had a good look at him yet* ... Still, he was giggling, and no alarm bells were ringing in my head (not that *that* meant anything), so I went for it. The next morning, I could see his face more clearly. It wasn't a look I would normally find very appealing.

We went for a run together through the public gardens. He seemed reluctant to wind his pace back from what to me was a sprint. Whenever I stopped to catch my breath, he paused the timer on his watch.

After a swim in the hotel pool, we showered and then drove into town in the rent-a-wreck he had hired.

'There's a cathedral tour starting soon,' he said.

'Could we eat first? I'm really hungry. I haven't had anything since breakfast yesterday.'

'But I've booked us on this tour.'

'Oh. Okay.'

The Anglican cathedral, which dated back to the mid-1800s, was beautiful, and it was a good idea to take the tour with a knowledgeable guide, but by the time we emerged into the square, a ravenous, weasel-like creature with sharp claws had taken up residence in my belly.

'I really need some food.'

He was looking at some notes he'd made. 'There's a café in the botanic –'

'Fine,' I cut in. 'Let's go.'

He paid for my sandwich and whatever was the daily special. 'What's next on the itinerary?'

'I thought we'd go paddling on the Avon.'

Apparently, it was my turn to pay.

It was actually rather pleasant on the river. The weather was glorious and there were a lot of punters about. He even did half the paddling.

We chatted, but there was no chemistry. Although he was fit, I didn't find him physically attractive. He pontificated and had yet to make me laugh.

'Fancy an ice cream?' I asked. Perhaps some sugar would lift my mood.

We found a dairy and he bought himself a double-headed cone. I chose a scoop of hokey-pokey and joined him outside where he was sitting on a retaining wall in the sun. He had a smudge of strawberry ice cream on the end of his nose. I started to feel a little ill. *Maybe I'm just tired. Yesterday was a big day. I didn't sleep much. I've run and swum and rowed. I need some time out.*

He consulted his list. A must-see scenic attraction some distance from town was next on the agenda.

'You go,' I said. 'Drop me back at the hotel and I'll have a nap.'

He looked flustered. 'That won't work.'

I hardly spoke as we drove out of town to a cable car that took us up to an information centre and viewing platform on the crest of a bluff. 'Great view,' I conceded.

'Let me get you a coffee.' He surprised me by reaching for his wallet, from which he extracted a coupon for a free coffee at this very attraction. The coupon was provided by our hotel, which I was paying for.

When we came down from the mountain, I insisted that I have something decent to eat.

'But we don't have time,' he said. 'I've booked a Maori concert and it starts in an hour. Do you have $20 for your ticket?'

We ended up getting a couple of falafel wraps in a dingy place on a busy highway.

Towards the end of the concert, he was among the audience members invited to join the performers in a traditional Maori *haka*, or war dance. I wouldn't have done any better in his shoes, but as I watched his awkward movements, I slumped further in my seat. *I am not with this guy.*

Later that night, when I awoke, he wasn't in the bed I'd reluctantly shared with him.

'I was arranging things in the car,' he said the next morning.

As we drove out of Christchurch towards the hills in the distance where we were entered in an orienteering event, I suspected that I'd dug a sizeable hole for myself. I had flashbacks to two years before, when I was stuck with someone I'd pinned my hopes on but soon found I didn't even like.

Orienteering involves using a compass to follow the clues given on a map as to the whereabouts of a number of small flags. At each flag is a hole-punch provided to mark a card. The winner is the first person to finish with all the checkpoints punched on their card.

As we proceeded through the course, running from flag to flag, my dislike of this guy I'd tethered myself to intensified. At one point, we had to do an out-and-back leg to one of the flags. 'You go,' I said. 'I'll wait here.' I needed some time out.

'But you won't get your punch!'

My expression must have conveyed what I thought about that, because he shrugged and ran off.

I lay down on the grass and looked up at the sky. *Hey, universe! What am I going to do now? I'm supposed to spend two weeks with this anal-retentive dickhead. I'm in the middle of nowhere. All my stuff is in the car.*

I abandoned the course and found my way to the tents where the finishers and their supporters were gathering. I was on a mission. In the crowd, unexpectedly, I spotted a woman I had met at an event in Albury, who agreed to give me a lift back to Christchurch.

'Oh, you're an *angel*. Thank you! I'll just go and get my stuff.'

'What happened to you?' he said, when I arrived at the car.

'I ditched it.'

'But you can't do that. If you don't officially finish, they'll think you're lost.'

'Listen, mate. I ditched it. And I'm ditching *you*. I'm aborting this holiday.'

He looked shocked. 'You *can't* pull out ... I've already paid for your ticket for the boat cruise on Milford Sound!'

I spent the night – only my third in the country since I'd arrived late on the Monday with a head full of dreams – drinking alone in my room at a budget motel near the airport and wondering if I would ever get my life right.

By the next afternoon, I was back in Sydney. Sunglasses shielded my bloodshot eyes from the summer glare as I lined up on the tarmac with other passengers waiting to board a small plane that would take me home to Albury. The aircraft appeared to be rocking in the strong sea breeze, and I kept shuffling backwards to allow other passengers to board ahead of me. Finally, I was the last one remaining at the foot of the steps.

'I can't do it,' I said to the flight attendant, who was standing by and gripping her hat. Her neckerchief flapped horizontally.

'I can't fly today.'

'You're sure?'

'Yes. I'm sorry.'

'No worries,' she said. 'We'll offload your bag.'

Ten minutes later, I was in the office of a representative of the regional airline changing my flight to the next day.

'You're anxious about flying?'

'Today, yes.'

'You know you can get counselling for that?'

'I'll keep it in mind.'

I REMAINED UNSURE of my footing through 1997. Without a new running goal, I wasn't training regularly. My internet romance had blown up in my face. No fantasy lover had appeared at my door, backlit by the sun and offering to be my hero.

In July, I attended a function hosted by the Chinese Chamber of Commerce in Melbourne to mark Hong Kong's return to China. The date had seemed far off in the future when I first fell under Hong Kong's spell in 1985; now, here we were already. *Life can slip away so quickly,* I thought. *I can't just wallow.*

'I'm going to move into town,' I said to my sister, when the lease on my flat came up for renewal. 'I need a change.'

'I didn't think you'd last long out here.'

'I'm not leaving Albury. Just the 'burbs.'

The logistics of creating a new home gave me a shot of energy, something to focus on. I enjoyed rearranging my possessions in a different space and replacing the daily rituals I'd developed in my old place with new ones to suit my new circumstances. It was similar to the principle I tried to apply whenever I had computer problems: unplug everything and reboot the system.

My new home was a two-storey townhouse half a block from the main street. I went to exhibitions and openings at the art gallery. The director contracted me to edit some papers from a museums conference and invited me to join the citizens' advisory committee. Through the gallery, I met other staff and local photographers, artists and collectors. I went to the cinema two or three times a week. My cultural needs were now being better met, but physical exercise had fallen by the wayside. And if I wasn't a runner, I reverted to being a drinker, with all the remorse and anxiety that went with it.

At the end of August, Princess Diana and her lover Dodi Fayed died in a Paris car crash. I watched television coverage of Diana's troubled life, which had ended so abruptly. It was a good excuse to mourn my dashed hopes for my own life, to let flow the tears that seemed to spill over from a deep well. I talked with a counsellor, who prescribed an anti-depressant. 'You're very hard on yourself,' she said.

I started again to attend recovery support meetings. One slogan became my mantra: *One day at a time*. I could relate it to running a marathon: the distance from where I was to where I wanted to be might seem interminable, but it was possible to get there if I proceeded one step at a time.

But it was hard to do it in practice. For the next six months, I was again in and out of the program. I'd be off the booze for a week or two, start to feel good, think that if I tried harder I should be able to drink moderately (*No more than three glasses a day*, I told myself), fail to stick to my self-imposed limit, feel like crap, try again to stop … repeat cycle.

How do normal people manage just to have one or two drinks, or none, and not be bothered? Why is it such a struggle for me? Why can't I do that?

CHAPTER EIGHTEEN

What was it about a new year that would see me pin my hopes yet again on a man to rescue me? This time, it was someone I'd known in real life for more than two decades.

'Hi.'

Just one syllable, but I knew instantly who it was. In 1974, when my flatmate in Sydney introduced me to the manager of the wine bar where she worked, he leaned across and kissed me full on the mouth. After the bar closed, he gave me a lift home, where I vomited into the gutter the cider and orange juice I'd been drinking all night. Not long afterwards, he moved in. After a tumultuous year, he returned to his marriage and his life resumed its original course.

We had stayed in loose contact during the intervening decades, but there had always been the fact of the marriage, and then of his children. We'd never really had an opportunity to see what we had. Now that he was on his own, we would try living together, we decided. The removalist who had moved me into the centre of town from the suburbs packed up my life again and set it down 400 kilometres away.

Four months later, the same firm moved me back to Albury. 'It's not you; it's me,' I said, handing over my set of keys to the house we'd shared for one winter. I hadn't been able to stay sober and I didn't want a witness.

'I'm going to save for a deposit on a house and put down some roots,' I said to Janet. 'All this moving is crazy, and so expensive. I'm getting whiplash. Maybe if I settle down, I'll get my act together.'

Six months later, she and I were standing in front of a 1930s-era, red-brick bungalow on which I'd made an offer to the real estate agent after it was passed in at auction. Situated just across the railway line at the eastern end of the main street, it had three bedrooms, a large living area, front and back yards, and fully established gardens with rose bushes and azaleas. This type of house – a family home on a quarter-acre block – had been foreign territory to me since I was eighteen.

The agent approached us. 'The owner's told me to sell it to the redhead.'

I looked at him blankly.

'That's you!' Jan said, elbowing me in the side. I'd had a henna colour put through my hair but hadn't yet adjusted my self-image.

'I've bought a house?'

'Yes, darling, you have. And we should celebrate. Come for tea tonight.'

That evening, I was chatting in Jan's backyard with Bill, her brother-in-law. I'd known him, and Jan's sister Barb, for a quarter of a century.

'Congratulations, Robbie,' Bill said, topping up my wine glass with a local chardonnay.

'It hasn't sunk in yet.'

'Bill!' Barb called from the back door. 'Come and take some plates out to the table for me, darl.'

'Now that you've bought a house,' Jan said, when we sat down to eat, 'you should get a cat.'

'I have a hard enough time just looking after myself!'

IN EARLY 1999, I found evidence of mice in the kitchen pantry of my new home. The solution to the problem, as Jan had predicted, was a cat. I named her Vita, after the eccentric English writer Vita Sackville-West.

There were flowerbeds to tend, rose bushes to prune, ivy to cut back and lawns to mow. It was the type of house where normal people might live. Perhaps I could pass for one? I got help with the yard and the house, and worked hard to pay for it all.

A client asked me to adapt a Canadian book for beginning runners who wanted to be able to jog 10 kilometres. I'd hardly run since the marathon two years before and welcomed the commission as a timely kick in the butt. But I needed to test the book's program on a novice.

'I'll try it,' said Barb. 'But I can't see me ever running 10K.'

'That's why you're perfect for this. It's a test of the program, not of you. We'll just follow what the book says and see what happens.'

We worked out a schedule of morning walking sessions that gradually introduced more and more running. It was the same principle as the 5K training program I'd used with Sarah in Hong Kong more than a decade before. I interviewed nutritionists, podiatrists, sports medicine practitioners and other runners, to give the book some Australian content. Right on schedule, to Barbara's shock, she jogged 10 kilometres at a steady pace.

'You did it!'

'Yeah, but I'm not doing it ever again! I'm happy to walk. You're the one that needs to run.'

I didn't seem able to maintain a routine on my own, though. And if I wasn't running, the wheels kept falling off the bus. A mood spell or a social event would tip me back into my old habits.

If I'd been drinking the night before, I would take an

inventory the next morning, apprehensive about what I might find. Sometimes I couldn't explain why things were as I found them. Why were the shoes I had been wearing lined up neatly under the bed in the second, spare bedroom? Why were all the lights on? Why had I put on a load of washing during the night? *Oh* ... I remembered that I'd stumbled to the loo with my eyes closed, but found when I opened them that I was sitting on the cane clothes basket in the laundry.

Vita's sex life was more active than mine and soon there were kittens. Brenda, who cleaned for me, took one. Janet took another, and I kept the third, which I named after Polly. Vita had watched by my side when I buried, with some ceremony and solemnity, the body of her fourth kitten, wrapped in a pink cotton table napkin. It didn't occur to me to have Vita or Polly desexed, and soon there was a third generation. I kept Vita's grandson, Lu. Barb and Bill took Bella. Polly and her two remaining kittens went to live on a cousin's rural property.

In the lead-up to 2000, I started to worry that the Y2K bug everyone was talking about might turn out to be a thing. I relied on email and the internet for my work. What if computers everywhere failed on the change of date from 19– to 20– and plunged the world as we knew it into chaos? I stayed home from a family party, filled the bath with water just in case the utilities failed at the stroke of midnight, and ate one of the many bags of cashews I'd stockpiled in my now mice-free pantry.

When nothing untoward happened after the clock ticked over to 2000, I pulled the plug in the bath, gave thanks to the universe for allowing life to go on as usual, and spent the day working at my desk. There was no phone call from a man from my past to upset my rickety applecart at the start of a new millennium, when the future seemed wide open.

During the Sydney Summer Olympics of that year, I was contracted by the official broadcaster to transcribe and edit the interviews conducted with Australian competitors when they exited the pool or were still catching their breath on the athletics track after their event. Within half an hour of my emailing the edited text back to the client, it was up on the website for the world to see. For the duration of the Games, I had to be available each day from early evening until midnight. I was on my best behaviour.

CHAPTER NINETEEN

'Don't lose her,' Dad said in a phone call from New Zealand just before I flew to Paris with my niece Chloe in March 2001.

'Don't you think that's my worst fear?'

It rankled that my father was still telling me, at age forty-eight, what to do. Thirty years before, when I left home, he had driven me to my college accommodation in Sydney. I'd been surprised to see his tears when he said goodbye after giving me a long list of instructions. I was too excited to feel any regret about leaving my family. I'd worked hard for the day when my father would no longer have authority over me. Four days later, after having too many ciders on a fresher-week harbour cruise, I lost my virginity to an architecture student who was attentive and sweet to me and held my hand for a time.

Although I still couldn't stomach my father's attempts to control me, his comment had touched a nerve. I was fully aware of the trust my family had placed in me whenever I'd taken their children overseas on my own. I was out of my comfort zone being a child's sole carer for an extended time, but I wanted them to see something of the world beyond the one they knew in regional Australia. It was also fun to get to know them better. Until recent years, I'd been living away from the family and hadn't been a part of the kids' day-to-day lives when they were younger. Travelling with and being responsible for a child also forced me to keep my drinking to the bare minimum, if I were drinking at all: two glasses of wine with dinner. It had to be two; there was never any point in having just one.

Chloe, now eleven, had mentioned Paris as the place she most wanted to visit. Unusually, in 2001, my finances were reasonably healthy. An author whose book I had edited for a client in Singapore and who had since become a friend was now living in Paris with his wife and young child. Michael would be only a local phone call away.

It was early on a Sunday morning when we arrived by taxi at the building in the historic Marais district, in central Paris, where I'd booked an apartment. No one came to the street door when I pressed the buzzer for the apartment. I double-checked my notes. The address and the apartment number were correct. I tried again. Still, no one appeared.

I didn't own a mobile phone.

'Clo, we need to find a café. I have to call Michael. Can you manage your bag?

'I'm hungry ...'

'We'll get you a croissant when we find a café.'

A few blocks away, a waiter was placing metal ashtrays on the small glass-topped tables that were lined up along the street-front.

I need a coffee and a cigarette ...

Chloe dumped her bag and slumped in a seat.

'S'il vous plaît,' I said to the waiter. 'Please, may I use your phone?'

I mimed holding a telephone to my ear and jabbed at the air with a finger.

He pointed inside.

'Stay here, Chloe. I'll order you a croissant. Don't move.'

My call woke Michael, who woke his French-speaking wife, who agreed to call the apartment owner.

'*Merci*. I'll call you back.'

I lit a cigarette and downed an espresso sweetened with a heaped teaspoon of sugar. Through the window I could see Chloe picking at a *pain au chocolat*. My heart was pounding from tiredness and jet lag, the strong coffee and the stress.

'He's waiting there for you,' Michael said, when I called him again. 'He said he buzzed you in, but you didn't come up. When you hear a click, you can open the door. Then take the lift.'

'*Oy vey*. Okay, I'm an idiot.'

After settling into the apartment, Chloe and I took a walk around the neighbourhood, which was close to the Pompidou Centre and its contemporary art collection. It was my first time in Paris, too. From the escalator that clung to the exterior of the building I could see the Eiffel Tower in the distance.

'Look, Clo ...'

She squealed when she spotted it.

'Happy?'

'Yes, Arnie Rob.'

We saw the sights together. She was a bright and creative kid, and fun company. Wandering the streets, enjoying being in Paris in the springtime, we created French personas for ourselves and played other games of imagination. At Disneyland Paris, Michael joined her on the scariest rides.

She could also be a pain in the arse when she dug in her heels. 'I don't *want* to go out. I want to watch TV.'

'We didn't come all the way to Europe for you to watch cartoons all day, Chloe – even if they *are* in French.'

At dinner one night at a restaurant opposite the apartment, my patience was exhausted after a long day of butting heads with a pre-teen. I needed to let off steam. 'I'm going for a walk for FIVE minutes. DON'T move. DO NOT leave this table. Not even to go to the toilet. Okay?'

'Okay.'

'Promise me. Not even if you wet your pants.'

She giggled. 'O-*kay*!'

I took a fast spin around the block to clear my head. She was sitting slouched in her seat when I returned.

'I'm sorry, Clo. You okay?'

'Can I have a crepe?'

'You can have whatever you want.'

Back in the apartment, I made inroads into a bottle of wine I'd stashed in the fridge, just in case. Going to the loo, I stumbled and fell heavily against a wardrobe, hurting my back. The noise woke Chloe.

'Arnie Rob?'

'It's nothing, Clo. Go back to sleep.'

We made two excursions through France by train: to Lausanne and Montreux, on the shores of Lake Geneva in Switzerland for a few days; and to England on the *Eurostar*, through the Channel Tunnel. In London, we rendezvoused with Sarah, who was visiting from Vancouver. She and I spent a few hours in a pub at our hotel, catching up on news of our lives over drinks, while Chloe watched TV upstairs.

At the Portobello Road market, Chloe and I bought wigs – hers electric-blue, mine purple – and wore them for a visit to Peter and Amanda, now living in rural England. They had grown to a family of six in the decade since our road trip together in Botswana and Zimbabwe.

On our final day in Paris, Chloe and I visited Père Lachaise Cemetery. I had wanted to see the final resting places of Jim

Morrison of The Doors, Colette and Oscar Wilde, and was thrilled to stumble across the grave of the writer Nancy Mitford's lover, Gaston Palewski.

On the way to the Metro afterwards, Chloe was dragging her feet. I knew that she was missing home and her family, and I was feeling the strain of having to be aware of someone else around the clock. We were due to meet Michael in the Marais for a farewell drink.

'Come on, Clo. I don't want to be late.'

'I don't want to go.'

'But we're leaving tomorrow. I won't see Michael again after this.'

'I'm tired. I don't want to go.' She came to a dead stop.

'Well, I don't care!' I shouted. 'Wherever *I* go, *you* go.'

An elderly Frenchman who was approaching and had heard my raised voice veered towards me and spat at my feet. I stared after him, mortified.

EARLY ONE WEDNESDAY morning a few months later, my sister phoned. 'Have you seen the news?'

'No. What?'

'New York … It's terrible. Planes flew into buildings.'

'What?'

I turned on TV and saw scenes of jetliners crashing into the World Trade Center towers in a fireball, of ash-covered grey people running in the streets, of an elderly woman somewhere in another part of the world looking jubilant.

I hadn't been to the mainland US, but I felt that I knew New York through books, films, music, photographs and paintings. Watching the coverage, I grieved for the physical city as well as for the people whose lives had been destroyed. For three days, I tried to comprehend the images I was watching over and over. My cats had never known me to stay in one spot for so long and tucked themselves around me on the couch. By the Saturday morning, only the multicultural broadcaster was still showing September 11 content and I called a halt to the vigil.

At a nearby nursery, I purchased pots of colourful flowers for my garden. And on the Monday, I got a puppy. Months later, I read that plant and pet sales in the United States soared in the aftermath of 9/11.

CHAPTER TWENTY

Charlie was a white and ginger Papillon. With her large butterfly-shaped ears, she resembled a cute mogwai from the film *Gremlins* before it got wet and turned vicious. Four months later, Butch, a Maltese terrier, joined my growing family. I named him for the boy who first kissed me at fourteen. ('Not like that,' he'd said. 'Open your mouth.' My practice kisses against the cool plaster of my bedroom wall hadn't prepared me for the real world.)

Vita wasn't impressed by the invasion of canines and started to spend more time roaming the neighbourhood. Her grandson, Lu, didn't seem to mind the extra bodies on the bed.

I was now the head of a household, with four animals to feed and care for, plants to water and sustain, lawns to tend, and a sizeable house to manage. Even with paid help, it was a handful and a good enough reason to hunker down in Albury. Besides, after September 11, I was in no rush to get on a plane.

Around this time, I met Sue, an artist who worked in a local picture-framing business. She wore her thick, silver–grey hair in a short, straight bob, and had a yelp-like laugh that made me feel good whenever I heard it. She and her husband, Neil, and their whippet, Woody, lived near me, and she knew everyone in the local art scene. We started to meet regularly for a drink after work, a walk with our dogs, an art opening or film, a meal.

My circle of friends expanded to include more artists, and

people who had lived in other cities, other countries. I'd found another tribe, beyond my family and the friends I'd made through running, and my social life bloomed. Albury had unexpectedly come to feel like home and was no longer just a place to hide out and recover from life elsewhere.

Sarah visited from Canada in March 2002. To amuse her, I invited a dozen friends and acquaintances with dogs to a Sunday brunch by the river. I called it a 'dogs' breakfast'. Each dog went home with a doggy bag containing small gifts and treats that I'd scrounged from local businesses. Someone had mentioned the brunch to *The Border Mail*, our local newspaper, and a reporter and photographer turned up. The following Monday must have been a slow news day, because a feel-good item about the gathering of about fourteen dogs for a riverside breakfast made it into the paper. My email address was included and enquiries came in about the date of the next breakfast.

'We meet on the second Sunday of every month,' I replied, picking a day at random. And so, a one-off gathering became the Albury-Wodonga Dogs' Breakfast Group.

AS MY FIFTIETH birthday approached, I decided to tackle my smoking addiction. Attempts over the past twenty years to quit using patches, acupuncture and other methods had all failed. I resolved in mid-June of 2002 to face the withdrawal head-on. *Just don't smoke, one day at a time.*

At around seven on a Saturday evening, I smoked the last cigarette in the pack I'd bought earlier in the day. Somehow, I got through the Sunday without buckling. The next morning, I read that a young writer I admired had died of lung cancer. Caroline Knapp's recovery memoir, *Drinking: A Love Story*, had made a big impression on me some years before. She had endured so much to get sober. She had written a book about her dog. And now, because of smoking, she had lost it all: her sobriety, her dog, her new husband, her life.

I vowed that if I craved a cigarette, I would think of Caroline; hopefully, she would be my angel and save me from myself. My discomfort from withdrawal gradually eased and I started to believe that I might never need to smoke again.

Drinking was another matter entirely.

The taxi drivers who occasionally dropped me home the worse for wear after a dinner with friends or family were the same ones who had delivered cigarettes to me late at night when I lived in an outer suburb. It's hard to stay under the radar in a small town. One night, at a party in Jan and Pete's yard around an open fire, I nearly toppled into the flames. I had fallen over in the gutter on other occasions when getting into a taxi they had called for me. Sometimes I couldn't remember coming home. We all drank at these gatherings, but I suspect that my friends worried I might be overdoing it.

Frightened by the memory gaps, by the thought that some damaged part of me that I kept under tight control may have surfaced, I would again front up at recovery meetings and stop drinking for a while. It would then seem either too easy or too difficult a change. If I got through the first week without much trouble and fell asleep without becoming anxious, I'd wonder if I'd been a tad premature. *I can do this anytime*, I'd think. *I don't need to do it right now.* Or, if my nerves were on edge and everyday life made me jittery, I'd chicken out. *I can't give up yet. I'll try again when I'm feeling stronger.*

It was the same broken loop I'd been stuck in for a decade and a half. Alcohol felt like my most reliable companion, despite the dysfunctional nature of our relationship. I didn't want to tell friends I was 'in recovery', as I didn't want to have to justify every occasion when I picked up a drink again. Each time I resumed drinking, I would be overwhelmed by a sense of relief mixed with fear. The first mouthful of cold white wine would course through me and out to my extremities like a transfusion. Until I fell and seriously cut myself, I was prepared to walk the razor's edge.

To mark my half-century, I held a 1960s-themed party in an art deco hotel lounge with a Motown tribute band. Three singers in sequinned gowns and wearing beehive wigs performed choreographed numbers by The Supremes and other girl bands of that era. It was the biggest celebration I'd ever organised for myself. I spent the evening with friends and family, dancing, laughing, talking, drinking champagne. I didn't get loud or embarrass myself, and the next morning there were no blank spots. It seems I had passed for normal.

'DO YOU HAVE a problem with alcohol?'

I had fallen in love with an artist and begun to let go of some control. I'd trusted him to lead me when we danced and to keep me safe when I perched on his bicycle crossbar, his arms around me, and he freewheeled down the slope near my house. But I hadn't trusted him to love me if he really knew me.

'Do you have a drinking problem?' he repeated.

The question hit me in the gut.

'What? No!' I was barely able to breathe.

'I think you do. You change when you have a drink. It's like you can't relax until then. I think you're dependent on it.'

'No! I work hard all day. It's the end of my workday. I just enjoy it.'

'I think it's more than that. And if you do have a problem, I'm not interested.'

His words clanged in my ear.

'I'm tired,' I said, and stood up. I wanted him to leave so that I could have a drink and numb the guilt that pushed up from inside me.

A few days later, I called him. 'Okay, I do have a problem with alcohol.'

An abyss opened up beneath me as I spoke the words. I wasn't sure I could get across it to the next sentence.

'I'm going to fix it.'

But it was too late for us. I was going to have to find a new boyfriend. Fearing to open my heart and be vulnerable, I had used alcohol as a buffer. I'd wanted him to love an edited version of me. He was looking for the real deal, and I wasn't it. Instead of taking his rejection as a prompt to do something about my relationship with myself, I drank to cover my embarrassment and anger at being spurned.

AROUND THIS TIME, I edited a book about buying and selling art. 'Take it up a notch,' the author said, when I mentioned that I had a small collection of works by local artists.

I thought about it for a day or two. I needed a new interest, something new to get passionate about – a new identity: *art collector*.

I made an appointment with a loan officer at my bank.

'I want to borrow a lot of money, please.'

'What do you want it for?'

'To buy some art.'

'Don't you mean a car?'

'No, I don't.'

'It's the first time I've heard that.'

The next day, he phoned to say the loan had been approved. I did some research, narrowed down my choices, and then purchased serious works by two of Australia's top photographers and a painting by a respected Indigenous artist. It seemed I could reinvent myself as whatever I wished, except as someone who could live life comfortably in her own skin.

FOR THE FIRST anniversary of the Dogs' Breakfast Group, Sue and I organised an exhibition at a local gallery of artworks about dogs. Many artists lived and worked in our area, and we pulled together a show of paintings, drawings, sculpture, photography and installations. In a performance piece, a Maltese terrier named Ivan, dressed in an Elvis-inspired sequined outfit, sat motionless atop a plinth. Only the occasional blink indicated that he wasn't made of plaster like a Jeff Koons sculpture.

Sue and I plugged 'The Dog Show' on a local radio station, and I gave away copies of *The Border Tail*, a new newsletter for the group's members that I'd put together with layout help from Polly in Hong Kong. Another feature article in the local paper spread word of the Dogs' Breakfast Group further around the region. A Melbourne newspaper wrote about us, which led to interviews with radio stations in Tasmania and Western Australia, and to a 'Live from the Albury-Wodonga Dogs' Breakfast' segment on Mother's Day with a station north of Sydney.

As Sunday mornings didn't suit everyone, I added a monthly Yappy Hour as an alternative: nibbles and drinks in the late afternoon at a scenic spot along the river or on the top of a hill that overlooked the town. 'You're just like a Border Collie,' a friend said of my latest new identity. 'A herder.'

Like the Women in Publishing Society had done in Hong Kong, the Dogs' Breakfast Group gave me a public profile that acted as a keel to keep me steadier than I might otherwise have been. But I wasn't out of danger. At a wake held in a hotel beer garden for someone I had known since I was a teenager, I drank myself drunk in public. The next morning, I had only memory fragments hovering on the edges of my awareness like shadowy eye floaters. I recalled trying to write my phone number for someone but being unable to remember it. Had I made a spectacle of myself? Could I look in the eye people who had seen me there? Fear and shame were a familiar breakfast cocktail.

When I ventured outside to walk the dogs, I saw the scarf I'd worn at the funeral caught in the branches of a bush a few houses downhill from mine. I could only imagine that, after I'd got out of my lift home (a taxi? a friend's car?), I'd teetered off-balance in that direction, become entangled in the foliage, then tottered scarf-less back up the slope to my door and oblivion.

Shamed by the thought that I might have been seen by my neighbours when I'd obviously had a skinful, tiring of the maintenance my home's multi-level lawns and flower beds needed, and ready for a change of scene after five years of being in one place, I decided to move house again. A change of location had worked for me before; hopefully, a fresh start in a place that was simpler to maintain would help me again. In the meantime, like the captain of a small vessel at sea reeling in heavy weather, I kept tight hold of the wheel and tried to keep the boat afloat until conditions eased.

IN MID-2004, I moved to the other end of Albury's main drag, Dean Street. 'You're a strange lady,' said the removalist who had overseen all of my recent relocations, when I phoned yet again to book his guys and a truck.

Vita wouldn't be coming with us. She had never accepted the dogs, and I'd had to find a new home for her after she began to live rough and came home one day injured and in pain.

My three remaining animals and I moved into my new place: a townhouse across the street from the botanic gardens. Lu had been used to scaling the side fence and roaming the neighbourhood and hated now being housebound in the centre of town. During the day, he sulked beneath the quilt on my bed; at night, he climbed the wooden slatted blinds.

'I can't stand it,' I said to Sue. 'I can't sleep.'

I found a new home for him in a neighbourhood that posed fewer hazards for a free-roaming tomcat. I was down to two pets, in a house with no yard to manage and two garden beds each no bigger than an ironing board.

ON 26 DECEMBER, the evening news programs reported that an earthquake in Indonesia had triggered a tsunami. Reports continued to come in, each time escalating the estimated death toll from the catastrophe that was devastating coastal communities right around the rim of the Indian Ocean, including on the low-lying coastline of Sri Lanka where my sister and I had holidayed in 1992.

The massive onslaught of water had obliterated villages, resorts, farmlands and families. More than a quarter of a million people who had been going about their everyday lives or were holidaying from their homes elsewhere in the world had been caught up in an inconceivable event.

I had every advantage in life, every comfort, extraordinary

opportunities. The disaster was a reminder to count my blessings – to not wallow in a self-constructed story that my life lacked something outside of myself that was essential to my wellbeing and happiness.

CHAPTER TWENTY-ONE

One afternoon, I ran into Julie, my former running partner and water aerobics instructor from when I'd lived in an outer suburb in 1996. We agreed to train together again. As I was no longer a smoker, it didn't take long to get my wind back when we started a weekly run through the back streets of South Albury in the pre-dawn quiet. Since we had last spent time together, Julie had completed a university degree and trained as a primary school teacher. Soon, I was also joining runs with my old training mate Robert and his new morning running partner, Diane.

It felt good to be back.

My latest home was perfect for entertaining friends and family. I'd turned the two-car garage into a library and home cinema; the house was filling with artworks. The internal courtyard was big enough to seat ten for dinner around the two large wooden tables I'd bought in Sydney eight or nine homes before. One half of a couple who were regulars at my dinner parties sometimes disappeared, after a few drinks, into a catatonic-like state from which she might not have emerged when the evening ended. My friends and I were concerned that she had a drinking problem. So far as I knew, I hadn't disappeared like that since the funeral wake two years before. The idea that I might do so again was terrifying.

MUM AND I were having our weekly dinner date at a Thai restaurant across the street from my house. There was great warmth between us, but my love for Mum was more cerebral than visceral, and hers for me the reverse. When I was a vulnerable child and she an overburdened young mother, I hadn't experienced the kind of mothering that would have created a deep emotional attachment between us. Mum had worked hard to meet her family's physical needs; there was little left over for her eldest child's emotional ones. I had found a refuge in my intellectual abilities. They set me apart in my family and brought me approval and validation outside of it. And I was sometimes arrogant and dismissive of what I saw as my mother's choice to live a 'small' life.

'You might have thought to bring the washing in, Rob,' Mum said one day when she arrived home after winning a golf tournament. I was maybe sixteen. It had rained and the two loads of clothes she had washed earlier, put through the manual wringer and hung out on the Hills hoist in the back yard were now sodden.

'Some of us have more important things on our minds than laundry, Mum.'

I didn't intend to hurt her feelings. I just needed to separate me from her, my concerns and my prospects in life from hers. Only later would I appreciate the strength of her character, her exceptional ability at any sport she played, and how much she loved each of her children.

She had little authority within the family of which my father was the undisputed head. 'Who made you the boss?' I'd asked him once as a teenager. He'd clipped me around the ear for my impertinence. Mum's father, too, had been a harsh disciplinarian. Had Mum recognised the 'type' when she met my father and experienced that feeling as love? My parents had married so young, they were hardly yet adults when they had me. Neither of them had much of an education. And in the 1950s, women had little power within the typical family in regional Australia. How had Mum felt, hearing her children pleading, screaming and sobbing when Dad caned us? I can't imagine what it was like for her not to be able to step between her husband and her child and say, 'Stop it!'

My mother's life and mine had now brought us full circle, back to the town we had both left in the 1970s. Our restaurant table was only a hundred metres from the former site of the hospital where she had given birth to me, when life must have seemed filled with promise for her and my father.

I clinked her wine glass with mine. 'Cheers, Mum.'

'Cheers, darling.'

JUST BEFORE CHRISTMAS 2005, I flew to New Zealand with Sarah, who was on a second visit from Canada, and Therese, whose dog-on-a-plinth, Ivan, had been a hit at 'The Dog Show'. We had planned a driving holiday in the North Island, including a quick visit to my father. Four decades after he had last laid a violent hand on me, I was still wary around him.

The morning after we arrived, I was making coffee in his small kitchen. My back was to the sink. He stood by the fridge, talking at me and blocking my exit. He wasn't intentionally cornering me, but my body and spirit hadn't forgotten what that felt like. The hairs on the back of my neck might not have been standing on end, but they weren't lying down either. I waited for a break in his monologue, said 'Excuse me' and ducked around him into the more open space of the dining room.

Dad was generally liked and was considered 'a good bloke' by his clients and his friends met through kayaking and tramping. I didn't begrudge him their regard; I was happy for him that he had several close friends and many friendly acquaintances. But his way of fathering me when I was a child had made loving him a challenge. Actions have consequences. It was a relief when I could give him a loose hug goodbye and my friends and I could get back on the road.

I'D CREATED A comfort zone around me in my new house by the botanic gardens. My friends were interesting, creative and fun, always up for a dress-up dinner or a themed film night. Regular running had made me fit and strong again. I was working full days as a freelance editor. The Dogs' Breakfast and Yappy Hour were well attended each month. Occasionally, I would be door-stopped by a news reporter and camera crew looking for an opinion on a local dog-related issue. I was *someone*.

But the monkey remained on my back. I kept reverting to wanting to drink wine alone upstairs with my dogs at the end of the day. This was *my* time, when I could disappear into my own head. The trick was to drink only enough earlier in the evening with friends to allow for that private ritual while keeping my total consumption under six glasses – or, if I had a morning run scheduled, under three glasses – or at most, four.

It was a balancing act, and occasionally I fell and would wake the next morning in fright. The process of recalling the evening before would be edged with dread. I tried to convince myself that memory gaps didn't necessarily mean I had done or said something I should be concerned about. Part of me didn't want to know. So long as my dogs were safe inside and I'd locked the front door, I could try to ignore the blanks and niggles that sometimes appeared at the edges of my awareness. I thought of my friend who sometimes went over to the dark side during a dinner party and wondered if I got that blank look on my face when someone was there to see it. It was safer to drink alone at home, unobserved, unjudged.

The best way I'd found to keep a handle on things was to keep setting performance goals. In March 2007, I flew to Singapore to meet with clients, and then to Hong Kong to run a half marathon. It was a decade since my last visit. Memories were embedded everywhere in the city. I saw my younger self weaving through the crowd for the Star Ferry, arriving at the Foreign Correspondents' Club for a WIPS meeting, climbing into a limousine outside an exclusive city club, eating dim sum in a Chinese teahouse, dancing at Joe Bananas. And I remembered the sensation of panic and claustrophobia and mounting anxiety that had overwhelmed me in my last two years there.

CHAPTER TWENTY-TWO

To mark the fifth birthday of the Dogs' Breakfast Group, I asked a photographer friend to take a formally posed picture of a group of members with our dogs. Jules composed the finished photo from individual shots of eight of us, dressed first in formal wear and then naked, with our eleven canine companions. *The Hunting Lodge* showed everyone posed formally and regally around a central naked figure. My dog Charlie sat on my bare lap, facing the camera and preserving my dignity. The work went on to be shortlisted for Australia's National Photographic Portrait Award and was hung with other finalists in the National Portrait Gallery in Canberra.

Butch and Charlie were at the centre of my life. I worked from home, so I spent all day with them. Social activities with friends often revolved around what we thought our dogs might enjoy. A sit-down, dress-up dinner party on the lakeshore under a full moon? *Yes, the dogs would love it.* A walk along the river? *The more dogs, the merrier.* A dog-themed film night in my home cinema? *We'll pause the movie midway so that the nine canine guests can take a wee break on the grass verge at the front of my house.*

If I took a wee break myself while working at home, Butch and Charlie would trot into the loo with me, stand on their hind legs with their front paws resting lightly on my knees and gaze at me intently. I spoke to and touched them constantly and slept with them at night. It was as if they knew everything about me. When their groomer's mobile canine beauty parlour rolled up at my house every week or so, they seemed to have anticipated Karen's arrival by some minutes. Like mini pogo sticks, they would jump around on their hind legs, their front paws raised, happy to see her. An hour later, they would be shampooed, blow-dried and sweet smelling. The familiar domestic routines reassured me that I was in control.

AN OLD FRIEND from my first days in publishing in Sydney came to stay for a night. Wisty had just completed a horse-riding adventure in the nearby Snowy Mountains area. I'd invited Therese, Genevieve and Trish and their dogs Ivan, Zsa-Zsa, Frida and Doris to dinner at my house to meet her.

After the meal, we were sitting around the table, having another glass of wine. With the exception of Wisty, we each had a small dog or two on our laps.

'Would you like a dog?' I asked her, as if I were offering an after-dinner mint.

She shook her head, then rubbed a finger slowly around the rim of her wine glass.

'I've got a big birthday in September,' she said. 'I want to do something special. There's a two-week guided walk in Europe I'm thinking about. Around Mont Blanc.'

'Sounds amazing.'

'It goes through Switzerland, Italy and France, over mountain passes.' She paused. 'Would you like to come?'

Her question took me by surprise. I gulped at my wine, then dabbed with my napkin at where I'd dribbled some of it on Butch's head.

'Sure!'

It was just the sort of challenge that would help keep me in check. Besides, I'd got the travel bug again. After Hong Kong back in March, I'd spent a week in Hanoi, in North Vietnam. I hated flying, but I was willing to endure it in order to spend time in places very different from where I now found myself. It was one thing to put down roots, but I didn't want to become root bound.

MY FIRST TREKKING experience morphed in the planning into a seven-week overseas working holiday. I gave myself an early birthday present of a MacBook Pro laptop. Therese and Ivan would move into my house. Butch and Charlie would board with Jules and his partner, Yvonne, and their Papillon, Shinji.

The Mont Blanc trail linked the seven valleys that surround Europe's highest mountain. The other walkers in our group were Britons, Americans and Canadians. On the day we all met for the first time at Geneva Airport, our guide introduced his girlfriend as our chef and driver.

'There'll be plenty of good food,' he said. 'You won't go hungry, I promise! There's also a spare single tent if anyone wants to pay a supp–'

My hand shot straight up. 'I'll take it!'

I hadn't been keen on the idea of sharing a tent.

'There's beer available,' the chef said, when we sat down together for dinner that night in Chamonix, in France, at the first of our many campsites.

'No wine?' I asked.

'Just beer.'

'That doesn't seem fair ...'

THE SCENERY ALONG our route was spectacular, with peaks, glaciers, mountain passes, forests and alpine meadows. We ascended/descended, or descended/ascended, up to three times a day over the next two weeks, with three scheduled rest days. I was fit from running, but the steep clambering was still taxing.

Life as a long-distance walker was simple: eat, walk, eat, walk, shower, eat, sleep. There wasn't time for anxiety to set in between when I crawled wearily into my sleeping bag in my little tent named 'Aspiring' and conked out sober.

Day-trippers would come up from the valleys to walk parts of the trail, looking far fresher than we did by week two. One day, a sun-bronzed, affluent-looking couple with a perfectly coiffed white standard poodle appeared from around a bend like an apparition.

During the second week, our group of hikers stopped for lunch at a hotel that had once been grand but was now decayed. I visited the old-style squat toilet. Around my ankles was one of the two dozen pairs of paper underpants I had brought along to cut down on laundry. Every time I pulled them down or up, they would stretch, becoming so voluminous by the end of the day it was difficult to stuff them back into my walking trousers.

In the stall, while trying to extract some tissues from my pocket to use as toilet paper, I overbalanced and fell forward. It seems I hadn't latched the door properly and it gave way under my weight. I pitched forward into the main restroom area, my big-girl pants still around my ankles, my bum bare.

'Thank you, thank you,' I said to the universe when I found the bathroom empty. I waddled backwards into the stall and firmly latched the door.

Later in the day, in a village market, I spotted a stall selling lace knickers. I bought a dozen pairs, including one in bright orange, and threw away what remained of my stash of disposables. At our group's farewell dinner later in the week, I would be named 'Best Knicker Shopper at High Altitude'.

On the final day of the walk, at lunch on a café terrace high above the valley, I drank a glass of wine before we began the descent to complete our circuit. A small voice drifted down from a hang-glider suspended in the clear blue sky far above my head: '*Bon appetit!*'

IN VENICE, ON a night lit by a near-full moon, I ran with an Italian mountain runner through the city's alleyways and across its bridges. The Dead Runners Society had a few members in Italy. I had made contact before the trek to say I would be in Venice and asked if someone might run with me. Cristiano had put up his hand. It seemed that I had only to ask for what I wanted and I would get it.

The thought of gliding along the canals alone in a gondola steered by a black-hatted gondolier wasn't appealing. Gondolas were for lovers or tourists. One day, I joined people waiting for a *traghetto* at a crossing point on the Grand Canal. The narrow commuter gondola had space only for a dozen standing passengers. After positioning myself, I found that I was facing in the wrong direction. Too afraid to turn around in case I upset the vessel and tipped us all overboard, I balanced as best I could, my feet spread, my knees trembling, a feeble grin fixed on my face. Six sure-footed Venetians stared through me as if I were invisible.

Early the next morning, I joined commuters waiting in the rain near St Mark's Square for a *vaporetto* ferry that was headed for the railway station. My destination was the espresso bar I'd discovered the morning before, near the Rialto Bridge, when I'd sought a strong coffee after failing to pass for a local in the *traghetto*. My café latte had been hot – unusual in Europe. I took the same seat at the same small table by the doorway.

'*Buongiorno, signora*,' said the waiter. 'The usual?'

ON THE ISLAND of Gozo, in Malta, I stayed at the Gharb studio of artist Norbert Attard. Norbert had been in Albury earlier in the year to produce a light show for the opening of the new library/museum. Therese and I had befriended him, fed him and taken him for drives around the local region. I hadn't imagined I would ever visit Malta, and yet here I was, just months later, working on my new laptop computer in the studio of an exciting artist.

One morning I ran past fields bordered by crumbling stone walls to the dramatic coastline where Homer's hero, Odysseus, was shipwrecked while returning home from the Trojan Wars. He remained on Gozo for seven years, a captive of his rescuer, Calypso, until finally he could resume his journey and return to Penelope, his wife waiting patiently for him in Greece. Looking out at the calm waters of the Mediterranean, where so much of Western history had begun, I wished I'd paid better attention during Ancient History classes in high school.

On another run, I padded through the sleeping village to the outskirts of the island's main city, named for Britain's Queen Victoria, my progress tracked by the barking of local dogs behind stucco villa walls.

From Malta, I flew to Rome, then home via Hong Kong. During the nearly two months I'd been away, except for the fortnight of the trek, I'd stayed on top of my workload without inconveniencing my clients. The internet, email and electronic files had changed everything. I was no longer reliant on couriers and physical floppy disks. My clients didn't need to know my location; their only concern was that their jobs were done on schedule and within budget. I'd found I could do that just as easily in Hanoi or in Venice, or on a small island in the Mediterranean, as from my home in regional Australia. I was surprised, too, by how comfortable I felt wandering around Europe on my own odyssey.

The two realisations offered intriguing possibilities.

CHAPTER TWENTY-THREE

The Mont Blanc trek had been demanding, but in hindsight the bar looked to have been set a little low. My father's daughter, I immediately raised it. In April 2008, I flew to New Guinea to walk the Kokoda Track. The slog across the country's backbone traced the muddy bootprints of the Australian and Japanese soldiers who had fought there in 1942. Among Australians, 'Kokoda' was a byword for courage and mateship. Fathers and sons, and macho football players, undertook the trek together as a bonding rite. I was a slightly built, middle-aged woman, a former pack-a-day smoker, still a problem drinker. Would I succeed where others who were younger, fitter, less burdened by a substance addiction and with more testosterone had failed?

Butch and Charlie would again stay with Jules and Yvonne.

'Are you *sure* you don't mind? Am I being an irresponsible parent?'

'Honestly, we love having them stay,' Yvonne said. 'Go! Shoo!'

Our group of twelve trekkers and three local guides flew in a light plane from Port Moresby to Kokoda village, the start of our route back across the Owen Stanley Range to Owers' Corner. I was the second-oldest, and nearly twice the age of the only other woman.

There would be no comforts or amenities or booze for the next two weeks. This was what I had signed on for: an extreme test of my character, abilities and guts. A dozen or so local men would carry our food, cooking and other equipment, tarps and tools. My small daypack held water, snacks, instant soups, rain gear, a toilet roll and tissues. (I'd learnt from the Mont Blanc trek that hard walking made my nose run.) I paid extra for a personal porter to carry my heavy backpack.

Our days quickly took on a rhythm. After breakfast of coffee and cereal, we walked, often in single file, under the tree canopy until a halt was called for an early lunch – invariably, saltine crackers with toppings of tuna, beetroot or peanut butter. By mid-afternoon, we would arrive at our overnight accommodation – if we were in luck, a large thatched-roofed room on stilts – where we laid out our mats and sleeping bags side by side. There would be time for a rudimentary wash before dinner of vegetables and pasta or rice. Night fell early, and the snoring started soon after.

Apart from tattered T-shirts and the occasional iron pipe or rubber hose, there was little to indicate that life for the villagers along our route had changed in tens of thousands of years. Sometimes we could buy a few bananas or peanuts, or a can of warm soft drink, to supplement the meals our porters prepared.

My porter stuck by my side for the five or six hours we walked each day, urging me on as I hauled my jelly-legs up yet another crumbling ridge. Standing waist-deep in a swift-flowing stream, he would hold my hand as I shuffled across tree trunks the other porters had felled and roped together to create a precarious bridge.

'Tell me about your family, Phil.'

We were looking around a battle site at Eora Creek, and I was thinking of the families, both Japanese and Australian, that had lost sons and husbands and fathers here.

'I have eight brothers and sisters. My mother is old.'

I imagined she was younger than I was. 'And your father? Is he still alive?'

'My father live with my auntie now.'

'What do you mean?'

'My auntie pay witchdoctor to put spell on him.'

'Really?'

'Yes. Not his fault.'

'Oh, that old black magic, right?'

Just then, my feet shot out from under me. I'd been picking my way down a steep embankment, finding handholds and then footholds. Phil, following behind, grabbed hold of my daypack to stop my slide.

On the trail, time as I knew it in my working life – billable units of fifteen minutes – ceased to exist. It was marked now only by each step and breath I took, and sometimes by the porters' voices singing together in harmony and then fading away.

One day, the noise of cicadas filled the air for some time, the sound swooping and diving and rolling in and around the treetops as if the spirits of the track were unleashed.

At Efogi, I looked for the memorial that Kokichi Nishimura, the 'bone man of Kokoda', had erected to honour his fellow soldiers who had fought and died on the trail. I had edited a book about him and knew that he had returned to New Guinea many times after the war to locate the bones of his fallen comrades and return them to Japan. I wanted to see the large stone he had brought from the island that had been the birthplace of many of the soldiers, but there was no sign of it on the memorial plinth.

'Phil, can you ask where it is, please?'

He wandered off.

A few minutes later, he was back at my side.

'The head man keep it in his house.'

'Can I see it?'

'I ask him.'

He returned accompanied by the village head, who placed a sizeable stone on the plinth.

'Just for you to see,' Phil said. 'He say it not safe to leave here.'

I put my hand on my heart. 'Thank you.'

During the second week, we encountered more groups of trekkers. We were all converging on Owers' Corner in time for the Anzac Day services on April 25. The heavy foot traffic and the regular afternoon rainfall were turning the clay track to sticky mud.

The two 'runners' who had previously gone ahead after lunch each day to secure us a hut at our next overnight camp now set off before dawn. On a couple of nights, we missed out and had to sleep on groundsheets under a canvas tarp. Village dogs clambered over our exhausted, sleeping-bagged forms, fossicking in the darkness for food.

The climb up to Imita Ridge, near the end of the trail, was laborious. At the top, I doubled over and clasped my knees.

'We made it!' I said, when I'd caught my breath.

'Strong *grrrl*!' said Phil.

I sat on a boulder for a while and had a little cry. Kokoda had been a tough slog, but I'd expected it to be worse. Barring an accident, I would be able to complete the walk. I *was* a strong grrrl. There was nothing to say I couldn't achieve whatever I set my mind to.

'Everest Base Camp, followed immediately by the Annapurna Circuit. Five weeks' trekking,' I announced a few weeks later to a friend in Albury who was also a Kokoda veteran. 'October. Five months to train.'

'You've got OCTD,' she said.

'What's that?'

'Obsessive compulsive trekking disorder.'

'That's like a positive addiction, right?'

THE WINTER THAT gripped Albury from May onwards felt severe, though it wasn't cold enough for snow. Perhaps steamy, tropical New Guinea had thinned my blood.

I was up early three or four mornings a week for a run with Diane, Robert's former running mate, and her friend Fran. They would drive to my house from their properties on the outskirts of town, where Di kept horses and dogs and Frannie raised cattle. We would run north for half an hour, or south along the river. Afterwards, we'd sit on tiny plastic stools at a coffee van and sip happily at our hot lattes.

At the end of winter, Di, Fran and I drove to Sydney for the City to Surf race. In the final stages, as I ran past the corner near the clifftop where I had lived fourteen years before, I dipped my head in acknowledgement of my younger self who had stood there watching the runners passing by and had vowed to be among them again one day.

CHAPTER TWENTY-FOUR

The flight into Lukla, in Nepal, required a very tricky approach through a canyon, with one shot at landing uphill on the tiny airstrip before a hard right-hand turn just before a cliff face. Ten days earlier, a plane identical to ours – a Twin Otter – had crashed and exploded on landing, killing all sixteen passengers and crew. I took half a Xanax with my breakfast coffee at the Kathmandu Guesthouse before we left for the airport. Once we were airborne, I gripped the seatback in front of me until we touched down in one piece.

The village, high in the Himalayan foothills, was the meeting point for our dozen trekkers from Australia, Ireland, Scotland and Canada, three local trek leaders and a pod of porters.

I carried a daypack and trekking poles. My duffel bag had been stuffed with others into a large woven basket held in place on a porter's bent back by a cloth strap across his forehead. The walk from Lukla to Phakding would take about three hours. The air was cold, with a whiff of animal dung from the droppings of pack animals along the path. I placed on a chorten the flat grey mani stone inscribed with *om mani padme hum* that I had brought with me as an offering to the gods of the trail and took the first of the many steps that I hoped would get me to the foot of Mt Everest.

I'd prepared physically and mentally as best I could. Setting challenging goals was the most effective way I'd found to control my drinking if I wanted to be able to have *some* alcohol in my life. One glass of wine had never been enough. But after two – the amount I thought a normal person would find sufficient – I always wanted more. I needed something to make it worth forgoing a third and then a fourth glass. That *something* was the natural high and sense of accomplishment I got from going for a long run or a hard walk. Feel-good and reward chemicals could be addictive in themselves and were sometimes an effective substitute for a nice cold chardonnay.

THE MODEST TEAHOUSE where we spent the first night of our trek to Everest Base Camp was luxurious compared to the amenities I'd experienced on the Kokoda Track.

'I'll have the pasta,' I said, scanning the menu.

'Boiled potatoes for me,' said the Irish medical student.

In this early part of the route, the steep, stony paths were trafficked by local villagers, porters, traders and other trekkers. Heavily laden pack animals – yaks and small ponies – picked a careful path. The sounds of the trail filled the air: the tinkling of animal bells, the flapping of prayer flags strung from inconceivable places, the *click-clack* of prayer wheels spun by passers-by, the steady chipping of tools against stone, the rushing water as we crossed over wobbly suspension bridges spanning milky green rivers.

It was a hard, seven-hour walk to Namche Bazaar, which appeared to cling precariously to the steep slopes behind the town. 'No hurry, no worry,' said Ram, our lead guide. 'At altitude, we take slow steps. We will stay two nights in Namche, to acclimatise. Tomorrow, you will climb higher, then come back down to sleep lower.'

The next morning, my fifty-sixth birthday, we climbed to a hotel perched at just under 4,000 metres, where we drank hot chocolate on a terrace with views of the world's highest mountain. I'd spent my birthday in worse places.

Back at the teahouse, after a steep descent, one of our trekkers became unwell and a doctor was called. High-altitude pulmonary oedema was the tentative diagnosis.

'I'm sorry,' said Ram. 'You must return to Kathmandu.'

David looked both ashen and relieved as he was bundled into a rescue helicopter. We waved him off and thanked the trail gods that it hadn't been us.

I went shopping for a present for myself: a necklace made of local turquoise. I liked Namche, which had steep winding streets and the funky feel of an outpost town. After a massage, I drank a whisky.

The next day, we entered Sagarmatha National Park. Everest came in and out of view in the distance. 'Tomorrow, we have one more acclimatisation day,' Ram announced that night at dinner in our teahouse at Denboche. Nearby Kala Patthar, at 5,500 metres above sea level, would be a hard climb, he said. 'Go as high as you can before you come down again. We will sleep here tomorrow night before we go on to Base Camp.'

THE AIR WAS so thin, the slope of the ridge so steep, I had to push myself up the gravelly path at a snail's pace. I was the slowest of the five who had got this far – four trekkers and Dinesh, Ram's assistant; the rest of our group had turned back. Finally, panting heavily, my legs feeling like concrete blocks and my nose streaming, I hauled myself the last few metres to the top. The others had taken up positions on a rocky outcrop, their bodies outlined against the deep-blue sky. No one spoke. I looked around, my breathing still raspy. The peaks on all sides, Everest among them, appeared close enough to touch. A glacier swept down from the sky directly across from us; at its foot was a lake the colour of my new necklace. Around us, prayer flags strung across the rocky terrain fluttered and flapped, destined to disintegrate from exposure to the elements.

By breaking down a daunting task into tiny faltering steps, I had transported myself to a place near the top of the world that literally took my breath away. The trek was still only in its early days, but the slog up to this sublime spot, where the air was thinner than any I'd ever breathed, was without doubt the hardest thing I had ever done.

In my daypack was a bag of chocolate-covered caramels. I offered them around, then put one in my mouth. The sweetness seemed to be accentuated by the rarefied atmosphere. As I surveyed the world from my perch, my heart full, my eyes watering from emotion and the exertion, I couldn't think of anywhere I'd ever been that was more beautiful.

Dinesh looked at his watch and got to his feet. I picked up a small stone and balanced it carefully on a teetering pile nearby, then dipped my head. *Thank you.*

Halfway down the steep, stony path, my feet slipped out from under me. I fell backwards, landing heavily on my left wrist. For a moment, I lay still. When I tried to stand, I felt faint.

'Dinesh, I think I've done something to my hand ...' My voice sounded far away to my ears.

He helped me to my feet, prodded the flesh around my wrist and flexed my hand. 'Can you move your fingers?'

'Yes.'

'Can you walk?'

'I think so.'

'Okay. We will walk slowly. Ram will know what to do.'

'Stay with me, will you?' I was suddenly fearful of losing my footing again.

At the teahouse, Ram looked at my now swollen wrist. 'There is a clinic an hour's walk from here. Dinesh, come. We will go now.'

The Himalayan Rescue Association's clinic at Pheriche was staffed year-round by volunteers. During the climbing season, it supported a temporary clinic at Everest Base Camp.

'I think you've got a Colles fracture,' said the visiting doctor from Colorado who examined my wrist. 'You need to have it X-rayed. We can't do that here. You'll have to go back to Namche or to Kathmandu. If it's broken, you may need surgery.'

My head spun. 'Are you saying I can't go on? Can't it wait? Can I go to Base Camp and then get it looked at when we get back to Kathmandu?'

'You need to have it X-rayed to confirm if it's broken,' the doctor said. 'I don't think you should wait that long. You should go back to Kathmandu as soon as possible.'

'Ram? What do *you* think I should do?'

My eyes pleaded with him.

'I also think you must go back to Kathmandu.' His knuckles were white from clasping his hands together tightly. 'You must leave in the morning. Dinesh will go with you.'

How quickly things had changed. From having been close to heaven, I had crashed back to earth.

In the morning, one of the women in our group helped me to wash and dress before I turned my back on Sagarmatha, Goddess of the Sky, and set off to return to Lukla, accompanied by Dinesh and a porter. Khagendra came up only to my shoulder and had

an elfish face, making him look like an extra from *Lord of the
Rings*. My duffel bag, which he carried on his back, towered
over him. Dinesh had his own pack on his back and my daypack
strapped to his chest. I carried one trekking pole. My left arm
was in a temporary splint held high on my chest by a triangle of
calico cloth.

Our return route was via Tengboche monastery, near a
spectacular peak I had seen in the distance two days before. I'd
been feeling sooky about having to give up on my plans, but the
sight of Ama Dablam, which is said to look like a mother hugging
a child, buoyed my spirits.

The next day, we crossed again the wooden suspension
bridges high above the Dudh Kosi River that we had navigated
the previous week. Dangling like tightropes, festooned with
wind-torn prayer flags, they swayed violently from the uneven
footfalls of people and pack animals. I held on as best I could
with my one free hand.

From Lukla, after an overnight stay, we boarded the morning
flight to Kathmandu. At the base of the cliff next to the
ramshackle air terminal, the pilot revved the engines hard and
then propelled our small craft at speed towards the edge of the
mountain. We lifted into the air just before everything fell away
to the valley far beneath us.

A few days later, I had surgery under general anaesthetic
to insert pins in my wrist. My forearm was encased in plaster.
The hospital required full payment before they would discharge
me, but I didn't have the money. Dinesh made a phone call, and
someone from the trekking company arrived on a motorcycle
with a bundle of cash. I promised to repay it from Australia.

When I arrived back at the Kathmandu Guesthouse from the
hospital, a blonde Englishwoman drinking a cup of tea in the

garden introduced herself as Wendy. She had heard about my accident, she said.

'Can I get you something? A hot chocolate?'

'Wine, please. White wine.'

'You sure? You don't want a cup of tea or something? You look very pale ...'

'I'm positive. Just wine, please.'

CHAPTER TWENTY-FIVE

During a transit stop at Singapore's airport on the way home from Nepal, I used the public internet to check my emails. There was one from Tom. My breath caught in my throat, my heart took two beats in one, and my uterus may have contracted.

Nearly two decades had passed since he had stayed with me in Hong Kong and I had thrown a wobbly because he was unavailable to me in the way I wanted. A lot had happened in that time. I had changed. Had he? Was the universe giving us another chance?

He was now retired and living back in Sydney. Where was I? he asked. What was I doing?

'I'm at Changi with a broken wrist,' I tapped out with one finger. 'Had to abort Everest Base Camp trek and have surgery in Kathmandu. I'm living back in Albury. I'll be home tomorrow. Call me.'

I'd known him for more than half my life – since we'd been in our twenties. We were both now edging towards our sixties. When we had met, my skin was young and didn't yet hold the dent when pressed. My breasts had sat higher on my chest, and my gums hadn't yet started to recede. He had been gorgeous, his hair thick and black, his sexual vigour youthful. We had been at the start of our careers. In the photos he emailed, his body was still trim, but I could see that life had happened to him, too, since I'd last looked in his eyes. There were lines and grooves on his face I'd not seen before, and his hair was now salt-and-pepper. Despite our past problems, the prospect of being with him again tugged at my vitals. Why would he reach out after so long if he didn't have enduring feelings for me? If *he* was willing to try again, then so was I.

A COUPLE OF weeks later, he pulled up in a four-wheel drive outside my house with a large dog beside him. He brushed his lips across my cheek, then stood back. The close hug I'd hoped for wasn't offered.

'This is Sonia,' he said, and scratched the back of the dog's neck.

'Hello, Sonia.'

I gave him a tour of my house, pointing out my growing collection of artworks featuring dogs and sometimes touching him lightly. Not wanting to assume that we would sleep together, I showed him the spare bedroom. In the kitchen, I poured a bowl of water for Sonia and put the jug on for coffee.

'I can't take the dog where I'm going camping with my cousin,' Tom said. A look of slight distaste flitted across his face when I spooned instant coffee into two mugs. 'You don't mind if I leave her here, do you, Rob? It'll just be for a week.'

He looked adoringly at his dog. I looked at my plastered wrist. My two dogs, sitting at my feet, looked from Tom to Sonia to me.

'I'm not sure how I'd manage. She seems pretty boisterous.'

'Nah, she's good. She won't give you any trouble.'

He gathered her up in his arms and bowled her the length of the tiled dining room. At the end of the skidding slide, she untangled her legs and bounded back to him for another turn.

It was obvious that she was besotted with him, and it seemed churlish of me not to find her totally adorable.

I made us dinner, and we sat in my back room and caught up on our lives. He seemed to have had a lot of girlfriends, as he called them. Each time he used the word, my foot jerked involuntarily, as if a doctor had tapped just beneath my kneecap with a tiny hammer.

By bedtime, when he hadn't made any sort of move, I said goodnight. 'Sleep tight, Tom.'

''night, Rob.'

The next morning, I awoke to find him standing at my open bedroom door with a towel wrapped around his waist, his hair standing on end and an overnight growth of bristle on his face. 'Come in,' I said, putting my head willingly back in the noose. *Come into my room. Come into my bed. Come into me.*

That night, I invited friends to join us for dinner to meet the man I'd fancied for three decades. He was personable, interesting and intelligent, widely travelled, liberal in his views and well read – and could be funny. Like Sue's laugh, his was a joy for me to hear. A good conversationalist, he was interested in others' thoughts and opinions. I knew my friends would like him. I also wanted him to appreciate them – the fun, interesting and talented people who were my comfort zone; to see that I had a vibrant life; that I had made a good choice in moving back to my home town.

After everyone left, Tom logged on to his laptop in my office and was soon engrossed in reading. I stood in the doorway, hesitant to ask for what I wanted. 'Well, good night, then.'

''night, Rob. I like your friends.'

The next morning, three dogs and I watched him pull out of the driveway and turn the car south towards the new expressway.

A week later, I handed him the bill for Sonia's holiday spent with my dogs' groomer, Karen, and her pack of boarders.

'What's this?'

'I told you I wouldn't be able to manage her, Tom.'

THE FOLLOWING MONTH, Therese and I flew in a tiny commuter plane to Canberra for a friend's birthday weekend. I'd invited Tom to join us from Sydney. If all went well, he and I might add on a short road trip. If all went *really* well, I hoped our life together might start. Where Tom was concerned, my heart trumped my head.

'Be cool, girlfriend,' Therese cautioned. She knew that in all the years I'd known Tom, I'd never felt on firm emotional ground with him; that it was all shifting plates and quicksand. But I couldn't help myself. Was I just re-enacting the dynamic with my father over and over? If someone who withheld love and approval like Tom did – like my father had – could show me that he loved me, could touch me with a loving hand, then perhaps I was worth loving. The notion seemed pathetic even to me.

At the arrivals terminal, Tom was engrossed in his iPad. He looked up when I greeted him, raised a finger to indicate he wanted to finish whatever he was doing, and returned his attention to the tablet. Therese and I stood by awkwardly, suspended, waiting. The peck on my cheek when he finally engaged with us was like the prick of a pin in a balloon. His casual greetings always put me on a back foot. I wanted more.

Things started to unravel the next day, though he seemed initially not to notice. I was used to making decisions for myself, usually with some confidence, but I started to dread trying to make any decisions or choices with Tom.

'There's a photography exhibition at the War Museum. I'd like to see it. Do you want to go?'

'Hmm?'

'Do you want to see this photography exhibition?'

Silence.

'Tom, did you hear me?'

'What?'

I was sick of repeating myself. 'Don't worry about it.'

'Steady on,' he cautioned, catching the change of tone in my voice.

We made it to the museum but wandered separately through the exhibits.

On a previous visit, I'd seen an impressive sound-and-light show. Tom seemed interested when I mentioned it. I staked out space for us by a railing that looked straight across to the suspended Lancaster bomber that was part of the show.

'Is this the best place to stand?'

No, it's the WORST place. That's why I chose it. 'I had a good view from here last time.' Were my teeth gritted? Why did I feel I was walking barefoot through prickles?

'I think over there is better,' he said, and moved away.

What was the point in standing my ground and watching the show alone? I followed him, feeling resentful.

'You're too sensitive. You take things too seriously,' he said, when he realised I was pissed off. He was right. I *was* far too sensitive. I wanted him, but I couldn't figure out how to stand up to him and not let him undermine me.

Once things had started to deteriorate, I couldn't reach out to him physically to try to re-establish a connection. His own flight response had kicked in when he sensed my anger and resentment. He shrugged off hugs. I couldn't hold his hand for more than the few seconds it took for him to disengage himself. Kisses were swatted away. If I touched his arm, he would move just out of reach. I felt more alone in his company than I did on my own. It was a repeat of the days we had spent together in Hong Kong. He had gone someplace where I couldn't reach him.

That night, it took some wandering around before our group that had come to Canberra to share our friend's birthday finally found a restaurant that would allow us to sit outside with a dog.

'When did this whole trip become about Sonia?' I muttered to Therese.

'You okay, girlfriend?' she murmured.

'Bloody Tom. It's too hard.'

She squeezed my hand.

I wanted only to drink cold white wine to numb my disappointment. As we had arrived late in the evening, we were rushed through our meal and I'd had nowhere near enough to drink before we had to leave.

'Should we pick up some wine and ask the others back to our room?' Tom said. It was a conciliatory gesture and I grabbed hold of it.

'Absolutely.'

For half an hour we searched for somewhere to buy wine. Then, when we found a place, he couldn't decide among the selection of wines on offer and we left the store empty-handed. I went into a meltdown.

'Tom!' I hissed. I was drowning in my feelings and he had deflated the only life raft within reach. We were both shocked. I apologised immediately, but it was too late. He had bolted back into his safe place inside and slammed the door. No one came back to our room with us. There was nothing to drink. Miserable, I got into bed. Tom and the dog watched television.

After he turned off the lights and stretched out on the far side of the bed, his back to me, I extended my good right arm, the one not in plaster, across the chasm that separated us and placed one fingertip against his skin. He moved, shrugging off the contact.

There was no further discussion about my joining him and the dog on a road trip. I couldn't bear to prolong the torture. When he dropped Therese and me at the bus station for our return trip to Albury, I walked away without a word or a backward glance. Therese's goodbyes would have to do for us both.

CHAPTER TWENTY-SIX

When I received an unexpected insurance payout for my broken wrist, I decided to take an extended overseas working holiday. It remained only to choose where in the world I wanted to go. The answer popped into my head like a tap dancer making a triumphant stage entrance from the wings. *New York City*. I'd never been there.

A random search of a website of apartments available for short-term lease turned up a one-bedroom place right beside Central Park, on the Upper West Side. Two hours' work a day would cover the rent. I was ahead on my mortgage payments. The photos clinched it: floor-to-ceiling bookshelves. My kind of place.

On my way to the East Coast, I could visit friends in British Columbia, San Francisco and Silicon Valley. Yin, whose China business books I'd edited in Hong Kong, was living in New York. A Dead Runners Society get-together in Missouri was being planned. I'd been online friends for years with many of the people who would be there.

While I was still in Australia, I joined New York Road Runners and the Hudson Dusters racing team. The Dusters, semi-serious runners, were members of the New York chapter of the Hash House Harriers, the international social running network I'd run with in Hong Kong in the 1980s. I sent in entries to various races scheduled for the summer months, including a half marathon in Brooklyn. If I ran it within a certain age-graded time, I would have a guaranteed place in the New York City Marathon. I'd never imagined I might have an opportunity to run one of the world's most iconic races, but suddenly it was within my grasp if I straightened myself out again.

I'd fallen back into drinking every evening on my own, my dogs the only witnesses. It had been years since I'd gone to a recovery meeting. I still hoped not to have to stop drinking entirely. Having specific training goals gave me the incentive I needed to pull back towards moderation.

In March 2009, two months before I would leave for the US, I flew to New Zealand with Christine, a friend and regular training partner. We were entered in an off-road half marathon that would be a good gauge of my fitness. It was also a chance to see my father. Chris was fun company and helped keep the mood light between Dad and me. I appreciated all the things he had done for us as children, and I could now forgive him his failings, but I was never fully at ease in his presence.

The half marathon, which wound up and down trails in a pine forest, was taxing, but I felt strong. The training I'd been doing in the lead-up to my New York adventure paid dividends.

Soon after the last stragglers crossed the finish line, the results were posted on a piece of paper nailed to a tree.

'My name's got a "1" next to it,' I said to Christine. 'What do you think it means?'

She looked over my shoulder. 'It means you came first in your age group, you nutcase!'

It seemed I was good to go.

THE LIGHTS OF the vehicle receded until I was alone. The only sounds were the padding of my feet on the bitumen and the occasional cries of wildlife. I was in the middle of a forest, in the middle of the night, half a world away from home.

Back in early May, when I'd just arrived on the west coast of the US and was still making my way to New York, I'd received an email from Tim of the Hudson Dusters. A team was looking for a few extra people for a long-distance relay to be held later in the summer in Vermont. I put up my hand and scored a spot on the New York Running Chicks and a Few Dudes team.

'You'll hear from the team leader soon,' Tim wrote.

I'd decided to throw myself headfirst into the experience of living for a time in New York, to say 'yes' to everything that appeared in my path that would require me to be my best self. If I acted as if I were more together than I actually was, it might become clear who I could possibly become.

Just days after I moved into the apartment beside Central Park, I ran a 10K race and was surprised to place sixth out of eighty women in my age group. This was New York City, not little old Albury in regional Australia. At a Hudson Dusters brunch in an Irish pub afterwards, I introduced myself to Tim, to Lauren, who had processed my membership application, and to Heather, who had brought along my team singlet.

'Don't forget to tick the team box whenever you enter a race,' Tim said. 'If you get an age-group placing, you'll earn us points.'

A few days later, in an evening 5K race through the Wall Street business district to Battery Park, I paced myself well, then sprinted as hard as I could the last couple of hundred metres to the finish line.

After I caught my breath, I headed for the subway through the dispersing runners and the tourists strolling along the waterfront. In the distance, the Statue of Liberty was illuminated against the darkening sky. I grinned at some passers-by, who nodded and smiled back.

When I arrived home, the results were up on NYRR's site. I had placed first in my age group and in the top 15 per cent of all the women in the race. I double-checked I'd read the results correctly, then let out a whoop. As a newly minted Duster, I was already earning points for the team. I deserved to let my hair down for a night. Two bottles of wine were chilling in the fridge. I broke the seal of one bottle and sloshed a generous amount into the glass I'd already chosen as my favourite.

MY NEIGHBOURHOOD ON the Upper West Side – apartment tower blocks mixed with nineteenth-century brownstones – was a melting pot of White, African-American, Hispanic and Jewish singletons, couples and families. There seemed to be dogs everywhere. In my building alone, there must have been a hundred or more. I wouldn't have to miss my two at home, who were tucked up with Jules and Yvonne for the Southern Hemisphere winter.

Between Central Park, across the road, and Broadway were Columbus and Amsterdam avenues, with everything a community needed: primary schools, a library, grocery stores, pharmacies, nail salons, banks, diners, corner delis, dive bars, liquor stores, and fire and police stations. I walked everywhere, getting a feel for my neighbourhood and the city.

Early on, I'd identified three or four places near home where I could buy wine. It was best to rotate among them, rather than be too much of a regular face in one store. There were always other unaccompanied women – well-groomed corporate types –

waiting in line to pay for the bottle of wine they clutched as if it were the hand of a best friend. None of us made eye contact.

My building, like many apartment blocks in the city, had round-the-clock concierge staff and security cameras. Whenever I was in the common area on my floor, I was visible on the CCTV cameras. When I took my rubbish to the trash collection room halfway along the hallway, I would place yesterday's *New York Times* and the bag of kitchen rubbish on top of the empty wine bottle so that it wasn't visible. Rarely were there other empties in the box reserved for glass items. *Doesn't anyone else on my floor drink? Just how conspicuous is my consumption going to be?*

The goal I'd set myself while in New York – to try to get entry into the marathon – helped me to moderate my drinking, but it was never easy. Sometimes, in the morning, I couldn't recall parts of the previous evening. If the empty bottle was still beside the rubbish bin, I was reassured that I hadn't ventured out into the hallway in my nightie to dispose of the evidence, risking encounters with neighbours and gossip among the staff. It was a long time since drinking had been a simple, social activity, rather than a secret, private one. I didn't want others to know how big a part alcohol played in my life and how much space it occupied in my thoughts.

CHAPTER TWENTY-SEVEN

Dead Runners from all over the country gathered in St Louis, Missouri, on the Memorial Day long weekend in late May for a world conference. DRS had been an online family for me since 1996, and I felt I was among dear friends.

A tall, good-looking man with a Southern accent stuck out his hand in greeting at the picnic that kicked off the reunion.

'Hi, I'm Rich.' The strength of his grip buckled my knees.

'Hi, I'm poor.'

Richard was in charge of beer and had brought along a large quantity of his special home-brew. 'I'm sure it's delicious,' I said, when he offered me a glass. 'But wine's my poison.'

The weekend was anchored around two races: a 10K and a 5K. I was the only entrant in my age group in the 10K event and automatically scored a first place.

A long-time Dead Runner from New England who had been undergoing chemotherapy had set her sights on completing the 5K event, which followed the 10K. I was among the friends who ran the course with her. I was learning that this widespread community of runners of all abilities was far from being just a 'virtual' one. Along with online training and other information and support, it provided real-world friendships, compassion and affection.

At the barbecue on the final night, Josh, a retired computer geek with a passion for astronomy, arrived late, one hand heavily bandaged.

'What happened?' I asked.

'Gunshot wound.'

'What?'

He had spent the afternoon at a shooting gallery with his brother who lived locally, and the gun had recoiled and torn the skin of his hand. He'd just come from the hospital.

'If you're in the States in the fall, stay a couple of days with us in Maine to see the foliage,' he said.

THE SUBWAY WAS packed with hundreds of runners headed for the start of the Brooklyn Half Marathon in Prospect Park. The race would finish on the boardwalk at Coney Island. If I crossed the finish line within 1 hour and 50 minutes, I would be eligible to return to New York later in the year to run the New York City Marathon. I studied the time splits I'd written on my forearm. I would have to be focused and maintain an even pace. Nervous, I lined up twice at the portable toilets before the start.

A visiting celebrity sang the national anthem to the runners assembled in the starting corrals. I, too, placed my hand over my heart, as much to calm its wild beating as out of any sense of patriotism. The anthem was sung before every NYRR race. I enjoyed the ritual, and it had been lucky for me.

After running on undulating roads around the park, we emerged on to Ocean Parkway. My confidence rose as I ran steadily along the long, straight course that would take us to Brighton Beach, New York's Russian enclave. When racing, I'm aware of an imaginary line just in front of me, like the tape the winner breaks at the finish line. I try always to nudge the line; if

I push against it too hard, I'll be short of breath and lose form. But if I can't 'feel' the line at all, I'm jogging, not racing. My mind is focused on how to move as efficiently as possible: *Can I extend my stride further, pump my arms harder, relax my shoulders more, move closer to the line?*

It was the same way I drank – always monitoring myself and asking: *Can I have another glass of wine, nudge the fine line between too little and too much, and not lose form?* In both cases, I sought the elusive 'zone' where there was no pain.

I tucked in behind a guy who was running at my goal pace and concentrated on staying a body length behind him: not so close that he might feel I was on his heels and crowding him, but close enough to be in his draft and pulled along by his effort.

Halfway through the race, my goal time seemed within reach; with luck, I might even shave off a few minutes and revisit my best time for the distance. I was working hard but breathing evenly. When we turned on to the wooden boardwalk, with the sea on our left, the rides of Coney Island's famous amusement park were visible up ahead. Now was the time to embrace discomfort. When I crossed the timing mat some minutes later, I knew I'd run the race to the best of my ability – at an even pace, always just this side of discomfort but not too comfortable, until I'd given it everything I had left when the finish was in view.

It wasn't enough. I missed my goal time by nine seconds. Somewhere along the way, my pace had slowed by an average of half a second per kilometre. It seemed I wouldn't be returning to New York in November to run the marathon after all. *Perhaps it's for the best,* I thought. *I can't just pop over to the States any time I want to run a race.* My real life was in Australia, not in New York, even though the city seemed to fit me like a glove. It had been a dream, but an impractical one.

BY THE START of June, I felt like I'd always lived in New York. I looked like any other local heading downtown on the subway, sharing a carriage with folks from the Upper West Side, Harlem or communities further north; with musicians dressed in evening wear and carrying instrument cases headed for Midtown to play in the orchestras on Broadway; with quartets of doo-wop singers busking for dollar bills; and with polite down-and-outs with convoluted hard-luck stories. Ordinary, extraordinary New Yorkers.

I'd met Holly, a photographer, when she was handing out copies of a self-published magazine at a photo fair in Brooklyn two days after I'd arrived. I emailed her the next day to invite her to breakfast. At Eisenberg's Deli, near the Flatiron Building, I felt like Dorothy from Kansas in the company of this brilliant artist with a wild shock of black hair and a twin obsession for jockeys and drag queens. She was a quintessential New Yorker: someone who had moved to the city from small-town America, intent on fulfilling a destiny initially only they could imagine.

My own dreams were taking wing, too. My friend Yin liked an idea I was developing with an illustrator in Australia and showed a sample to a literary agent she knew. He emailed me: 'If you'd like to talk about a book project, I'd be pleased to discuss the possibilities.' I loved the feeling that doors might open wherever I directed my energy; that this incredible city seemed to love me. I was experiencing and achieving far more during my visit than I could have imagined was possible.

SOON AFTER THE Brooklyn race, I headed north with my New York Running Chicks and a Few Dudes teammates in two vans to take part in the Green Mountain Relay, the 200-mile, twenty-four hour event in Vermont that I'd signed on for back in early May. Our team leader was a bubbly marketing professional from Queens – another quintessential New Yorker.

We would each run three times. Sometime between two and three in the morning, I was running alone in the dark through a forest. The only illumination was my headlamp, which cast a small circle of light on the road just ahead and attracted a swarm of insects. One of our vans, carrying my now tired, sweaty and smelly teammates, roared up out of the gloom behind me and slowed alongside.

'You okay?' the driver asked. 'Got everything you need?'

'Yep. I think so.'

'Good. Well, we'll see you in about five miles.'

The van pulled away to wait at the next changeover point where I would hand over to the next runner. It felt good to be a part of something larger than myself, to feel a connection with people I'd had an opportunity to know through indulging a positive addiction.

Later in the month, when the moon was full, I invited Holly and two of the relay Chicks to a picnic on the pedestrian walkway of the Queensboro Bridge, high above the East River. I'd picked up finger food from Zabar's Deli, and served wine in heavy stemmed glasses from the apartment.

'This is the craziest thing I've ever done!' said one Chick.

On those Sunday mornings when I wasn't racing in Central Park, I sat among the congregation in a small Baptist church in Harlem and listened to the gospel singing. Alongside me were old men dressed in suits, their wrinkled wrists protruding from cuffs now too large for them. Women wearing smart outfits and extravagant hats cooled themselves with paper fans that bore the name of a local funeral parlour.

In the same way that the slowly turning ceiling fans provided some relief from the humidity, the joyous singing of the choir, the rhythmic clapping of hands, and the uninhibited vocal responses of the congregation helped the members of this community to cope with whatever life threw at them. Some of the people present would have lost family members to addiction, and on the Sunday morning in the summer of 2009 just after Michael Jackson died, he was simply another lost son.

ONE MORNING, I was in the reading room of the New York Public Library copyediting a book about brand management for a client in Singapore. An email arrived from Tim. 'The Dusters have been offered a place in this year's marathon. You've earned us points while you've been here. It's yours if you can get yourself over to New York Road Runners today to register.'

In a flash, I was out of the library and in an uptown subway train headed for the NYRR offices, located in a brownstone around the corner from the Guggenheim Museum on Fifth Avenue. I knew it well from picking up race bibs there before my races and Perspex age-group awards afterwards. When my registration for the marathon was finalised, I was able to transfer it to the following year, 2010. It seemed I was destined to return to New York after all.

Just before my flight back to Australia, Dusters Tim and Doug and two Dudes from the Vermont relay team joined me for an evening run across the bridges of the lower East River. During the summer, I'd learnt too late of an attempt on a Guinness World Record for the biggest gathering of people running in their underwear. I had decided to stage my own 'Three Bridges Underpants Run'.

Like a superhero, I wore over my black running shorts the orange lace undies I'd bought in the Swiss Alps two years before. As we ran back and forth across the Brooklyn, Manhattan and Williamsburg bridges, overtaking locals commuting home on foot from their offices in the city, Orthodox Jewish men with long side curls and dressed identically in high black hats and long coats, and out-of-towners snapping photos of the skyline, no one gave my knickers a second glance. I was just another New Yorker.

We finished the run on Delancey Street, on the Lower East Side, as the evening settled over the city and street lights illuminated the bridges behind us. Doug had suggested a nearby bar with a small garden that served craft beer. While we waited for a break in the flow of traffic, I stepped out of my superhero knickers and tucked them into the zippered belt that hung around my hips.

For now, my work here is done.

CHAPTER TWENTY-EIGHT

Albury was still hunkered down for the last of the winter when I returned from New York. I reclaimed my dogs and house and picked up my life where I had left off. Di and Fran still met at my place for early morning runs. Therese and Ivan still came for dinner and a film a few nights a week. I still worked out of my office facing the botanic gardens. Late in the afternoon on Sundays, I still went to the cinema at the other end of the main street, with a friend or on my own. On Monday nights, my mother and I still had dinner at the Thai place across the street. And most nights, I still wanted to finish my day alone in my bedroom with my dogs, the television, and as many glasses of cold white wine as I thought I could get away with.

New York seemed like a dream.

One night, after Therese and Ivan had left, I drank a fourth glass of wine, though I'd resolved not to have more than three. I clipped the dogs on to their leash and zippered myself into a warm jacket for a quick walk before bed.

A block from home, a car slowed alongside me.

'You are so fucking ugly.'

The passenger's insult skewered me like a spear. It was likely intended just to amuse the driver, but I crumpled in pain. I heard laughter as the car accelerated away, before the shock and the thumping pulse in my temple blocked all sounds of the night.

What has he seen?

Charlie was pawing and sniffing at a patch of grass beside the path. Butch was motionless at my feet, gazing up at me intently. I looked away; it was too much, all this scrutiny.

I turned back, aborting our walk. The serrated edge of my house key bit into my palm. At my door, it took three stabs before I could insert the key in the lock.

I don't want to feel this.

'Sorry,' I texted to Diane. 'Won't run tomorrow. Sore knee.'

My need for numbness – to not feel my feelings – was greater than the shame of lying to a friend. I took a new bottle of wine from the fridge, broke the seal and poured large dollops into the glass I'd used earlier. The first cold mouthful tasted like the answer to any question I could ask.

When I came to, I was on top of the bedcovers. Butch was asleep on the pillow beside me; Charlie was at the foot of the bed, awake and watchful. The overhead light and the television were on. The glass on the bedside table held three mouthfuls of wine. Was it the remnants of the first glass from the second bottle, or a second or third glass?

I heard Di and Fran's cars pull up in front of my house. It wasn't yet dawn. When they saw my light was on, they might ring the doorbell. I'd have to answer it. But my clothes were dishevelled, and I could smell the stale wine on my breath and skin. I couldn't bear for them to see me like this, to know this about me, to witness my shame.

Holding the quilt to my chin, I lay motionless, frozen, my ears straining.

I don't want to feel this. I'm small. Eleven? Twelve? My parents have gone out. We have been left alone at home. I'm woken from sleep by a hand. I don't know whose it is. Something is wrong. This shouldn't be happening to me. I keep my eyes closed tight and try not to breathe. I feel only the hand, touching me in a way that feels wrong. I lie motionless and pretend I am dead. I try to disappear far inside myself where I can't be reached. When it seems that I will burst from holding still, something changes. The hand has gone and I am alone. I'm safe now. I can breathe again.

Finally, my friends' voices faded away. I was unseen, safe, and could breathe again.

I HAD ACHIEVED so much in the past two years: I had clambered over mountain passes in the European Alps, run beside the canals of Venice, waded ankle-deep in mud across the spine of New Guinea, spun prayer wheels in the high Himalaya. I was a decent runner for a woman of fifty-seven. I'd been a success in New York. I was self-employed, busy socially, known in my local community. But my reliance on alcohol to fill the void and blot out painful memories was threatening to engulf me.

Success in meeting challenges I'd set myself was usually worth forgoing the extra glasses of wine I always craved after I'd had a first one. But it was a nightly trade-off, and sometimes morning seediness and trembling hands were a price I was prepared to pay for the numbing effect I sought. I seemed unable to experience any constant comfort, to reconcile the person who functioned well in the world with the one who sought oblivion. Ashamed, I couldn't look in the mirror for long enough to know what others could see. Was my shell cracking apart? Was my fear etched on my face, my jitteriness in my own skin apparent now even to a passing stranger?

The gap between the parts of me I was comfortable with others knowing and the side I wanted to keep hidden from view was growing, and I seemed to be falling into it.

Every step I had taken in the sixteen years since my near breakdown in Hong Kong had led me to where I now stood: at another turning point. New York had given me a glimpse of a different life, a different me, and I couldn't let go of the thought that I could leave everything behind, start over yet again and be *that* person.

I now had dogs, a mortgage, a sizeable art collection. But there were no children or grandchildren, or even a partner, to consider. I had lost Tom. Through the running, art and dog scenes, I had made close friends and many acquaintances, but I hadn't found a way to fix what was wrong with me. It didn't matter what some feral punk, a stranger to me, had chosen to see. What was important was how I saw myself.

I could imagine a different future from the one that seemed to be slouching towards my doorstep in Albury. I'd returned to my home town fifteen years before, promising to give it a year. I now wanted something different. It seemed that I was good at travelling; that it mostly brought out the best in me. What if I upped the ante right off the scale and detached myself from the ties that had been keeping me tethered, and just sailed free? The logistics involved in this would force me to be careful of my physical safety, which could help me to sort myself out, heal what needed to be healed, and ditch the most damaging of my addictive behaviours. I'd moved from home to home so many times in the past forty years, the prospect of not having a permanent address didn't bother me. New York had shown me that I could make temporary homes that worked for me. I enjoyed routines, but I also quickly became restless. I was still young and fit enough to meet people through running and hiking. I'd found that saying 'yes' to opportunities that presented themselves opened unexpected doors.

I could stay where I was, huddled in my upstairs bedroom every night, numbing my feelings with white wine and trying to straddle the growing gap between the person others saw and the one I was when alone. Or I could embark on an open-ended adventure, a hero's journey, and perhaps become the woman I had the potential to be.

'I'm selling up and leaving Australia,' I announced to my friends and family in late 2009. 'I don't know yet where I'll go or whether I'll be back. I'll see what happens.'

PART THREE

Excess baggage

CHAPTER TWENTY-NINE

Ubud, in Bali's hilly interior, was my first port of call on becoming a nomad in late May 2010. I'd visited the town a number of times and hoped it would ease me into my uncertain future.

The driver who collected me from the airport set down my luggage on the front porch of a small villa, unlocked the carved wooden doors and handed me the keys.

'*Terima kasih*,' I said, and gave him some rupiah notes.

'*Terima kasih, ibu*. Good night.'

The property was on the edge of a rice field. Garden lights outlined a pathway bordered by flowering shrubs. Frogs croaked insistently. The air smelled earthy, with hints of jasmine and motorcycle exhaust.

The room was dimly lit. Beneath the steeply pitched roof was a double bed swathed in mosquito netting. A vase with a sprig of bougainvillea stood on a bedside bamboo table. The floor was bare tile.

When I started up my laptop and logged on to the internet, there was an email from a client with a draft of their latest monthly report. *Aiyaah*. I was exhausted, but Polly in Hong Kong would need the edited file from me by morning to do the layout. Sleep would have to wait.

The swivel chair at the small desk wouldn't stay elevated. I piled cushions on to the seat and perched myself atop the stack for a better view of the keypad. Suddenly, something scampered above my head. A noise sounded like teeth or claws tearing at the bamboo poles that supported the roof. My heart thudded. It seemed too loud for a gecko. In Asia, a house isn't considered a home without a resident gecko to catch bugs and bring good luck. I could only imagine that my visitor was a giant monitor lizard shredding the roof of the villa, like in a scene from a B-grade horror flick. I abandoned the desk for the bed and sat huddled under the mosquito netting. Finally, the job was done, the noise had stopped and I could slither exhausted between the sheets.

I had no template for how to live the life of a permanent traveller, though my constant relocations from house to house in Sydney in my twenties, and then from city to city in my thirties and forties, pegged me as a gypsy. Ever since I'd left my father's house, exultant at finally being beyond his control, I'd relished the freedom to change my circumstances whenever they no longer suited me. But I had always had a home address, a key to a door, a landline telephone number. Now, I would be living temporarily in hotel rooms or someone else's apartment or house before moving on. I would have to find 'home' in myself, so that, like a snail, I could take it with me wherever I went.

I had an itinerary of sorts for the rest of the year. I hoped to be open to whatever and whoever came along. Instead of hiding away in my bedroom in Australia, I would engage with the world – be my best self, the strong woman I had it in me to be. Far from running away from life, I would run towards it. Soon, I would deal with the drinking. I just needed a little more time.

ON THE WAY to breakfast at a nearby *warung*, I saw a Western woman jogging along the roadside towards me. When I greeted her, she stopped for a chat. Dee was from Perth, she said, but was a frequent visitor to Ubud.

'I've sold up,' I said. 'I can work from anywhere on a tourist visa.'

'Digital nomadism's definitely the go.'

She agreed to meet for a run together the next morning. It was the first day of my new life and already I'd made a meaningful connection.

After breakfast, I unpacked. It had been hard to know what to take on the road for a journey that might have no end. I needed clothes and footwear for different climates, occasions and activities. For luck, I'd packed the orange lace knickers I'd worn over my running shorts in New York. I'd divested myself of my house; everything else, I'd sold or given away or stored in a shed on Di's country property. Butch and Charlie had new homes with friends they had known all their lives.

A ping from my laptop was Polly's email with formatted pages of the report. After checking them and sending them on to the client, I set out to walk the short distance into town. Vegetable plots were scattered along the roadside. Statues of mythical beasts, their loins covered with black-and-white checked cloth that symbolised balance and harmony, guarded family compounds set behind grey walls. I was careful not to step on the small daily offerings to the spirits, made of banana leaves, frangipani blossoms, rice grains and incense, that lay scattered on the ground.

A family rode past on a scooter. The father wore a white shirt over a batik sarong, and a white handkerchief tied around his head. A boy perched in front appeared dressed for school in a short-sleeved shirt and high-waisted blue shorts. A woman in a lime-green *kebaya* tunic and sarong tied at her waist sat sideways at the rear, her ankles crossed. Her sandal-clad feet looked dry and cracked. An infant lay swaddled in a cloth she'd slung across her chest. It was a world away from the four-door sedan that was the vehicle of choice for families where I'd just come from.

THE NEXT MORNING, my new friend Dee and I ran for an hour out towards the Tegalalang rice terraces, then back to town, where the roadside was lined with *penjor* poles, made for a recent festival. The tall wands of bamboo fronds decorated with coconut leaves had begun to deteriorate from exposure to the elements.

At Kafe, I felt a little scruffy in my sweaty running clothes. Many of the other customers might have passed for models in a photo shoot about 'new age' glamour. Man buns were popular, as were very long hugs. Taking a bite of my toasted sourdough with smashed avocado, I suspected that, in such company, my chakras might be conspicuously out of alignment.

Three days later, I had a lunch date with Cat Wheeler, whose book I was reading about her life as a *tamu*, or foreign guest, in Bali. Dee was joining us. I had decided that if I wanted to form attachments as I flitted from place to place, and not just skate across the surface, I would have to put myself forward, get in the faces of people I thought I might like and ask to spend time with them.

CHAPTER THIRTY

At the start of June, I arrived in Kuching, the capital of the former British Crown colony of Sarawak, now a Malaysian state on the island of Borneo. The place had once been home to headhunting tribes, 'white rajahs', and a client of mine who assured me I would enjoy it. 'Kuching is different from anywhere else,' Abdullah had said. It seemed like a sufficiently exotic location to kick off my big adventure in earnest.

My hotel was on the edge of Chinatown. I unpacked my few belongings, checked that I could get online, then headed out for a walk. Jalan Padungan was lined with shophouses – two-storey reinforced-concrete structures painted in garish purples, greens and mustard-yellows. At street level were small businesses, with residences above. It all looked ramshackle and lived-in, and I loved it on sight.

Cars and motorcycles streamed in both directions, separated by a row of mature trees. Four young Malay women wearing *hijabs* (the traditional Muslim head covering), long-sleeved T-shirts and skinny jeans sipped pink, milky drinks at an outdoor café. A group of Chinese-Malaysian kids in blue-and-white school uniforms chatted noisily in English outside McDonald's.

A buckled slab of concrete spanned a deep stormwater drain between the footpath and the road. As in Ubud, walking could be hazardous, and I picked my way carefully. An Indian-Malaysian family posed stiffly for a photograph in front of a large concrete statue of cats clustered on a traffic island.

The Sarawak River was muddy looking. Broken tree branches tumbled in the current. At a wooden jetty, the boatman of a small craft with a peaked roof smoked a cigarette while waiting for passengers. I could hear the puttering engine of another *sampan* crossing from the opposite shore, where a huge structure with a roof shaped like a parasol dominated the skyline.

In India Street, behind Main Bazaar, late-afternoon shoppers browsed through the bolts of sari fabrics on display and cooled themselves with brightly coloured drinks from small carts. It was like India, but without the cow manure underfoot.

Inside a large Chinese temple where elaborate tableaux were devoted to statues of deities, the air was thick from the incense coils that hung smouldering from the ceiling. The smells took me back to an earlier time in my life, when I'd been enchanted by Hong Kong and had followed an impulse to move there.

The call to prayer came from a nearby mosque. I had first heard a *muezzin* in Yogyakarta, in the late 1970s, during an overland journey from Bali to Jakarta with a Javanese musician. We had detoured to Muntilan, his home village near the ancient Buddhist temple complex of Borobudur. There, his mother, a batik artist, had held my hands and looked into my eyes. The only word we had in common was her son's name.

ONE MORNING ON the Kuching waterfront, I met Sim, a Malaysian-Chinese woman, who invited me to join her regular running group. We ran through the empty city streets, across a wide bridge and back through a dusty *kampong* to a small wharf opposite our starting point. A *sampan* carried us back across the river, squeezed in among some local commuters. A woman wearing a mauve *hijab* that left just her age-freckled face exposed sat opposite me on the hard, wooden seat. I was wearing shorts, a loose-fitting shirt from a race I'd run in New York the year before, orange socks and lime-green running shoes. My outfit was immodest by her standards, but she gave me a friendly smile. Two skinny young men were deep in conversation in Bahasa Malaysia. My colleague had been right: I liked his home town very much.

AN ARTICLE IN *The Borneo Post* announced that the Society of Sarawakians Writing in English would be holding a writing workshop in Miri, in the north of the state. As I would be in the area at that time and had determined to make local connections wherever possible, I emailed the SOSWE secretary, offering to help out.

'I'll be in Kuching this week,' Jennie replied. 'We can meet.'

For afternoon tea at my hotel, she wore a sixties-style shift dress that ended well above her knees and a floppy, large-brimmed hat. I could see that she enjoyed putting together a 'look'.

'How can I help with your workshop?' I asked.

'I think you could talk about your work and your life.'

Aiyaah …

'It will be *very* informal. No pressure.'

A day or so later, I was again looking through *The Borneo Post* at breakfast when I noticed another article about the SOSWE event. This time, I was named as a special guest speaker. Unaccustomed as I was to public speaking, I was nervous at the prospect of being on show. At the same time, this is what I had wanted from my new life: to find out who I was and what I was capable of.

In the north, just before I spoke at the event, where I had my photograph taken with the mayor and helped to hand out prizes to senior high school kids who had excelled at English composition, I trekked with a group for four days through Gunung Mulu National Park. One day, we travelled by longboat down the Melinau River to the start of the Headhunters Trail. Walking the dank-smelling track through the forest to our camp for the night, it was easy to imagine a victorious war party making its way home to the longhouse with fresh trophies of the heads of their enemies for drying and display.

I had been unsure about making an all-day return climb the next day to the Pinnacles, razor-sharp limestone formations near the summit of Gunung Api. After reading the information board at camp (a warning described the climb as being 'very, very high risk' and had thirteen exclamation marks), I decided not to attempt it.

'I don't want to knowingly put myself at risk,' I said to Han, our guide. 'I've only just started my travelling life. I don't have anything to prove.'

I did only the first stage of the climb. It was long and steep, and the hard effort felt good. 'Good luck!' I said to the braver members of the group who were going higher. Then I slid and scrambled my way back down the track. After a dunk in the stream to wash off the sweat and grime, I walked alone for two hours back along the Headhunters Trail. I was nervous, but it seemed I had to prove to myself, if to no one else, that my caution didn't derive just from being a coward.

The next morning, we carried on by boat to a traditional communal longhouse, our accommodation for the final night of the trek. We were to be guests of an Iban tribe that still followed age-old traditions. There would be a feast, with *tuak*, a traditional alcoholic brew made of fermented rice. It was a unique opportunity – a *privilege* – to be hosted by such people, but I was apprehensive about drinking anything unfamiliar in an environment where I had no control. In the years before I had fully understood the extent of my problem with alcohol, I'd drink anything. Now, frightened of what might happen if I varied my rituals, I was much more cautious, much more private. I didn't want to be seen to have a problem if I went into a brownout after drinking a strong spirit. But I also didn't want to offend the hosts by refusing it.

'I'd like to get to Limbang today,' I said to Han on an impulse. 'Is it possible?'

He rubbed the bridge of his nose and then went off to talk with some people from the longhouse. When he returned, he was smiling. 'The headman will take you in his longboat to a small town an hour away. From there you can take a bus. There is a small charge.'

As the tribal chief and I made our way downriver, the only sound was the puttering of the engine and the wash of water along the sides of the narrow craft. I imagined crocodiles slithering into the river from the banks. For me, it seemed like a place where there was only ever today, measured by the passage of the sun across the sky. Tomorrow – that elusive day when I would say 'no' to any type of alcohol, not just to *tuak* – didn't exist here. Only a vapour trail indicated the presence of a world beyond this one.

CHAPTER THIRTY-ONE

Sim mentioned that a charity run was being held on my last weekend in Kuching. I found the details online, including a phone number for entry enquiries. 'It's only open to Malaysians,' the race organiser said when I phoned.

'I really want to enter it. I write a column about running for an Australian newspaper, and this would be a great story.' A local free paper in Albury had given me space for a fortnightly travel column, which I'd called 'My Own Two Feet'.

'I'll see what I can do.'

When he called me back, it was with good news. 'My boss will make an exception for you. You can enter as an international media guest. Guests and VIPs are eligible for the 3K event.'

I knew there was also a 7K course. 'But I really want to enter the longer event. I'm an experienced runner.'

'I'll see what I can do.'

An hour or so later, he rang me back. 'I have more good news. Despite your age, my boss will make another exception for you.'

I'D BECOME FRIENDLY with a Malaysian-Chinese woman, tiny and impish, who owned a laundry just around the corner from my hotel. Emily nicknamed me 'Beep Beep' when she learnt I was a road runner. One evening, she invited me out for a casual meal with her friend Rita, a massage therapist. We ate at a hawker centre, on the perimeter of a daytime car park, where dozens of food vendors specialising in different traditional Malaysian dishes operated side by side. Afterwards, Emily introduced me to her brother, James, a photographer and producer of music videos.

Just before the charity race, I was a guest on a morning radio show. The presenter, Jennifer Lau, had read in *The Borneo Post* about my involvement with the SOSWE event and invited me in for an on-air chat. I'd already met the guest who preceded me, an architect, at a dinner held by a local artist I'd introduced myself to recently. I could hardly believe I'd arrived in Sarawak only three weeks before.

THE EVENING OF the race was hot and humid. I ran conservatively for the first few kilometres and then increased my pace. There was no water available along the course. On the homeward leg, I wobbled and nearly fell.

The next thing I knew, I was sitting on the ground, against an earthen bank, vomiting and panting. Men dressed for prayers at the mosque hovered over me. Someone was fanning me with a piece of cardboard. A group of women stood silently to one side, watching.

Eventually, the nausea passed and my breathing slowed. My lower back hurt. I had a lump on a knuckle on my left hand and some grazes on my legs.

'I need to finish the race.' My voice was croaky.

'What race?'

'Where are the other runners?'

'What other runners?'

I needed to get to the finish line, where Emily, Rita and James were waiting for me. I was a guest for whom exceptions had been made; I couldn't just disappear.

'Please, could someone take me to the river?'

'Go to your hotel,' a man said, not unkindly.

They didn't know what to do with me. I was obviously distressed, looked dishevelled in shorts and a soiled singlet, and smelled of vomit. I was too weak to walk unassisted.

After some discussion, two men came forward, half-carried me to a small car and deposited me in the back seat. Within minutes we were on the waterfront, where runners and spectators were milling. I had been less than a kilometre from the finish line when I had somehow passed out while still on my feet.

'Thank you.' I'd barely shut the door when the car pulled away.

I located a first-aid table, where one of the attendees found a chair for me and agreed to take my race number to an official at the finish line. Though I hadn't completed the race, the organisers would need to account for me.

A glass of water was produced. After taking a few sips, I had time only to lean forward and spread my feet before I vomited all over the pavers. The first aiders looked unsure of what to do next.

'My friends will be looking for me. Could someone ask the announcer to say something, please?'

'I'm a special guest,' I added feebly.

A few minutes later, at the conclusion of a Taiwanese pop song, I heard a male voice address the crowd: 'Mr James Lo? James Lo? You are needed at the first-aid station. Your wife is unwell.'

Apparently, I had acquired a husband in Kuching.

Soon, my friends were by my side. 'What happened?'

'I don't know. Dehydration? Heat exhaustion? I blacked out. I still can't keep any fluid down.'

'You should go to hospital,' Rita said. 'I'll call an ambulance.'

'You'll need some ID,' Emily said. 'We'll go to your hotel and get your passport and credit card.'

When the ambulance arrived, a paramedic helped me on to the stretcher in the back. The pop songs had been replaced by announcements of the placegetters in the race. As Rita settled by my side and took my hand, my name was announced as the winner of the 7K race in the international media guest category.

At the hospital, I was attached to a drip to rehydrate. At around midnight, I was discharged. Emily, who had kept me company, drove me to my hotel. My skin was still smeared with dirt and dried perspiration. I smelled bad, and was exhausted and very frightened. I'd expected to run a quick evening race; instead, I had lost consciousness. How close had I been to having heat stroke? Disoriented and delirious, I'd apparently stumbled across busy roads before collapsing some distance from the course near a backwater of the river.

The expanse of time between when I wobbled and when I regained consciousness was a blank. What must I have looked like, weaving like a drunk through traffic and up a dusty back road? Had I fallen? Why was my back sore? I had felt this confusion before, when I was unable to put flashes of memory into any logical sequence. Today's fugue-like state had been caused by dehydration, not by alcohol, but the fear felt the same.

Instead of showering and getting into bed, I opened the bottle of wine I had stashed in the minibar before the race and filled a glass nearly to the brim. Holding it to my lips with both hands, I sipped quickly at the liquid until the panic began to subside.

I WAS IN Hong Kong for July to register a new business that would service my non-Australian clients and separate that income stream from Australian-sourced income for tax purposes. My home for the month was the Helena May, in what had once been Sarah's room in the garden court. I sensed my own ghostly presence in the room by the stairwell where, twenty years before, I had chain-smoked, drunk scotch and stared at the television every evening after I'd split from my business partners.

One weekend, I went with Polly by jetfoil to Macau. In the mid-1980s, the Lisboa hotel and casino had been the city's only high-rise building, and cycle-rickshaws and pony carriages were a common means of transport. Now, reclamation had created space for the dozens of spectacularly kitsch casinos that were a magnet for gamblers from mainland China.

On the Sunday morning, we took a walk. The air quality was poor and the sky an opaque grey. I poked at the ground with a stick as I walked, my thoughts drifting.

'I forgive you for leaving,' Polly said, suddenly.

When I had abandoned everything in Hong Kong in late 1993, I had left my remaining share of our office set-up expenses unpaid. Polly had never mentioned the debt.

'Thank you, Pol.'

'It was a long time ago.' She sighed. 'You weren't happy. You're better now.'

Not quite, I thought. *But soon.*

I STAYED ON my feet for most of August, walking in the Piedmont region of northern Italy with a Dead Runner friend, Giorgio, and across England on a guided walk – a distance of around 300 kilometres. Late one afternoon on the edge of the

Yorkshire Dales, our group of coast-to-coast walkers gathered for drinks in the bar after arriving at our night's lodgings. Although I was some days into a two-week hike, I wasn't on holiday. When I checked my emails, there was an urgent job – the same monthly report I'd had to work on the first night of my new life, back in late May.

Everyone was rather jolly by the time I could join them again in the bistro. I downed two large glasses of wine with my scampi and chips, then had a couple more in the bar afterwards. I'd been chatting with Hannah, Jo and Tony when, suddenly, I sounded like I was speaking in tongues. It was as if a switch had been flipped and I'd gone straight from being merry to being *drunk* drunk.

My friend Michele was awake, making notes in her journal, when I tumbled through the doorway of our shared room, fell straight into bed and passed out.

In the pre-dawn, my cell phone rang. "Lo?' I croaked, pulling the covers over my head so as not to disturb Michele.

'Did you get my email?' Polly said. 'I need you to check the pages.'

'It's the middle of the night, Pol!' I whispered. 'I was going to do it before breakfast.'

'I need them now.'

'Bloody hell.'

I grabbed my laptop, a blanket and pillow and crept out into the dimly lit hallway. For the next two hours, I sat on the floor, my back against the wall, squinting at the formatted pages on the lookout for typos and whimpering for a coffee.

For much of that day, I kept to myself. I was embarrassed and frightened. I hadn't even had all that much to drink. Why had I slid over into la-la land? At the end of the walk, I threw the pebble I'd picked up beside the Irish Sea, on the other side of the country, into the North Sea. How much longer could I keep myself afloat before I, too, sank like a stone?

CHAPTER THIRTY-TWO

'I love New York,' I said to the Bangladeshi taxi driver who picked me up at JFK Airport. Across the East River, the spire of the Chrysler Building shone in the sunshine like a golden pagoda.

'Everybody love New York!'

It was early September. The same apartment beside Central Park that had been my base the year before would be home while I prepared to run the New York City Marathon. It usually takes sixteen weeks, starting from a good base, to prepare to run a race of this distance; I'd have only eight.

The night before a Fifth Avenue Mile event, I went to bed without having had any alcohol at all. I wanted to give the race my best shot. But without any wine to take the edge off, I had trouble falling asleep. My heart raced, and I changed position restlessly, becoming anxious about having another panic attack like the one I'd had in Hong Kong. Turning back on to my right side, I opened my eyes and saw in the gloom by the window a spider the size of my outspread hand. It took my breath away. I couldn't take my eyes off it for long enough to blink. Slowly it made its way behind the slatted window blind, while I stared at the wall in horror.

If there IS a huge spider in my room, I am totally going to shit myself, I thought. *Or if there isn't, but I'm seeing one, I am so fucked.*

In the dead of night, the second scenario seemed slightly

preferable to the first, but I didn't have the courage to check behind the blind and confirm whether I was suffering from arachnophobia or alcohol withdrawal. I tried to keep one eye open, in case the spider was real and reappeared, but sleep overtook me and spared me further terror. The next morning, I took the absence of any sign of a spider as a sign that I really needed to get serious again about trying to quit drinking. It wouldn't matter how far I walked, or how many races I entered, or how fast I ran them, I couldn't get away from the fact I had a problem with alcohol. My new life was extraordinary. Why was I sabotaging it?

After the race, I checked online for recovery meetings in my neighbourhood and saw there was one at a church not far from me. When I arrived there the next day, a dozen Hispanic women were talking together in the vestibule.

'Is this where the meeting is?' I asked.

'Meeting? No, there's no meeting,' someone said.

I had got the details wrong. Relief coursed through me. The universe had spoken: I didn't have to fix myself right now. Not today. I'd been given a reprieve.

While I continued to tie myself into a knot trying to find a way to drink without all the psychic anguish that accompanied it, I set new physical challenges that rewarded my efforts with feel-good chemicals. I accepted that I could get addicted to just about anything, not all of them harmful. Positive addictions could meet some of my needs, too.

Over three days, I walked right around Manhattan, staying as close to the waterfront as possible. Tamar, a teammate from the Vermont relay of the previous summer, joined me to run the first stage, from the Staten Island Ferry Terminal up the western side of the island to Harlem. On day two, my photographer friend

Holly and I followed the riverside path from Harlem up to Inwood Hill Park, at the top of Manhattan. In the early 1600s, it was here the Dutch bought the island from the local Indian tribe for a pittance. This far north, the city sounds were muffled, as if the park lay under a heavy cloak.

In Spanish Harlem, on the east side, after Holly peeled off, I lost sight of the river in a poor area riddled with public housing projects. A youth wearing a hoodie slouched towards me, the crotch of his baggy jeans hanging low on his skinny frame. When I asked him for directions, he pointed to a cross street up ahead. 'Turn left up there. You'll see an overpass. It'll get you to the river.'

'You're welcome, miss,' he said, when I thanked him. He stuck his hands deep in his pockets and slouched away, leaving me feeling unexpectedly cheered.

The following afternoon, battling a strong headwind coming off the East River, I returned alone to my starting point – via Midtown, then beneath the bridges I had run across the previous year with my orange knickers on show, and down through the financial district. I was depositing memories all over the city, like a dog marking its territory.

As a nomad, I didn't want just to accumulate ready-made experiences. I wanted to create my own relationship with a place. Running and walking were ways to do that – to go off the beaten path, to spend time with people, to experience their home in the way *they* did, to create memories and to be a part of others' memories, to be seen and to leave a trace of myself behind.

AT THE START of the 41st New York City Marathon in early November, I wasn't confident I would make it to the finish line.

My preparation had been erratic. There had been too many mornings when I'd concealed an empty wine bottle beneath yesterday's *New York Times* and breathed easily only after I'd deposited it in the trash box along the corridor from my apartment. Still, I'd been able to keep my drinking under some control. I hadn't been really drunk since the coast-to-coast walk in England. On that measure, I wasn't doing too badly. The marathon was important to me. I wanted to enjoy the day and to complete what I'd set out to do. I'd been willing to make the trade-off.

The ferry to the race start passed Ellis Island and the Statue of Liberty. I thought about the millions of people who had travelled to the United States in the hope of making a home there. But I was learning that home isn't necessarily a physical place. If I could be at home in my own skin, I could be at home wherever I was in the world.

When I crossed the finish line after running from Staten Island to Brooklyn, through Queens, up the East River on Manhattan to the Bronx, and back down through Harlem to Central Park, I hadn't just got to the end of a 42-kilometre race. My new life had shown me I was capable, determined and strong. Despite the cracks in my shell, it seemed there was a chance that I could put myself back together and become whole again.

Clutching the medal that hung around my neck, and with a smile plastered across my face, I hobbled the twenty blocks up Central Park West to my apartment. New Yorkers are always generous in affirming other people's efforts, but on marathon day they are without equal: fellow finishers exchanged proud grins and weary nods; passing drivers rhythmically tooted their car horns; and strangers on the street cooed congratulations and offered high fives.

CHAPTER THIRTY-THREE

A major annual festival was in progress when I returned to Indonesia in December. Ubud's roads were congested with noisy processions of locals dressed in their best traditional outfits and bearing on their heads ornate constructions of fruits and flowers intended as temple offerings to Bali's many gods.

Through Cat, the writer I had lunched with in May, I met Gede, a reliable and affable driver and guide. One afternoon, he and I followed a funeral procession to the site of a double cremation. There, the shroud-wrapped bodies were transferred from ornately decorated wooden caskets to the cremation towers, where the souls of the departed could be released to the afterlife. Far from being a solemn occasion, the buzz in the air was like that at a sporting event, with hawkers selling snack foods and drinks to the crowds of spectators. Little had changed since I'd witnessed a similar ceremony here in the 1970s. I stared, transfixed, at the blackened legs and feet that protruded from a shelf of the tower and wondered again at how fluid was the notion of 'normal'.

FOR A RETURN visit to Kuching, I made my home at the Batik Boutique Hotel. The owner, Jackie, was a Malaysian-Chinese entrepreneur and keen hiker. Jo-Lynn, the shorts- and thongs-clad manager, also encouraged guests to join in hikes, waterfall climbs and overnight visits to remote Indigenous communities. One weekend, on a walk to Jangkar Falls, my foot slipped while I was picking my way across a stream. I fell forward and banged my chin hard against a boulder.

'You'd better get that X-rayed,' Jo-Lynn said, when we returned to town. 'I'll take you to Normah Hospital.'

Nothing was broken. It was my second visit to a hospital in Kuching and a second lucky escape.

The Malay woman who cleaned my room at the Batik invited me to join her and her husband at a café that was renowned for its spicy Sarawak laksa. They arrived for our date on a motorcycle, Mas dressed in black leggings and a colourful patterned tunic top. Her hennaed hair glistened in the sunshine. Jun's hair was snow-white and hung to his shoulders.

A few days later, they introduced me to the surreal world of Kuching's karaoke bars. A *sampan* deposited us on a dock beside a weather-beaten shack with open sides that was a popular mid-afternoon karaoke venue. My new friends seemed to know everyone. When a middle-aged Malay man wearing a pink shirt tucked into his jeans took to the small stage and began to sing a ballad, three women of an age to have teenage grandchildren line-danced in formation in front of him, their *hijabs* fluttering in the breeze from the river.

Mas and Jun had been together for decades but acted like young lovers. I envied them their sureness of each other. 'We don't take things too seriously,' Jun said, his eyes twinkling. 'Life is to be enjoyed.'

I WAS STILL busy with my work and thrilled to be meeting a lot of new people, but without a serious running goal I was a little adrift and again relying too much on my own most constant companion. I worried what Mas thought when she cleaned my room each day and found yet another empty wine bottle. Despite her Western-style fashion choices and uncovered hair, she was a devout Muslim and never drank alcohol.

On the first day of 2011, I vowed once more to stop drinking. To my mind, all the ones in 1/1/11 represented a unique opportunity to reset the way I did things and begin life anew.

The next day, I went for a run along the waterfront. Happy to have started off the new year on the right foot, I trilled '*Pagi!* Good morning!' at every passer-by. From a café near Main Bazaar, I bought roti flatbread fresh off the griddle to eat as I strolled home, floating on an exercise-induced cloud of wellbeing.

Jackie introduced me to her friend Josephine, a beauty therapist. I had booked a waxing session with her, but Jo looked me over and announced that my nipples were lower on my chest than they need be. 'Your breasts could be plumped up a bit. I've got just the thing.'

Jo's home salon resembled a medium-sized intensive care unit but smelled of lotions and potions. While she applied molten wax to my nether regions, I lay hooked up to a kind of breast pump. The regular, gentle chugging reminded me of my Uncle Frank's dairy farm, which I had visited regularly as a child. I would hover at the edge of the milking shed, careful not to step in fresh cow manure, and watch Frank attach to his cows' teats suction cups similar to those that were now attached to mine.

The following Saturday, Jay, a Canadian forestry expert who had retired to Sarawak, led a hike in search of a lost antimony mine. It sounded like something out of *Raiders of the Lost Ark*, but instead of locating an abandoned mineshaft, we spent three hours wandering through a leech-infested swamp. The peace of the forest was shattered by our intermittent screams when yet another leech attached itself to a body part.

Walking behind Jackie, I had a disturbing sensation in the region of my crotch. I put my hand down the front of my walking trousers, pinched hard, and pulled out a small, black, squishy mass. It seemed like the tail end of something.

On hearing my scream, Jackie turned back. She dropped to a crouch in front of me and brandished a can of some kind of critter zapper. I pulled down my pants and poked my pelvis in her face. She pointed the nozzle at my privates and pressed hard, releasing a stream of vapour.

My screams turned to giggles. 'Thank god I've just had a wax!'

IN INDIA, TWO months after I'd stopped drinking, a glass of wine again seemed like an excellent idea. I thought I was becoming free of the burden of my addiction to alcohol, but it had only been waiting stealthily for my resolve to weaken.

I'd rendezvoused in Chennai, on the east coast, with Uma, an artist I'd met in Malta during my Mediterranean odyssey in 2007. From there, we'd flown across the country to Mumbai, where I was entered in a half marathon with a Dead Runner friend, Sanjay. Uma and I shared a twin room at the colonial-era Taj Mahal Palace. The hotel had been targeted by members of a Pakistan-based Islamic terrorist organisation in a series of attacks in November 2008. Two years later, security in and around the hotel was still tight. During the siege, Sanjay had been 'Our Man in Bombay', posting to the DRS list updates on the events as they unfolded.

'This is where they came ashore,' he said, when we were walking to the expo venue to pick up our numbers and T-shirts for the race. 'More than thirty people were killed at your hotel.' I knew that over a hundred had also died at the railway station, in the Leopold Café and at the other targeted sites.

That evening, Sanjay and his wife, Reetu, and Uma and I settled in for a pre-dinner drink at an outside table at the Bombay Cricketers Club, another relic of India under the Raj. I had intended to order a sparkling water, but the setting was so delightful, the evening air so balmy, the lawn so lushly green under the lights, I couldn't withstand the 'yes' that rose from my toes when I was offered a glass of wine. The first mouthful of sauvignon blanc washed away any remaining defences in an instant. A second glass followed without even a whisper of caution from my inner navigator.

The next day, Uma and I had lunch at the Leopold Café, which had been operating since the early years of the Raj and was today busy with tourists.

'It's hard to imagine someone appearing in the doorway with an automatic weapon and just opening fire on people.'

I reached for my glass of wine.

'People like us, without a care in the world ...'

My voice sounded wistful and somehow distant, as if I were floating outside of myself and listening in.

On my last night in India, Sanjay and Reetu took me to dinner at their favourite bistro to celebrate my having placed fifth in my age group in the race.

'Try the fillet steak,' Sanjay urged.

'Isn't it from a sacred cow? Won't lightning strike me dead?'

'Trust me.'

'It's on your head, then, if I get bad karma, Sanjay.'

The evening was fun. They didn't mind my intrusive questions about how they had met. After we said our goodbyes, I walked along the waterfront to the Gateway of India, where beautifully dressed families strolled, enjoying the gentle breeze.

I wanted a nightcap. Uma had left, so I would have privacy; the race was over; I was moving on tomorrow. I could let my guard down. It hadn't been as hard to stop as I'd expected. I would just set my mind to it again at a more convenient time.

Walking across to the hotel's security check, I winced when a passing pony harnessed to a gaudily decorated tourist carriage stumbled heavily while trying to keep its footing on the uneven road.

CHAPTER THIRTY-FOUR

During the long drive from Kuala Lumpur International Airport down to Malacca, on the strait that separates the Malaysian peninsula from Indonesian Sumatra, I passed the time by chatting with the Malay taxi driver.

'I have ten daughters,' he said, when I asked about his family. 'And three wives.'

'Were you trying for a son?'

'Still trying!' His twinkling eyes met mine in the rear-vision mirror.

'How do you keep all your wives happy?'

'I stay three nights with each one. No arguments that way.'

My home for the next ten days was a heritage building in Chinatown that had been converted to a boutique hotel. Jonker Walk and the Malacca River were close by. I'd hoped to make inroads into my workload; however, the Christmas carols being piped into my room all day made it difficult to concentrate.

'Are the carols really necessary?' I complained to the manager. 'It's nearly the end of January!'

'Our guests enjoy them.'

'Well, I'm a guest and I'm not enjoying them at all. I think it's time to give them a rest.'

I was more irritable when I was drinking again. If I couldn't control myself, I could at least try to control everyone else.

Again, each morning, I had to dispose of an empty wine bottle. In Kuching, Mas's good opinion of me had mattered; in Malacca, I just blanked out the person who emptied the bin and cleaned around me while I worked at the desk in my room. I spoke to none of the other guests, who seemed mainly to be young lovers or adulterers from KL or Singapore.

Having jumped back on the drinking carousel in India, I couldn't just hop off it again immediately. I would have to wait for another auspicious date. It wouldn't need to be another new decade, or even a new year, but certainly the start of a new month. Or at least a Monday.

MY SMALL HOTEL in Chiang Mai, in northern Thailand, was a ten-minute walk from the ancient town centre. The morning after I flew up from Malaysia, I slipped out of my sandals at the entrance to the small breakfast pavilion in the garden, walked up the wooden steps and entered the room. A new place. A fresh start.

'Good morning,' I chirped. Four couples turned their heads.

'Morning,' said two of the four older Western gents. None of their young Thai male companions returned my greeting.

Ah, I thought. *This could be awkward.*

The following morning, Mike, an Englishman aged in his seventies, invited me to join him and his local partner at their table. 'What brings you to Chiang Mai?' he asked, buttering his toast.

'Dental work.' I grimaced.

'We get a lot of visitors for that.'

'Do you live here?'

'Oh, yes. We have an apartment in the garden. But Dom wants

to study at university. We'll probably go back to England this year.' Dom gave me a shy smile. 'It's his birthday this week. We're celebrating at a restaurant. Would you like to join us?'

'I'd love to!'

Within a week, Dom had become my early morning training partner. We would run into the centre of town before it was light, follow the course of the original city wall and moat, then head home in time for breakfast with Mike.

To celebrate Dom's learning to drive and getting his licence, Mike hired a rather nice car so that Dom might drive them to a resort near Lampang, a town popular with local tourists for its pony-drawn carriages.

'I sat in the back the whole way,' Mike wrote in an email. 'I had Dom's motorcycle helmet, just in case, but I didn't need it.'

MY DAYS WERE structured around dental appointments and work. I'd found a couple of local restaurants that I returned to regularly, and a small supermarket where I could buy wine. Nervous about the dentist smelling alcohol on my breath, I limited myself to two glasses on nights before a scheduled appointment, then took half a Xanax to ensure I'd sleep. On my 'free' nights, I self-prescribed a full bottle and omitted the pill.

A month had passed since the leech incident in Sarawak, and I was having uncomfortable sensations in my groin area. Googling 'leech in vagina' was a very bad idea. I heard that a nearby hospital had a good reputation among local expatriates and fronted up to get my itch checked.

At the general admissions desk, I couldn't make myself understood. On a piece of notepaper I drew a diagram with a stick figure, and an arrow pointing from a thick black squiggle to the crotch area. The girl nodded as if this was something she saw routinely and pointed to a sign that said 'Obstetrics and Gynaecology'. There, I again produced my drawing. A nurse showed me to an examination room, handed me a robe, and waved her hand in a way that I understood to mean I should remove my clothes.

A young male doctor knocked and entered.

'How can I help you?'

'Um. I was in Malaysia ... in the jungle ... in a swamp. And there were leeches. And, um, I think one might have gone in my ...' I pointed to my crotch. 'In my vagina.'

His cheeks flushed pink.

'Ah ... I will look. Sit in the chair and put your feet here.' He flapped a hand at a pair of stirrups.

When I clambered up and assumed the position, he motioned for me to scoot further down so that my bum overhung the edge. Then, seating himself on a stool between my spread legs, he switched on a headlamp, picked up a probing instrument, leaned forward and started to poke around in my innards.

After a few minutes, he sat back and smiled broadly.

'Good news! No leech!'

I realised I'd hardly been breathing, when air rushed back into my lungs.

A HALF MARATHON I'd entered in Lampang was a fundraiser for a local pony welfare organisation. It was still dark when our small group of runners, including one or two other Westerners, set off. An hour later, monks and locals were making their way to a nearby temple and the gentle sound of bells filled the air. People I passed in the villages along the course called out to me, gave me a thumbs-up, or placed their hands together and dipped their heads in greeting. I dipped my head in return, my heart full. Despite my ever-present anxiety when I was drinking again, physical exertion could produce a state of contentment. Special moments such as these didn't happen if I turned over in bed and went back to sleep. On a dusty back road in northern Thailand, at the start of a new day, I was momentarily at peace with myself and with the world around me.

THERE WERE NO more niggling sensations in my vagina until an email from Tom appeared unexpectedly in my inbox. We hadn't been in contact since the debacle in Canberra at the end of 2008, over two years before. We soon made plans to take a camping trip together in Australia in a few months' time.

'Are you insane?' might have been a reasonable question for anyone who knew me well to ask.

'Probably,' would have been a reasonable response.

In the more than thirty years I had known him, Tom had never made me feel loved or safe. But he sometimes made me feel desired. And he seemed to find something in me he hadn't found in anyone else. He didn't know what to do with it, or with whatever feelings it produced in him, but it pulled him back to me and me to him, again and again. Despite our mismatched needs – mine to be held, his to keep himself apart – I was addicted to the rush I felt whenever he reappeared on my radar, and was compelled to be with him again.

CHAPTER THIRTY-FIVE

When I arrived in Switzerland at the start of March, denial of my problem with alcohol sat like a thick layer of skin between the person I wanted to appear to be on the outside and the one I tried to keep hidden. The tension between the two manifested as a tremor in my hands and tightness in my jaw.

It was still very cold in Lausanne, with a winter haze blanketing the French Alps across Lake Geneva. I was staying in an apartment owned by Françoise, whose other home I rented when in New York. From the dining-room table, where I often started work before dawn, the lights of Evian-les-Bains were visible across the lake.

Each day, I was impatient to finish my work tasks and head out to explore the town and nearby villages. One day, a cluster of swans sailed alongside me, providing company as I walked by the lakeshore from medieval Lutry back to Lausanne. The weather had cleared, providing glimpses of the Alps. How privileged I felt to be here, in such a beautiful place.

One weekend, a new friend and I took a train excursion to the ski resort of Zermatt, at the foot of the Matterhorn. From there, the *Glacier Express* whisked us across nearly 300 bridges to St Moritz. The day was clear and sunny, the sky a deep blue against the stunning snow peaks.

'Did you talk with your friend?' Liliane asked.

'Yep. It seems he has a short memory. It seems we both do.'

I had no plans to stop my nomadic wanderings. My itinerary seemed to write itself, and I was intrigued by where my life was taking me. But where did Tom fit in? Why did I instantly imagine that we might put our lives together, when experience indicated we were incompatible? Was it just a matter of trying harder? What was standing in the way if he wanted me and I wanted him?

AFTER THE WINTER haze lifted, I walked alone for five days along the shore of Lake Geneva, staying the night in pubs along the way. My small backpack held only my laptop and a few changes of underwear and T-shirts. If I kept the lake on my right and put one foot in front of the other for 80 kilometres, I would get to where I wanted to go. If only all of life were so simple.

On the afternoon of the third day, the weather turned misty, then drizzly and grey. Rounding a corner of the lakeshore path, I came upon a man dressed in a black suit and holding aloft a tiny umbrella. He was standing motionless on a concrete slab that poked out into the water. I snapped a quick photograph before he could sense my presence. I couldn't imagine why he was there, dressed so formally and sheltering beneath an umbrella the size of a dinner plate. There was a whiff of performance art staged by the universe for my pleasure alone.

The final morning dawned pink and blue. The lake was mirror-like, reflecting the mountain peaks and sleeping swans. A large metal fork stuck up out of the shallows – a surreal installation artwork. Colourful flowerbeds and bamboo sculptures lined the path. From Montreux, the weather for the final stage to Villeneuve couldn't have been more beautiful.

Hang-gliders floated above me, their colourful canopies startling against the vivid blue sky. It reminded me of the voice that had called '*Bon appetit*' from a glider high above a terrace as I drank a glass of wine at the end of my trek through the Alps in 2007. I was now just across the lake from those same mountains. My life had brought me almost full circle.

I didn't want the walk to end. I loved spending days on my feet, making steady progress towards a goal I'd set myself, enjoying the solitude, lulled by the rhythm of walking, alert to my surroundings, delighted by the sights and encounters along the way.

On my final night at the apartment in Lausanne, I drank one of the two bottles of wine I'd bought in Villeneuve. The second was a thank-you gift for Françoise.

'I hope you enjoy this,' I wrote her in a note. 'I walked a long way to get it for you.'

When I threw my empty bottle into the deep recycling dumpster, the glass shattered loudly, rattling my nerves. I resolved once again to try not to drink, at least for the next month.

CHAPTER THIRTY-SIX

I had planned to attend the Anzac Day remembrance services at Gallipoli, at the entrance to the Dardanelles, in Turkey. My grandfather had fought there in 1915, in extreme conditions, with other soldiers of the Australian and New Zealand Army Corps. Like the Kokoda Track in New Guinea, the site is an iconic one for Australians – perhaps because we wonder how brave *we* might have been had we been in those soldiers' muddy combat boots.

In Istanbul, where I'd spent the past three weeks in a small hotel in the tourist area of Sultanahmet, I found when I arrived at the ferry terminal that the service to Bandirma had been cancelled. High winds had made crossing the Sea of Marmara hazardous, but no alternative arrangements had been made for the bumped passengers.

Nearby, an attractive man wearing a smart suit had been making calls on his cell phone. 'Are you also trying to get to Bandirma?' I asked.

'Yes. I'm giving a lecture there.'

I was intrigued. 'Would you like to share a taxi?' I asked impulsively. I had no idea what such a journey of hundreds of kilometres might cost.

'The university is sending a car and driver for me,' he said. 'But I could give *you* a lift ...'

A university may have been looking after *him*, but it seemed the universe was looking after *me*.

We had a very pleasant drive to Bandirma, where I said goodbye to my charming rescuer and continued by coach to Canakkale. On board, a bow-tied attendant provided moist towels, cold drinks and snack foods with a smile. It was just like flying, but without the turbulence.

Located at the narrowest point of the Dardanelles, Canakkale was the main jumping-off point for Gallipoli. My hotel was filled with Anzac Day pilgrims from Australia and New Zealand, including a group of noisy high school kids staying on my floor.

'Ashley! ASHLEY!' An adult – a teacher or a chaperone – was yelling in the corridor outside my room. The screams and shouts continued unabated.

After trying for some time to lose myself in a book, my tolerance deserted me. I leapt off the bed and yanked open my door. The noise was coming from the room directly opposite, the door of which was open. I crossed the corridor and walked straight into the room. Sprawled across the twin beds were six teenagers, their faces now turned towards the madwoman who had appeared in their midst.

'Could you POSSIBLY keep the noise down?' My head was shaking. Eye contact was made among the group and some eyebrows were raised, but no one spoke. 'THANK you!'

A ruckus then erupted in the room next door, where I could hear a television tuned to a cartoon channel. A squabble between two or three young boys had turned to shouting. There was a scream, then crying.

'Johnny, put your knickers on!' a man shouted. 'Where are your knickers? Have you got poo on your bum?'

My face scrunched up. *I need a drink ...*

ON THE EVENING of April 24, I was bussed with some other hotel guests across the Dardanelles to the site of the Australian Dawn Service on the Gallipoli Peninsula. For the next eighteen hours, before the system spat me out again, I was grateful only that it wasn't raining and no one was shooting at me.

Hunched beneath the blanket I'd been handed on the coach, my teeth chattering from the extreme cold, I became more and more miserable as the night crept imperceptibly towards the dawn. I bought hot tea, but my hands shook so much I couldn't get it to my mouth.

Following the service, which was live streamed to Australia, we were herded and corralled, and herded yet again, for another six hours before finally rejoining our coach. As we boarded, I looked back across the scrubby terrain and saw hundreds of empty buses inching their way towards the pickup point.

It took me some time to regain my sense of perspective. My grandfather and other soldiers – Allied and Turkish – had suffered in that place under appalling conditions. It seemed fitting that I, too, should be miserable there.

Still needing to thaw out, I located a *hammam*, a traditional Turkish steam bath, in a back street of Canakkale. After changing into a short cotton robe, I walked into the room I'd been directed to, then backed straight out again.

'Oops!'

Three young men with mats of chest hair and handkerchief-sized towels draped over their groins reclined on an octagon-shaped marble platform in the centre of the room. I thought I'd entered the men's steam bath by mistake, but the gent who had been assigned to wash my hair and massage my scalp with great vigour waved me back inside.

The fine young Turks adjusted their towels and continued

their conversation, casting a glance in my direction whenever I yelped. I was slapped and poked and prodded and lathered and massaged. Finally, a bucket of hot water was dumped over my head to rinse off the suds. When I emerged into the reception area, my face was flushed red and my knees were weak, but I was now warm and very, very clean.

At a café the next morning, a girl of about fifteen with a wild mass of dark curly hair placed a small metal pan of cheesy scrambled eggs and a basket of simit bread, similar to a poppy-seed bagel, in front of me. 'This looks yummy,' I said. I'd not weakened and drunk any alcohol since leaving Switzerland and my appetite was good.

'What country are you from?' she asked.

'Australia. But I don't live there now. Is this your family's restaurant?'

'No, I'm helping my friend.'

'What's your name?'

'Egem.'

'What do you want to do when you leave school?'

'Study medicine. I want to be a brain surgeon.'

I put down my fork and dug in my bag for a name card. It showed me holding on to the spire of the Empire State Building and brandishing my laptop.

'King Kong,' she laughed.

'Friend me on Facebook,' I said. 'We can stay in touch. I might need you one day.'

I HAD SCHEDULED a week free of work in England to walk the Cotswold Way with Jo and Tony, friends from the coast-to-coast walk in England the year before. The marked way went from near Stratford-upon-Avon in the north down to Bath Cathedral, through wooded glades smelling of wild garlic, up and over rolling hills, and across meadows and farmland dotted with historic houses. I loved the mix of solitude and company on long-distance walks. Daily life was simple: keep putting one foot in front of the other, savour the sights and smells and sounds along the way, eat hearty meals, and fall asleep easily on hitting the sack.

Peter and Amanda, whom I'd now known for nearly a quarter of a century since we'd first met in Hong Kong, drove from Cheltenham to Little Witcombe, along the route of the walk, so that we could have a pub dinner together.

'Mineral water? You're not ill, are you?' Pete said, when he asked what I wanted from the bar. 'I've never known you to turn down a drink.'

Far from being unwell, I felt fit, healthy and happy.

STILL FEARFUL OF flying, I preferred short hops to long hauls. My two-week return journey to Kuching therefore included some days on the ground in Luxembourg, Berlin and Singapore. I attended a client's work conference, advised a hotel manager on how to improve his establishment's customer service, checked out Checkpoint Charlie, where West had once met East, walked a midnight half marathon, and started drinking again.

In Singapore, dawn had been only an hour or two away when, after completing the half marathon, I asked my taxi driver to stop at a convenience store on the way to my hotel so that I could buy wine. Hopping back in the cab, I clutched the bottle to my chest and tried not to hear the small voice inside that was asking: 'What are you *doing*?'

BACK IN JANUARY, I'd met a bunch of runners on the Kuching waterfront. I'd exchanged business cards with Min and become friends on Facebook with his wife, Samantha.

'See you at seven where we met last time,' Sam replied, when I messaged her to say I was in town. 'We'll have breakfast afterwards.'

It was as if we were already old friends. Min, an architect, was training for the Kuala Lumpur Half Marathon, and soon he and I were running together about three mornings a week. Sam also took part in races, but got by on 'a wing and a prayer' rather than a training program. They immediately included me in dinners at their house with their teenagers, Sara and Sean, and their friends Belinda and Eng Hooi, both teachers, and architects Ivy and Swee, and their sons, Nick and Kieran. I couldn't account for the warmth these people showed me. They didn't know me at all, and yet they drew me instantly into their intimate circle as if I had always been a part of their group and an auntie to their kids. They enjoyed wine and must have thought me a wowser based on how little I drank at their dinner tables.

'I'm knackered,' I'd lie, and retreat early from company so that I could drink alone in my room at the Batik.

Each time I'd been in Kuching I'd had reason to go to a hospital. *Why stop now?* I scheduled a full wellness check at the same hospital where my head was examined after I'd crashed onto my chin in a streambed earlier in the year. If drinking was impacting more than just my mental health, perhaps it would show up in my test results and frighten me into quitting. My upcoming rendezvous with Tom seemed unlikely to be an alcohol-free zone, but after that?

'Your cholesterol is a bit high, but otherwise everything is fine,' said the head doc after all my test results were in. 'You're very fit for someone your age. Whatever you're doing, keep doing it.'

Bugger.

I was soon back to drinking six glasses of wine – a bottle and a half – every night if I didn't have a morning running date with Min. But disposing of the evidence was again becoming a logistical nightmare. Sometimes I'd have two glasses at the bar downstairs, so as to reduce the number of empties upstairs. But still they accumulated. *What must Mas think when she empties my waste bin?* It was becoming harder to look her in the eye.

One day, I stuffed two empty bottles in a backpack and left the hotel before it was light. In a deserted laneway behind a large hotel a few streets away, I threw them into a dumpster that was overflowing with kitchen rubbish. My skin felt clammy. The thumping of my heart muffled the sound of traffic, the voices of hotel staff making preparations for breakfast, and the call to prayer from the mosque across the river.

CHAPTER THIRTY-SEVEN

Tom and I had planned a bush-camping holiday at the start of June in the nether regions of Queensland. I'd had another series of appointments with Josephine in Kuching, so my own nether regions were spruce and my breasts again slightly perkier. But I was apprehensive about our reunion. I always had trouble controlling my frustration with Tom after a few days. I was like a predictable geyser at a thermal tourist attraction: *Here she goes, folks. Right on schedule. Got your cameras ready?* Would this time be different? How would we manage together for two weeks? I wanted so much for him to let me inside to where he was hurt, and for him to see me, hear me, love me. There were times when I had hated him for the way I felt around him, but I had never been indifferent. I wanted him still, as I always had.

In the arrivals hall at Brisbane Airport, I spotted him immediately. His hair was now white, standing on end as if he hadn't patted it down after scratching his scalp vigorously. I wasn't a fan of the salt-and-pepper beard, but I found his low-maintenance, unselfconscious style manly and sexy.

'Hi.' There was no hug.

In the car park, he stuffed my suitcase in his vehicle, which was packed to the gills with camping stuff.

'Are you sure you've got everything we'll need?' I teased, touching his arm lightly.

'There's no room for your backpack in here,' he said. 'You'll have to put it in the front, under your feet.'

'These are for you.' I held out my gifts: a Swiss Army knife with a multitude of functional attachments that I had bought for him in Zermatt, and a fine malt whisky.

A robotic GPS voice guided us through Brisbane's suburbs, filling in spaces in our conversation. Looking at his profile, I could still detect the younger man I had fallen for the moment we met. When a wave of affection rolled through me, I reached across and laid my hand on his thigh. After a few seconds, he readjusted his position and my hand fell away.

'How's Sonia?' I asked. When I'd last seen him in Canberra, he had been attentive to the dog's every need. I'd been envious, wanting him to be like that with me.

'She's fine.'

We turned into a driveway and came to a halt in front of a showroom. 'I want to check out some stuff for my big trip,' Tom said, unbuckling his seat belt. 'Come and have a look?'

I had imagined he might invite me along on an extended four-wheel-drive trip he was in the early stages of planning, but by the second morning even a short holiday together seemed like a mistake. I had rolled over in bed in our motel room and draped an arm over him. I don't know why I imagined he might welcome my touch. Immediately, he flung me off, as if I were a Huntsman spider that had just scuttled across his bare flesh.

'To-om! Why did you do that?'

'We're too old for all that lovey-dovey stuff!'

'How can you say that?'

The 'lovey-dovey stuff' was what I had hoped for, had flown from the other side of the world for.

Denied permission to touch him, I took my bruised heart for a run through the town. The place wasn't yet awake. Only a couple of scrawny dogs were up and about, padding along the dusty verge of the roadway and watching me.

'Good run?' he asked, when I arrived back.

It seemed we weren't going to mention the spat.

'Yep.'

'Hungry?'

'Yep.'

'We'll go and fill up the tank and get some breakfast, then.'

Tom was an intrepid camper, preferring wild camps with no facilities to anything serviced, including showers, toilets, water supply, and – horror of horrors – other campers. I preferred to have a few comforts, but it was his show. He knew what he was doing, and I was happy for him to make the decisions.

The first night in the bush was a reminder that even if he seemed to be open to suggestions, he wasn't really.

'Where do you think we should set up camp?'

His question surprised me. I looked around at the rather bare landscape. Across the way were the low hills that we'd driven in through. There was a clump of trees by some worn grass patches.

'Oh, I don't know. Over there?'

He glanced to where I was pointing and shook his head.

'Over here's better.'

Why did you bother to ask me?

'Can you hold this for me?'

'Sure.'

I grabbed the end of the flysheet, or whatever it was.

'Not like *that*! Like *this*.'

'I don't know these things, Tom. You just need to tell me. Don't be unkind.'

'I'm not. You take things too personally.'

Peace was restored over dinner and a shared bottle of wine. Perhaps our skirmishes were to be expected after nearly three years apart. He was curious about my life as a nomad, about the places I'd been and the people I'd met. He thought me courageous. His stories of his own intrepid adventures in the world's most remote places were fascinating and entertaining, as always. There was nowhere I'd rather be than where I was: sitting in the glow of a campfire in the middle of nowhere with a man I wanted, and hearing his laughter. When we clambered up into the rooftop contraption that was our tent in the sky and I knew he would touch me and make love to me, my heart was full.

AT BREAKFAST, TOM produced a thimbleful of rocket fuel from a complicated espresso maker that reminded me of the device a gynaecologist might use to inspect my cervix.

'I really like a long black coffee in the mornings,' I said casually. 'The next time we come to a store, I'll get a jar of instant.'

'We don't have space in the vehicle for things like that!'

When I used a scouring pad to clean an encrusted pan we had cooked with the night before, he was aghast. 'Don't you know not to use a scourer on Teflon?'

'I forgot! I was just trying to help. When you criticise the way I do things, I get nervous.'

'Oh, grow up, Rob.'

I was back to feeling unsure of myself and wary of him.

That afternoon, we took a long walk through the bush. On a gravelly beach by a shallow stream, we lay on our backs, pedalling our legs in the air as if we were bicycling through the sky, and chatted easily. Birds chortled in the branches high above us. For a time, all was right with the world.

'Look out for firewood,' he said, when we were walking back to camp.

When I saw a large dry branch, I grabbed one end and dragged it along behind me.

'What've you got that for?'

'You said to gather firewood.'

He snorted.

As it was unwieldy and hadn't passed muster, I left it beside the track after he went on ahead.

When I caught up with him, he asked where it was.

'I tossed it.'

'Why?'

'You didn't seem to think it was any good.'

He shook his head as if my behaviour perplexed him.

On a long walk the next day, Tom again drew far ahead as I picked my way gingerly across slippery rocks in a stream. It's not a walk I would have taken on my own, and yet I *was* alone. My boots had poor grip. When I had lost my footing in a stream in Sarawak, I had been lucky not to break my jaw. I was nervous now, and resented Tom for not staying close by.

Over the past few days, despite the peace that came with the onset of evening, I had been hurt by his criticisms and rebuffs. I knew I was a disappointment to him, too. I wasn't experienced or confident in this environment, and I did take his comments very much to heart. A mature response might have been for me to say: 'Fuck off, Tom. You're being a total prick. Don't be such an asshole. Cut me some slack here.' But I didn't have the courage. Instead, I retreated into silence.

We barely spoke over dinner that night. Small black insects flitted in the light cast by a kerosene lamp that sat on the esky lid beside an open wine bottle. The sky was alive with stars, but misery engulfed us both like a shroud.

'The next town we come to, you can just drop me off.' My voice sounded flat. 'I'll find my own way from there.'

He reached for the wine, topped up his glass and set the bottle back down. His face was stony. My glass stood nearly empty. I grabbed the bottle and poured what was left into it. I had stopped trying; I now wanted to stop feeling.

When we arrived at a one-pub town in the middle of nowhere the next morning, he waved a small white flag.

'You okay?'

'Yep. You?'

'Yep. Okay, then.'

He adjusted his sunglasses and reset the GPS.

We headed further into the hinterland. I felt relieved, but I knew it wouldn't be easy. I was on my guard, expecting a skirmish whenever we negotiated a decision on the smallest matter.

One night, in the middle of nowhere, I started to wash my hair in the camp shower that Tom had rigged up beside the car. I hadn't properly understood the shower mechanism and ran out of warm water while my hair was still covered in shampoo. It seemed I was stupid.

When I started to cry, Tom found the grace from somewhere to heat more water. While I sat on a campstool at his feet, he poured the water over my hair to rinse out the suds. It was one of the most intimate things he had ever done for me. Peace descended for a few hours on our little camp under the huge expanse of night sky. We gazed upward and talked softly to each other. Perhaps it hurt Tom as much as it did me to have the relationship we both seemed able to imagine keep imploding.

WHILE TOM PACKED up the car after breakfast, I ran back along the rough track we had driven in on the afternoon before. I needed time to myself. I don't know what I would have done had I encountered a wild animal or a snake or a serial killer. I was uncomfortable in the bush, especially when alone, but I needed to find my own centre again, just as I had done on the Headhunters Trail in Sarawak the year before.

At the spot where we had agreed to meet, I sat on a rocky outcrop waiting for the vehicle to appear. When I saw it bouncing towards me trailed by a cloud of dust, and then his suntanned face and cocky white hair behind the wheel, my heart jumped. Despite everything, he was lodged under my skin. I vowed to try harder not to let him upset me.

Towards the end of the trip, after we had left the parks, I had a chance to check my emails. The newsletter job that I worked on every month with Polly had come in.

'I need to do this, Tom. We'll have to stay at a motel tonight.'

'I don't want to stay in a motel!' he said.

'Well, *I* do. I need the internet, and I need somewhere where I can sit and work for a few hours.'

While I edited the report, Tom watched the news on TV and drank a couple of shots of the malt whisky I'd given him. 'Do you want one?' he offered.

He's trying, I thought. 'Not just now. But I'd love a glass of wine when I'm finished.' I hoped he might pop down to the motel's reception area, where I'd noticed there was a small bar, but he remained stretched out on the bed.

We ate at a nearby Asian place that had a few laminex tables and no alcohol. I was now seriously craving a drink.

When I unscrewed the top of the lovely cold bottle that I picked up downstairs on the way back to our room, Tom might have heard my sigh of relief. He poured himself another whisky.

'Would you like one?' I asked, when I'd finished my first glass and was pouring a second. I hoped he might decline, leaving it all for me. He'd seemed unimpressed by the label.

'Okay,' he said.

After we'd finished those, I drank the one remaining glassful and he reverted to whisky.

'You did a good job on this,' he said the next morning, picking up the empty wine bottle. If I'd been holding it, I might have thrown it at him.

FOR THE REMAINDER of my stay in Australia, I rented a serviced apartment not far from my old house in my home town. I'd been gone for a little over a year. 'Are you back already?' people said, surprised to see me.

'Just visiting.'

I'd sold my house there, but otherwise my days looked much like they had before I'd become a nomad: I worked long hours, saw friends, borrowed my dogs for walks, went with Mum for meals at our favourite Thai place, and ran in the early mornings with Di and Fran. The old routines were familiar and enjoyable, but I wasn't tempted to call Albury home again. I had become addicted to creating life on a bigger canvas using broader brushstrokes.

Tom invited me to stay in Sydney with him for a few days. His emails since our trip had been affectionate. We'd upset each other – he'd been critical and lacking in empathy, and I'd wobbled and wept and whinged – but there was still something we both wanted.

'He's a *man*,' a friend said. 'They're all like that.'

He went to a lot of trouble: the fridge was filled with yummy food; there was wine; he was kind. On my last night, he ran a deep bath for us. He placed tea lights around the rim of the enormous tub, added aromatic oils to the water, put on some music, and poured us two large glasses of red wine. I leaned back against the side of the bath and rested one foot on his chest. His hand kneaded my toes. Although he was uncomfortable with being touched in random ways, he loved sex, massages and baths. I felt sensual, seductive and slippery.

My head dropped back and I closed my eyes, happy to be in this moment with him. There was a sizzling sound, then a sharp new smell. The back of my hair had brushed against a candle flame and caught alight. Quickly ducking my head, I slid down the bath on my bum like a ship being launched on its maiden voyage from a slipway. Tom's grip on my toes tightened while my free foot shot straight up the other side of the tub.

CHAPTER THIRTY-EIGHT

From the window of my plane, as we banked over Manhattan and turned to fly down the length of the island, I could see the apartment building beside Central Park that would again be my home in New York.

I had been half holding my breath in Albury, waiting to return to the city where I'd decided I would finally confront my dependence on alcohol. It was time. There was no joy left in my drinking. For weeks, sometimes even for months, I managed to drink in social situations, or even on my own, without slipping over the edge and getting drunk or feeling anxious if I went to bed under-medicated. But that way of drinking wasn't normal or enjoyable for me. It required rigid control. And I could no longer guarantee my behaviour after even one drink, because alcohol changed me into someone who wanted to keep drinking.

My choice to live a nomadic life made me especially vulnerable. My future might be very bleak if I continued along the path I was headed down. For over two decades, I had been trying to manage how much I drank. My addiction made it harder for me to handle, calmly, kindly and with grace, the day-to-day frustrations that are a part of life. It was certainly a factor in my relationship with Tom. Because I was ashamed of myself, I was overly sensitive to his comments and criticisms. I doubt that he intended them to hurt as much as they did. His insensitivity and emotional distance arose mostly from *his* issues, not from mine. But how could we begin to be intimate if I didn't want him to know the real me?

I sought isolation, yet felt lonely and apart. I knew I was a good person in my heart – but somewhere along the way, I had become lost. I resented feeling invisible, and yet I didn't want to be seen too clearly. I set high standards in all aspects of my life. I had always pushed myself to perform to the best of my abilities, but I was ashamed of who I had become and fearful of what lay ahead. The crutch that I had used to hold me up was again pulling me down. I couldn't keep putting off admitting that my life had become unmanageable.

As if to underline the dramatic change I was preparing to make, New York experienced an earthquake. No damage was done, but it was an unexpected jolt. Later, when a massive hurricane bore down on the city, I took it as confirmation that the time had come for me to surrender.

I stocked up on all the necessities for weathering the hurricane over the weekend – food, batteries, bottled water, candles – and three bottles of a Chilean white wine. I would have exactly the amount I wanted to drink over the two nights of the lockdown. It would require restraint: if I drank more than half of the second bottle on the first night, I wouldn't have the six glasses I needed for the second night and would have to reschedule the whole rigmarole. If I could drink exactly the amount that I needed to achieve conscious numbness, I could say goodbye to my increasingly unreliable companion of many years with some dignity before starting my sober life.

I had resolved many times to quit drinking, but I'd never been able to stay sober for longer than those eleven months back when I was in my forties. Finally, on the brink of my sixties, I surrendered. It was the end. Ahead lay a different future, one that didn't include alcohol. What might it look like and feel like? I had no idea, but I would make my way towards it one sober day at a time. I would likely always have an addictive personality, but I would deal with that as best I could. Not all addictions need be as destructive as alcohol was for me.

During the weekend of my last drinks, a busy workload kept me occupied during the daytime. At night, I was aware of every ceremonial sip of wine.

Hurricane Irene ended up being a fizzer. The TV news channel tried to keep the fear going: *Irene is the size of Europe; Irene is unprecedented in its potential to damage cities all along the Eastern Seaboard*. But the reality didn't live up to the hype. Monday dawned calm and bright. The storm had passed.

I had located a meeting nearby of a recovery group and had rehearsed in my mind what I would do: outside my building, I would turn left, walk to the corner, cross the road, turn right after two blocks and descend to a basement meeting room. I was past debating with myself the pros and cons of continuing to drink. I would take the steps I had identified and keep things simple.

Fifteen minutes before the meeting was due to start, I took the empty wine bottles to the trash room.

That's the last time I'll do that.

I walked down to the lobby, exited the building and turned in the opposite direction from the one I had rehearsed.

PART FOUR

A different future

CHAPTER THIRTY-NINE

When I turned right, instead of left, my mind was filled instantly with loud chatter. It was as if I had stuck my fingers in my ears and was chanting *LA-LA-LA-LA!* so that I couldn't hear the small, sane voice asking: *What the FUCK are you doing?*

Halfway along the block, I stopped walking. *You know what lies ahead if you keep going in this direction, trying to manage the unmanageable*, the voice said. *More fear, more shame, more remorse, more unhappiness.*

I recalled the dream I'd had in Hong Kong so many years before. *Just take the first step.* Don't think too far ahead. Don't worry about how to deal with whatever might happen. Everything will be okay. One thing at a time.

From somewhere came the willingness to turn around, retrace my steps and then carry on as I'd rehearsed. I took a seat in the basement room and closed my eyes. *Please help me to do this*, I whispered to the universe.

I had gone as low in my own estimation as I was prepared to go. My life hadn't ended in the gutter, though I'd sometimes fallen in one. I hadn't lost a driver's licence for drink driving, or a husband and children through alcoholic neglect. I didn't need a stint in detox or rehab. I still functioned well in areas that were important to me. But every drink came at a cost. It eroded my dignity and self-respect. It caused me to lie; to feel shame and guilt, anxiety and fear; to withhold my real self from people I loved and wanted to be loved by.

Enough, already, said my inner New Yorker. It was time to accept that, from here on, I wouldn't be able to live an authentic life, comfortable in my own skin, if alcohol were a part of it. There could be no more moving the day of reckoning to the first day of next year, or of next month, or of next week. Tomorrow was of no use to me. I had only today. It was time to make a new path to a different future.

Like a diver on the ocean floor who could see, far above, the shimmer of sunlight with its promise of air, I would have to ascend from the depths slowly and patiently if I were to decompress safely.

Recovering from the physical dependence would be the first hurdle; far tougher would be breaking the emotional reliance on a decades-long habit.

AFTER THE MEETING, I approached the woman who had told her story to the people in the room. 'Today is my first day. I identified a lot with what you said.'

'Keep coming back,' she said. 'There's a great women's meeting on the Upper East Side tomorrow. I'll be there, if you'd like to check it out.'

'Okay. Thank you.' It was a relief not to have to think further ahead than the next day.

At the Tuesday meeting, someone mentioned a recovery group for writers that met the following evening in my neighbourhood. *I can manage not to drink until then.*

At the Wednesday writers' meeting, I was told there were four meetings held in that space each morning. The walls of the room were plastered with slogans: *Take it easy. One day at a time. Do the next right thing.* Hope found a toehold in my heart. At 8.45 am the next day, I raised my hand for the first time in that little room and identified myself as a beginner needing help. I had found a home group.

For the remainder of my stay in New York, I sat for an hour in that room each morning. People in different stages of recovery talked about what it had been like for them, what happened and what it was like now. Some had recognised and accepted their problem when still young, or early in their drinking days, and had rerouted their life's path away from active addiction; others had rebounded from a bottom so low they must have broken the hearts of people who loved them. Every story gave me courage and hope.

Three days without a drink became a week, then a month. One day at a time, I might never again need fear the answers to questions I had been asking myself for too many years: *Did I drink last night? How much did I drink? Do I remember everything? Did anything bad happen?*

I gave myself over to the group. These were my people. I did as they suggested, including throwing out the Xanax I'd used to quell my nerves when flying. It seemed that any mood-altering substance could potentially lead me straight back to self-medicating, instead of experiencing my life face-on, unfiltered. Everyone who shared their story could teach me something about how to sit with today. They could show me that sober was a place I wanted to be. And by arriving every morning and taking a seat alongside an old-timer or another beginner, I also helped them. I wasn't just taking, but giving, too.

Help from the universe also arrived in the form of an invitation to join a group of runners who met at 5.30 most mornings on

Fifth Avenue for a circuit of Central Park. Up until now in New York, I'd run mostly on my own. Having regular training partners was good discipline as I prepared to run my fourth marathon, but the hour spent talking and laughing with Maria, Joanne and Lissy, Duster teammate Heather and Hasher Joe, and with Sun, Natalie, Sarah, Andrea and Stephen, was its own reward. By mid-morning, I would be at my desk, my body, mind and spirit tuned up and ready to focus on the work tasks I'd set myself for the day.

A FEW DAYS before the Niagara Falls Marathon, on my fifty-ninth birthday, I had dinner in Toronto with Bella, my friend of more than twenty years.

'You're really not drinking?' she asked. 'Is it hard?'

'I've been trying to manage it for twenty years. You know what that's like. But in August, I just accepted it was over. Now I don't debate it with myself every day. I feel I've stepped out from under a huge weight.'

Since the waiter had brought us our drinks, she hadn't let go of the stem of her wine glass. 'I want to stop, but I need to feel stronger first.'

I'd said the exact same thing countless times.

THE LAST PART of the marathon course was beside the river that would soon plunge over the massive falls. After the final turn, I ran towards the rainbow – my second in a marathon – that hung low in the sky ahead.

Running another marathon was a timely lesson in learning to take things one step at a time. I had stopped drinking two months before, but I'd only just started to unlearn old ways of thinking and behaving. True freedom was a long way off, if I could achieve it at all. I just needed to keep making my way slowly towards the shimmering light of sobriety while life continued to happen.

The first test wasn't long in coming.

CHAPTER FORTY

Three men were in my face. In the seconds since I'd noticed them up ahead, they had apparently leapt through the air, like ninjas, right into my space. I knew instantly that I was under threat. One of them yanked at the black leather pouch that I wore across my chest, pulling me off my feet and breaking the strap. Then, they were gone.

The bag contained cash I had just withdrawn from an ATM, my camera, phone, keys to the New York apartment, debit and credit cards, and a security device I needed for online banking. By some miracle, I wasn't carrying my passport. It was November 2011. I'd been alcohol free for three months and had arrived in Valparaiso, on the coast of Chile, just two hours before.

When I arrived back at my hotel, Enrico, the manager, was dealing with another guest whose handbag had been stolen during check-in. It seemed cruel to have to tell him I'd been mugged.

'*Merda!*' he said. 'The police have just left. I'll call them again.'

After I'd told my story to an officer, I started contacting my banks in Australia and Hong Kong. The Skype connection was poor. Frustrated, I shouted at people who were trying to help me, but I was mostly angry with myself. Why had I gone out with items I didn't need and that would now be difficult to replace?

I'd lost the Hong Kong debit card I used to fund my day-to-day life. Without my bank's security device, I couldn't transfer funds to an Australian account that I could still access. I'd had to cancel one credit card, and the other had little available credit.

After a few days of hardly venturing out into the city I'd hoped to get to know well over the next two months, I decided I would start afresh in the capital, Santiago. The streets there were untainted for me and I'd have the support of English-language recovery meetings. Pre-payment of an Airbnb apartment used up most of my remaining cash, but the owner, Maria, was kind when I told her of my situation. 'I'll be in Valparaiso to see family on Sunday,' she said. 'Join us for lunch. We will look after you. And you will come to Santiago soon. Don't worry. Chile is a wonderful country.'

One morning, I ran along Valparaiso's waterfront, past the naval base and the port, with Maria's ex-husband escorting me on his bicycle. It was a relief to laugh again, and to talk of things other than my predicament. Before I moved on to the capital, he again rode shotgun while I ran for an hour to Vina del Mar, where we ate gelato in the sunshine. Workers busy preparing the resort for the summer season were a reminder that this challenging time would pass and better times lay ahead.

SANTIAGO'S MIX OF colonial-style buildings, arts and café precincts, and modern infrastructure was instantly appealing. The Mapocho River, runoff from the nearby foothills of the Andes, was the colour of chocolate milk. At night, I could hear the rush of fast-flowing water beside my apartment building.

Maria watched out for me. 'Come dancing,' she urged. She was taking tango and marenge classes. I felt too inhibited, and instead went running in the mornings along a narrow strip of parkland between the river and the roadway. My nerves were still fragile.

One day, I heard a screech of brakes and then a tremendous collision behind me. I quickened my pace and didn't turn to look. I feared that I would see something I couldn't then un-see.

The sense of community I found at recovery meetings with local people, expats and travellers helped to offset some of the vulnerability and anxiety I was feeling about my financial situation, which was still precarious. I wasn't tempted by self-pity to take a drink. A single drink was of no use to me. I would then only want to have another and another and another, and I might never again find the willingness and the courage to stop. But it was a stressful time to have to get through in very early sobriety. A replacement debit card that finally arrived from Hong Kong was for a long-dormant account. I was still unable to do any online banking. Trying to sort out the mess over Skype produced only tears. I needed *something*, if not the oblivion of wine, and treated myself daily to cherries and gelato, which were cheap, sweet and delicious.

A new friend arranged for me to use a private room with speakerphone in the local branch of my Hong Kong bank. The call quality was better than phoning from my laptop, but when my call was transferred to yet another operator at a call centre possibly somewhere on the far side of the Gobi Desert and I again had to explain my situation to an operator whose English I couldn't understand, it was too much. The young man keeping me company patted my hand awkwardly as I banged my head slowly on the polished surface of the oval conference table.

It was time to take a different tack.

'I'm getting nowhere trying to sort things out through call centres,' I said to Polly in Hong Kong. 'I need a case manager. Could you go to my bank and ask them to put someone in charge of things?

'I don't think that will help.'

'Please, Pol. Tell them I've been trying for five weeks to get some action.'

Only when Polly took charge did the bureaucratic wheels finally begin to turn.

BY MARCH 2012, I was again in Sarawak. My banking issues were finally resolved. I was now six months sober and no longer had the daily problem of trying to conceal from my friends in Kuching the extent of my drinking. In the absence of a local recovery community, and to substitute a positive addiction for a negative one, I'd set myself a tough physical challenge: to run twelve half marathons during this year when I would turn sixty. I'd already ticked off three events: in New York in a blizzard in January after I'd left Chile; in Austin, Texas, during a Dead Runners Society weekend in February; and in humid Kuala Lumpur on my arrival back in Asia after a short stay in Australia.

In Kuching, on mornings when Min and I had a running date, I would wait by the front door of the Batik hotel and watch, enchanted, the predawn goings-on in the shophouse opposite. If the ground-floor dispensary that operated through the night had not yet pulled down its metal shutters, cars would regularly pull up and customers would dart across the street seeking the Chinese herbal potions concocted there. Above the shop, like in a split-screen movie, a woman prayed and performed devotional exercises before an altar. When Min rounded the corner on his bike, I would feel another surge of happiness.

One morning, we were running along the deserted Main Bazaar. Dawn was approaching. The *muezzin* called the faithful to prayer at a mosque across the river. Our footfalls were in sync. From Min's iPod I could hear Billie Holiday singing softly. Contentment swept over me like an ocean wave rolling gently on reaching the shoreline. What a weight had been lifted when I finally faced the truth about myself. No longer burdened by a secret life, by shame and the fear of being found out, I could be fully present in myself and comfortable with being seen for who I was on the inside: a flawed, funny, sometimes fretful woman who was trying to deal with the cards she had been dealt in the best and most honest way she could. Sobriety didn't guarantee that the future wouldn't continue to present as many ups and downs as a possessed playground carousel, but I felt sure that I was on my way at last. One step at a time, I would learn how to fully experience the incredible life I'd been given the opportunities and imagination to create.

By quitting drinking I had removed the main impediment to living comfortably in my own skin. However, friends in recovery had suggested I also adopt some sort of spiritual practice that might make me more resilient whenever things went wonky. I wasn't religious and didn't believe in a Christian God. I had trouble even with the concept of a higher power, except when I gave thanks to the universe for landing my plane safely after a bumpy flight. I didn't pray or meditate. But I tried to observe and acknowledge my feelings, rather than just be consumed by them. Whenever I recognised that what I was experiencing was happiness or contentment or gratitude, I put it into words: *I feel happy. I feel content. I'm grateful.* It was as if I had turned on a switch and, as time went on, those moments of witnessed wellbeing occurred more and more frequently.

Emily included me in her family's celebration of the Ching Ming festival, a religious observance that was far removed from anything I'd known when growing up in Australia. During the festival, Malaysia's Chinese communities visit cemeteries to tidy the graves of their ancestors. As it had been at the cremation ceremony in Bali, the atmosphere was that of a fairground, with thousands of visitors gathered around the family plots. Smouldering incense sticks wafted curls of smoke into the air. Food and rice wine were offered to the departed; and paper replicas of luxury cars, high-denomination bank notes, or mobile phones were burned so that they might reach and comfort the ancestors in the afterlife. Many families set off firecrackers.

I saw that such practices provide comfort to people who believe in them. Everyone has hardships to endure. That is the nature of a human life. We must all come to terms with our own lives in a way that gives us strength and courage to carry on. I was starting to better understand that my thoughts and beliefs could influence how I felt about whatever was happening. My feelings didn't need to be the boss of me.

OVER FOUR CONSECUTIVE weekends, as part of the challenge I had set myself, I ran half marathons in Bali, New Zealand, Canada and the United States. In each place, I spent time with family and friends. The physical world had seemingly shrunk, but my own world had expanded in ways I couldn't have imagined when I set off from Australia two years before with my laptop, running shoes, a favourite pair of orange knickers, and a hurt I'd hoped to find a way to heal.

CHAPTER FORTY-ONE

Manhattan was again my base for the northern summer months of June and July. The freedom that came from no longer having to drink was exhilarating. The more relieved I felt of the need to keep my inner life hidden, the more I was aware of and responsive to the everyday world around me. Smells and sounds, the currents of energy on the streets, were more accessible to my senses than when I'd dulled and numbed them with alcohol.

On the Upper East Side one day, after lunch with my friend Yin, I noticed a man and a woman in their thirties crossing the road hand-in-hand to my side of the street. I was struck by the woman's face. She had a simple, natural beauty that was very compelling. *He must love to look at her*, I thought.

They turned into the flow of people just ahead of me and were separated by oncoming pedestrians. Instead of changing his course to reconnect with her, the man walked alone to the curb, where he stopped to wait for the walk signal. *Perhaps he expects her to come to him*, I thought. Instead, the woman hesitated, then veered away. On reaching the curb, she stopped and looked straight ahead. To any other onlooker, they appeared now to be strangers. When the light changed, she stepped into the street, holding her head high. He looked across at her, and I sensed that he understood he had slighted her.

On reaching the far corner, the woman continued on her own

path, her arms swinging purposefully. It was as if he no longer existed for her. He slowed to allow the people separating them to pass, and then crossed to her side. Still, she didn't turn to him. He reached for her left hand. Interlacing his fingers with hers, he slowed the movement of her arm until her hand again lay still in his. They had exchanged no words in the three minutes or so I had watched their little drama unfold and be resolved on the streets of Manhattan.

BEING MORE MINDFUL of when I was feeling happy didn't mean I didn't often still resemble a two-year-old having a temper tantrum. Sobriety wasn't all sweet surrender and serenity, by any stretch. I often felt irritated, disappointed, hurt, misjudged, mistreated, ignored, invisible. Now I had to sit with the fallout whenever I got caught up in those uncomfortable feelings instead of just acknowledging them.

In July, I flew south to meet Renee Petrillo. She and her husband, Michael, had left Arizona, bought a catamaran, and set sail for the Bahamas and the Caribbean. I'd felt a kinship with Renee after reading *A Sail of Two Idiots*, her book about their adventures at sea and their new life on land in St Kitts and Nevis. I'd emailed her, and she'd responded.

A 10K run together around Basseterre, St Kitts's rather ramshackle capital, cemented our friendship. We had much in common: a love of running and hiking; a tendency to take leaps into the unknown, based on little more than gut feelings; an acquaintance with life's darker side. I was pleased I had made the trip to get to know her a little.

A few days later when I was checking out of my hotel, I queried a telephone charge on my bill.

'I'm sure I didn't make this call,' I said, jabbing my finger at the amount.

'If it's on your bill, you must have,' the receptionist said.

'If I have no memory of it, I must *not* have. The bill must be wrong.'

'It's not wrong, madam.'

His certainty made me bristle. 'It's a large amount. Don't you think I'd remember it? I'm not paying it.'

'But you *have* to pay it!'

'I'm *not* paying for a call I didn't make!'

The manager was summoned.

'Madam, it's clear that you made this call.'

'I didn't.'

We were at a standoff.

'Delete it from the bill,' he finally instructed the receptionist.

'*Thank* you.'

I went outside to wait for Renee.

Oh, bugger.

I remembered, then, that I'd had a long chat two days before with a local pilot on his cell phone about what it might cost to fly by small plane to the nearby French–Dutch island of St Martin to buy a baguette. Renee had raved about the bakeries there, but 2,000 bucks was a little too much to pay for a sandwich lunch and I'd let go of the idea, along with any memory of having made the call. I was too embarrassed to go back inside and admit my error.

'I was wrong,' I emailed the hotel, when I was home in New York. 'I'm sorry. How can I pay you?' There was no reply.

Some days later, I was on Broadway headed for a cinema near the Lincoln Center. A man sitting against a shopfront held a hand-lettered cardboard sign that said he and the large dog by his side were homeless and hungry. I reached into my bag, counted off the amount of the unpaid telephone charge and handed him the notes.

He looked puzzled.

'It's a long story. Get your dog something nice.'

CHAPTER FORTY-TWO

When I arrived in Iceland at the start of August, it was just a month short of a year since my last drink. Eleven months had been a crunch point when I'd first quit in 1994. I'd thought, then, that perhaps I hadn't tried hard enough to be a 'normal' drinker. It took another seventeen years of falling on and off the wagon before I was again able to stop. I would soon turn sixty and didn't want to squander any more time on trying to manage the unmanageable, but it was a choice I faced every day. Just because I hadn't had a drink yesterday didn't mean I might not choose to drink today, because my problem wasn't alcohol; it was *me*.

Alcohol was just one of my many addictions. I was an addict by nature. I had emerged from childhood missing something at my core and had early found that emotional pain was best endured numbed. I could get as addicted to mushroom soup or salted caramel frozen yoghurt as I'd been to chardonnay or cigarettes or the boyfriend's cocaine. I'd been addicted to Tom for more than three decades. They were all manifestations of the same thing.

But as my first sober anniversary approached, I began to understand that I was changing on the inside. I no longer felt so acutely the loneliness a child feels in a household where a father's love is conditional, a mother's love is spread too thin, and a stranger can touch them in ways they don't want to be touched.

I no longer felt lonely in the way I had in my twenties and thirties, when sex was often a means to feel loved. I no longer felt the loneliness I'd known in my forties and fifties, when the most important relationship I would ever have – the one with myself – was dishonest. Though I was following a solitary path towards my sixties, it wasn't a lonely place to be. The more I accepted that *all* of my childhood and later experiences were what had made me a *strong grrrl*, the more I was able to be fully present in my friendships and relationships. It was early days, though. In Iceland, as in the Caribbean, it was clear that I could still be a dick.

Mid-month, I took a break from work for a trek near Eyjafjallajökull, the glacier-covered volcano whose eruption in 2010 had brought air traffic in Europe to a standstill. Late in the afternoon of the first day, our group, mostly Scandinavians and Italians, arrived at a mountain hut where we would spend the night. When I stood on a bench seat to claim an upper sleeping bunk, the other end pitched upward, like a seesaw, and threw me off. The heavy slab of wood slammed down on my calf, pinning me to the floor. The pain and shock knocked the breath out of me. No one even looked in my direction. Finally, a Danish woman responded to my whimpers and asked if I needed help.

I continued for the rest of the trek to feel invisible within the group, as if I existed only beyond its outer edges. My mood became as dark and oppressive as the glacier that sat like a massive storm cloud on the horizon. We walked through a landscape of ice and snow, black sand, mud pools, thermal springs and glacial moraine. I might have better appreciated its harsh beauty had I been able to escape myself. Was it finally hitting home that I was going to have to feel *everything* acutely?

On the third night, having been unable to connect with anyone, worried about a numbness in my leg, and rattled by lack of sleep after two nights of incessant, cacophonous snoring from one of the Italians, I had a meltdown. Earlier, a tiny woman had climbed down from her bunk, padded across to Snoring Man, and poked and prodded him, to no avail.

Without warning, a rumble rose in my gullet and exploded out of my mouth like molten lava. 'Somebody kick that guy in the head!'

No one spoke. The words banged around inside my skull. My stomach lurched. The barrage of snores continued. I shrank so far into myself, I thought I might never come out again.

Two days later, when a local bus trundled across a stony riverbed and arrived in the tiny settlement where we were to spend the night before heading off on a circle trek further into the wilderness, I seized on the chance of escape it offered. There seemed no way to turn things around. No one was speaking to me. I couldn't stand myself. By leaving, I would be doing us all a favour.

The black mood that had engulfed me for much of the past week began to lift as the bus drew closer to Reykjavik. By the time I arrived back at the small apartment I was renting next to Hallgrims Church, I had forgiven myself. I was a very flawed person, not a bad one. I had to learn how to manage emotions triggered by feeling invisible, fearful or resentful, now that I couldn't just try to drown them in alcohol. My sorrows, like the artist Frida Kahlo's, had learnt how to swim.

Reykjavik now seemed familiar and welcoming. I was thrilled to be back. The city was funky-looking, with colourful corrugated-metal-clad buildings set against fifty shades of grey sea and sky. There was an art-house cinema, a photography museum, and places I liked to eat. I'd been attending recovery meetings and had found a running mate.

I'd met Maggy my first week in Iceland at a geothermal public pool that was the gathering place for social runners. Unsure of the protocols, I'd arrived early. An athletic-looking woman had pulled into the parking lot on a bicycle. Her thick black hair was arranged in a fabulous, complicated construction that could pass for textile art. Thinking she looked like she might be a runner, I introduced myself. We were both entered in a half marathon at the end of the month, and soon we were training together in the early mornings. As she shared her favourite running trails along the coast with me, we talked about life, the universe, and everything that had brought a young single mother from southern Africa and a postmenopausal singleton from regional Australia to the northernmost capital city on the planet.

At a recovery meeting held in a white house by a manicured pond, an American who was in Iceland to work on a movie looked puzzled when he and I both introduced ourselves to the group as visitors. 'You look familiar,' he said. We realised that our paths had crossed on many mornings in New York when his home-group meeting ended and mine started. My world was both expanding and contracting.

Maggy took me to a doctor, who looked at my leg and suggested I stay off it. 'I wouldn't run, if I were you.'

I decided to ignore him. The Reykjavik Half Marathon wasn't just any race; it was to be my eighth half marathon for the year. My leg was numb at the impact site, not painful. I didn't want to lose momentum.

The race was fun, my leg didn't bother me, the course was beautiful, and I placed third in my age group among female runners from all over northern Europe. It seemed I had returned mostly intact from my sortie over to the dark side.

Daylight had decreased by three hours since I'd arrived in

Iceland, and the days were now noticeably colder. On the first anniversary of my last drink, Reykjavik was jolted by an earth tremor. It was a reminder that the ground beneath my feet could shift at any time.

CHAPTER FORTY-THREE

'Do you still want to help with a dog?' asked Gloria, a concierge in my building in New York. I'd just arrived back on the Upper West Side for a five-week stay after a month in Florence, Italy. During my last visit, I'd asked her to let me know if anyone needed occasional help with walking their dog.

'Absolutely!' I chirped.

'This is the number for Mrs D. Give her a call.'

Baxter, a Havanese–poodle cross, had separation anxiety and his barking when left alone was annoying the neighbours. Mrs D and I agreed that she would bring him to my place for a few hours a couple of days a week. He could hang out with me while I worked, and she could spend time off his radar.

'Is it okay if I take him for a walk in the park?'

'You can try.'

Towards the end of Baxter's first visit, I attached his lead and checked that I had a poo bag or two. 'Aren't you a lucky boy, having Central Park just over the road?'

At the entrance to my building, I tried to turn towards the corner and the park, but Baxter thought differently. He plumped down on his haunches, looked me in the eye and refused to budge. However hard I tugged on his leash, he was determined not to head in the direction I wanted.

'Okay, Baxter. *You* take *me* for a walk. Where do you want to go?'

He got to his feet, turned right and took off, pulling me along behind him. Five minutes later, we arrived at the entrance to a large pet store.

'*Woof.*' He looked pleased with himself.

'I thought that might happen,' said Mrs D, when I handed back her dog and his new squeaky toy.

I'D EARNED ENTRY to a second New York City Marathon by finishing nine New York Road Runner events and volunteering at another. My ninth half marathon for the year, on Staten Island in October, indicated I was in reasonable shape for the bigger event.

A week before marathon day, Hurricane Sandy slammed into New York and New Jersey. I hunkered down again, as I'd done for Hurricane Irene the year before when I'd ritualistically severed my ties to alcohol. This year, I was spared the inner turmoil and apprehension I'd felt then. This time, the tempest was all on the outside.

Uptown, it wasn't immediately apparent just how much damage Sandy had caused. There were fallen trees in our neighbourhood and in Central Park, and subway services were disrupted. The internet went off for a day. Downtown, it was a very different story. Storm surge, with waves reaching record heights, had caused major flooding. There was no power, which meant no working elevators in high-rise buildings, no lights, no communications, no transportation.

But lower Manhattan wasn't even the hardest-hit community: Staten Island, Queens, the Jersey Shore, and other nearby places were reeling. The damage was unprecedented, and the city wouldn't recover overnight. Many communities still had fuel shortages and power outages. People had died.

New York Road Runners and Mayor Michael Bloomberg tried to push ahead with the marathon, calling it 'The Race to Recover'. But the wider community was opposed. It wouldn't feel right to go ahead when parts of the city – some of them on the marathon route – were still in shock and needed all the available resources to assist their recovery. With just days to go, the decision was made, for the first time in its history, to cancel the event.

In its place, I ran a 25K race in County Cork, Ireland. Although I was fit and ran well, I didn't get too cocky about nabbing first place in my age group, being the only entrant in the category. My prize of a basket of cosmetics for ageing skin might be useful, now that I was officially a senior citizen.

CHAPTER FORTY-FOUR

I was in a taxi headed for the airport in Kuala Lumpur, Malaysia, when thunderstorms rolled in. 'How much to drive me to Penang?' I was entered in a race there the following morning.

'To Penang?' The driver squinted at me in the rear-view mirror. 'Almost 400 kilometres, miss!'

'I know. What would it cost?'

'Very expensive, miss.'

'*How* expensive?'

We settled on the equivalent of many hundreds of dollars to cover his return journey as well. I didn't care. My fear of flying had kicked in on seeing the bank of dark clouds. In the past, I would have taken a Xanax. Sobriety didn't come cheap.

The driver made a few calls on his mobile phone. 'Miss, okay if my brother take you? He is very good driver.'

'You can't?'

'My son has birthday. I promised to take him to KFC.'

By the time our deal had been negotiated, the storm system had rolled away and the sun was poking through the clouds. While all was now calm in the heavens, I feared for my life as my substitute driver swerved in and out of traffic for five hours on the busy freeway that headed north through Peninsular Malaysia.

The event in Penang was another reunion with Min and Samantha. I hadn't yet caught up on sleep after the long flight from Dublin and fell into bed straight after dinner. In the tropics, races start well before dawn to avoid the heat and humidity, and I'd managed only about an hour's rest before it was time to head out. Music still spilled out of karaoke bars as we plodded along the otherwise deserted streets to the start.

Sam would cross the finish line with a tiny lost kitten tucked into her cleavage after hearing its plaintive mewing beside the course. I finished with another notch in my belt. Two weeks later, in Singapore, I placed first ahead of the six other women in my age group in my last race for the year.

I'd achieved my goal of completing twelve half marathons in the year I turned sixty. And I hadn't picked up a drink. *Yay, me!* As I became more used to feeling my feelings, I realised that my fear and anxiety had diminished, and happiness, contentment and gratitude were taking up the space they had vacated. The light that had seemed so distant when I started my ascent from the depths now shone brightly.

My self-esteem had taken a great leap forward, just in time for another reunion with Tom.

We had been in touch intermittently since my hair had been singed in his bathtub the previous year. For this visit to Australia, I was based in Melbourne, but I'd planned to spend Christmas in Albury with family. Tom suggested he join me there. Something always pulled me back into his orbit. *This time* it might be different. *This time* it might be what I want it to be; he might be the man I want him to be; I might be the woman he would love.

My phone pinged. 'Cmin in2 town now. Art gall 10 mins?'

I had been expecting his text message, but my heart still bounced in my chest. He was riding his motorbike to Albury from Sydney, a journey of about seven hours. He would stay with me at my hotel.

He pulled up beside where I was waiting on the main street, turned off the ignition and stepped off the bike. I wanted to wrap my arms around him and hold him to my heart. As was his way, he brushed his lips across my cheek and then stood back. Aching to fill the space between us, I touched his arm awkwardly.

As seemed to be my pattern with Tom, my peripheral vision disappeared. His mussed silver hair, sun-browned face and tidy, muscular body filled my visual frame. He still affected me like no other man.

We spent the afternoon walking through the botanic gardens and along the river, where I used to walk my dogs. At one point, for a few seconds, Tom rested his hand lightly on the back of my neck. The gesture was intimate, affectionate and unfamiliar. I couldn't remember his ever touching me in quite that way before. I may have sighed as happy chemicals did a celebratory dance in the pleasure centre of my brain.

Later, we joined Jan and Peter at their traditional Boxing Day backyard cricket party. Tom, beer in hand, chatted with Pete, who was tending a large side of lamb on a spit roast in the garden. I sat in the shade with my oldest friend, watching our men.

'He seems nice, darl,' Jan said. In all the decades I'd known them both, it was the first time they had met. I watched idly as she tapped her cigarette against the ashtray that was balanced on the arm of her director's chair. It was ten years since my last cigarette.

That night, in our hotel room, I found myself gazing at Tom's upper lip, the shape of which I had always found sexually thrilling. He was saying something, but it was as if the sound had been turned down.

'Sorry. What did you say?'

'Would you like a whisky?'

'Oh, thanks ... no. I don't drink anymore. I told you that.'

'Not at *all*?'

'No. It's fine, though. You have one.'

When I had last seen him, I had still been a month away from quitting. Now, I had no compulsion to drink. I felt calmer, and less vulnerable emotionally. I didn't need wine as a buffer against him. When I waved him off the next day, I was a happy woman. Perhaps some sort of future together wasn't totally off the cards.

Before returning to Melbourne, I caught up with my local hairdresser. When I mentioned that Tom had just been in town, Angela paused from dabbing paste on to my roots with a pastry brush. 'I can't believe you got together with him again after that awful camping trip!' She held my gaze in the mirror. 'Aren't you ever going to learn?'

'There's something about him, Ange.'

'Something about *him*? There's something about *you*, girl. You're one crazy woman!'

IT WOULD HAVE been a simple matter to resume my former life in Australia. Tom and I were getting on well. Apart from the books and race medals I kept at the apartment in New York, and the X-rays and medical records from all my hospital visits that Emily stored for me in Kuching, I had everything I owned with me. I was enjoying seeing friends and not having to make excuses so that I could go off on my own to drink, or worrying that I might drink too much and 'disappear'. If I had left Australia in May 2010 intending to travel the world for a couple of years, I would have been able to tick that experience off my list and count myself extremely lucky for the people I'd met and the places I'd been. There were memories enough to last the rest of my life.

I had even faced my demons and quit drinking. But it didn't cross my mind to stop wandering the world. A six-week stay in Australia was simply another piece in the bigger picture of my life.

CHAPTER FORTY-FIVE

Sobriety now fitted me like its shell fits a snail.

Each morning, just before dawn, I ran back and forth along Dewi Sita Street, near Ubud's royal palace. Stray dogs and poultry scavenged in the dust. The reflexology and aromatherapy clinics, the boutiques selling Balinese clothing, hand-made soaps, leather goods and crystals were shuttered, their customers still sleeping in their resort hotels. Within a few hours, the street would be congested with motorbikes, taxis, minivans and tourists.

A stream dipped beneath the roadway before disappearing from sight around a corner. Three women stood knee-deep in the water, grooming themselves and their infants. Later, they would huddle on the wooden steps of a café, palms extended in the hope that a passer-by might offer some rupiah notes.

After the midway point of each pass of the street, I leant forward for the slight climb to a temple complex at one end or a soccer field at the other. I drank from the water bottle I kept stashed under a banyan tree by the field, where schoolkids arrived – on foot or on the back of a motor scooter – for sports training. A minivan owner hosed down his vehicle parked on the roadside. A father carrying a baby and holding the hand of a toddler strolled slowly along the footpath, stopping every now and then to allow the child to rest. Two young men waited for their lift to arrive, to take them to their jobs. An old man wearing the traditional Balinese wrapped skirt walked his dog on a leash. A Lycra-clad cyclist pedalled hard up the hill near the temple as he completed another circuit.

We greeted each other: '*Selamat pagi.*'

These people couldn't know how much pleasure it gave me to be one of them, one of the regulars in this place, an extra in *their* story, someone they were now used to seeing each morning: the foreign woman who jogged up and down the cracked roadway, in a kind of rapture, as the sky lightened.

A short walk away was the basement area of the main market, where traders gathered early to sell their fruits, vegetables and flowers. Long shafts of light penetrated from above, lighting the scene like a painting by Caravaggio. I perched on the bench seat of a small café with my breakfast of gritty Balinese coffee and hot banana fritters and quivered with happiness. Afterwards, at a nearby recovery meeting, I would find community with people from all over the world who had known my struggle and now also felt the freedom that came from acceptance.

One morning, I saw a white terrier dart into a dirt laneway near the inn where I was staying. It was unusual to see this breed alone on the streets of Ubud. It reminded me of my dog Butch and, curious, I followed it. The dog scampered away, but my eye was drawn to a sliver of a playing card lying in the dust. It showed two red hearts. Nearby was a full-size card, the eight of hearts. From my years in Hong Kong, I associated the number eight with abundance and good luck, despite the failure of the business venture I'd embarked on after 8/8/88. It seemed like a sign of some kind.

A couple of mornings later, in the same laneway, I found a third card. It was the Joker, the 'wild card' associated with endings and beginnings, unexpected events, transformation and destiny.

I wondered if it had to do with Tom, who would soon be joining me.

Then I met Paul.

THE COOL AIR felt welcome on my skin, which was grimy with sweat after the two-hour climb in the dark up an uneven track to the crater's edge. I could hear one or two low voices; most people sat in silence and gazed out towards the glorious sunrise. Mt Batur was an active volcano, but the only rumbling I could hear was from my stomach.

Mid-morning, in a café near the soccer field back in Ubud, I ordered another coffee from the waiter who was clearing my breakfast plates. I placed my laptop and papers on the table and signed on to start work. A group of people sat down nearby. From their conversation, I gathered that the man seated closest to me had just returned to Bali from the States. Later, we started to chat. Paul was friendly, confident and charming. Our conversation flowed easily. He gave me his phone number, saying something about getting together for a board game. 'Call me.'

I phoned him a few days later. 'Do you want to have that game sometime?'

'Sure. Now? I'll pick you up. Where are you?'

At the villa that he rented on the edge of town, we sat at a table on a verandah that overlooked a rice field. Paul set up the Scrabble board and letter tiles. He was gently flirtatious and I found him appealing. I liked that he made me feel I was funny and attractive, and that he was interested in what I had to say.

G-R-A-T-E-F-U-L.

Laughing, I laid down my tiles, building on one that was already on the board. I had covered two red double word score squares and earned a bonus for using all seven of my tiles. I was indeed feeling grateful as I looked across at this man, a decade my junior, who was making my skin tingle.

'Let's go and eat,' he said, after a second game. The hills in the distance were now in late-afternoon shadow. We had been listening to a jazz album as we played, and the silences between us had been as comfortable as our conversation.

As I swung my leg over the seat of his motorbike and settled behind him, he reached down and ran his hand down my calf. I rested my fingers on his shoulders and leaned in close to him.

The next day was Valentine's Day.

'How're you doing?'

I'd been swimming lazy laps in the pool by my room. 'I'm good. You?'

'Do you like gelato?'

'Do I like gelato? I *love* gelato!'

'Cool. I'll pick you up out the front of your place in half an hour, okay?'

'Okay! See you soon.'

When I walked out through the restaurant at the front of the inn to reach the street, I waved to the staff – Ardani, Ary, Sekar and pregnant Yanti – who were chatting at the bar. Paul pulled up on the other side of the narrow street, smiled, and patted the seat behind him. I timed a gap in the traffic and darted across to his side.

'Hi!'

'Hi!'

He handed me a helmet.

'You okay?' he asked over his shoulder a couple of times as we rode out into the countryside, his left hand resting lightly on my leg.

IT WAS CHALLENGING to get in any long runs because of the state of Ubud's streets and the lack of parkland. I loved the meditative aspect of my morning runs up and down Dewi Sita Street, but I wasn't getting much training benefit from them.

I had a chat with Gede, the driver I'd come to know, who provided a solution. He would pick me up an hour before dawn and take me across to the coast. There, I could run around the golf course at Tanah Lot, a temple complex on a small island that was accessible only at low tide. Afterwards, we would eat breakfast at a small family-run *warung*. Or I would run multiple circuits around the moat within the Tirta Empul temple grounds. Gede would wait patiently by the car, unfurling and retying his long silver–black hair in a loose bun and talking softly on his phone.

One morning before dawn, we drove out into the countryside for 21 kilometres – the distance of a half marathon. From there, I ran back to town, the roadway initially illuminated by the glow of the car's headlights behind me. When it grew light, Gede pulled ahead and guided me through tiny villages where I was greeted with smiles and waves. We came upon a bunch of school kids running an early morning race. For a few metres I joined in, to shouts of laughter, before stepping aside and cheering them on as they streamed past. An old woman smiled and raised both thumbs in salute as I ran through her village at six in the morning. Later, in Ubud's market, Gede and I ate *pisang goreng* as the traders haggled with their first customers of the day.

My body was happy to be at rest. My mind was at peace. My spirit was elated by the experience Gede and I had created together that morning, by first imagining it and then making it happen. Now that I no longer awoke in fear after a night of drinking, anxious about what I might find or recall, I was more aware of my surroundings, of things that were not me. I was better able to see beauty in the ordinary, everyday world, and to consciously acknowledge the pleasure I felt in noticing small things: a shaft of light in the market hall, the taste of hot banana, the wrinkles on the face of the flower seller, the sound of laughter.

CHAPTER FORTY-SIX

Why had Paul come into my life and created such an impact? I knew that he had worked hard to find balance and peace, that his steadiness wasn't due to any lack of imagination but to knowing what he needed in order to live a good life. He was much further down the road of self-awareness than I was, and it's possible that he appeared in my path as an example. In Ubud, it's easy to think in such new-age terms. But this interpretation was complicated by the physical attraction between us. I sensed that I now had an aura of health and vitality that had been missing when I was drinking, when my inner light had been dimmed by shame. I was also flattered by the attention Paul was paying me, and I enjoyed his company and the sparks we ignited. But, with Tom due to arrive in mid-March, I hadn't been looking for a lover.

A spiritual psychic I visited in Ubud suggested that I take up singing to unblock my throat chakra. I knew that my throat was often scratchy and tight, and that I kept some emotions bottled up. When Emily in Kuching had done a drawing of what she called my 'aura', she'd had difficulty with the area around my throat. 'Be careful there,' she had cautioned.

So, singing was on my mind in early March when I flew back to Kuching for a minibreak. I wanted to see my friends there, have another annual physical check-up and obtain a doctor's letter confirming I was fit to run the races I planned to enter in

Italy and France. As usual, I would make my home at the Batik.

On my way to the hospital one day, I was chatting about singing with the taxi driver, who remembered me, he said, from the year before. 'Do you sing?' I asked.

We were passing through an area of low-lying Malay compounds near the river. Min and I sometimes ran there.

'Yes.'

'Would you sing something for me?'

In a beautiful, gentle voice, he sang a Neil Sedaka love song. I tried – and failed – to imagine Tom crooning to me that I was the answer to his lonely prayer.

Inspired, I agreed to make my singing debut with Mas and Jun at the *kampong* food court across the river that was a late-afternoon karaoke venue. Jun bought a round of bubble teas, and we settled at a table where a few dried-up egg noodles and scraps of sauce remained from someone's lunch.

A tall Malay man approached our table. His large stomach pushed against the white-and-fawn checked cotton shirt he wore untucked over his old-man trousers. He spoke to Jun. They both looked at me, and Jun said something in reply. Mas started giggling. Jun removed his panama hat and fanned his face. His dark eyes behind heavy-framed glasses danced with mischief.

'What?' I looked from him to Mas and back again.

The man walked away and Jun replaced his hat. Mas's shoulders were shaking with laughter.

'He asked me if you're unattached,' Jun said.

'What did you say?'

'I told him you're my second wife.'

It seemed I had acquired yet another husband in Kuching.

Soon, it was our turn to sing. I put my arm around Mas and held on to her tightly. She had dressed up for our date: a black-

and-yellow patterned dress over leggings, a white headband and sunglasses. We had chosen to sing 'Que Sera Sera', which I knew from my childhood. My mother had hummed along to it playing on the radio while she dragged sodden clothes from the old copper boiler, mangled them through the wringer, and I then helped her to hang them out to dry. It was the song I had played as browsers turned over items that I'd placed on a table for sale when, at fifty-seven, I sold and packed up my house and prepared to start a new life as a global gypsy. It was a song whose message of trusting in the universe's inscrutable processes I both wanted to believe and rebelled against. From a young age, I'd determined that my fate lay in my own hands – that I couldn't really trust anyone but myself. I'd had a hard time ever since then, including in recovery, with the concept of relinquishing control. Yet, I sensed that the universe wished me well and was on my side. I hoped that the audience in this not-very-salubrious establishment would be forgiving of my lack of talent.

The following day, I could hear off-key singing at karaoke hour as I was walking along the waterfront. It hadn't occurred to me that my amateurish rendition of Doris Day's classic song might be heard by townspeople far and wide.

I now had a Kuching life that awaited me whenever I arrived in Sarawak. My friendships with people there were growing stronger. I loved to sit waiting for Min to arrive for our pre-dawn runs through the quiet inner-city streets or along the riverfront. The herbalist's shop across the road still operated through the night. Cars still pulled up a few steps from me, disgorging someone in need of a remedy who would dash across the divided road, then return minutes later clutching a small, brown paper-wrapped parcel. Upstairs in the shophouse, the woman still performed her morning devotions in a kind of shadow play.

The moist, warm air would sit lightly on my skin. My heart would lift when Min appeared at the corner on his bicycle. We would head out on our run together, the sky in the east beginning to lighten. Somehow, through running together on many early mornings, in the dark, in the quiet, as day was breaking, we had created a space together that was uniquely ours.

One morning, we were jogging along the roadside on our way to Sexy Popia, Min's name for a favourite *warung*, for breakfast with Samantha, Ivy and Swee. I was in a cocoon of contentment and happiness. For that hour, I had no wish to be anywhere other than where I was, somewhere upriver from the South China Sea coast on the island of Borneo, or with anyone other than Min.

'I love you, you know.'

'I know,' he said gently.

'I really appreciate you. I love that you're in my life.'

'I know.'

THE TAXI DRIVER who had sung for me drove me back to the hospital for the results of my tests. I felt well and had no concerns about my health, now that I no longer drank.

'You have osteopenia in your left hip and osteoporosis in your spine,' the doctor said. Her hair and neck were covered by a *hijab* and her face was unlined. She looked about twelve. Her voice was warm and concerned. 'You're a runner?'

'Yes.'

'Be very careful. No falling!'

CHAPTER FORTY-SEVEN

'Change of plan, Rob,' Tom said. We were in the car on the hour-long drive from Bali's airport up to Ubud. I was sitting in the front with Gede, to allow Tom to stretch his legs in the back after his flight from Sydney.

'I won't be staying with you the whole time now. Marie's flying up. I'll spend a few days in Sanur with her.'

I stared at him open-mouthed for a second or two, then turned away. His words bounced around inside my skull. I knew who Marie was. I knew she was an old girlfriend. I knew she had arrived from Europe for a visit in mid-January. He hadn't mentioned that she was still with him. It was a lot to take in.

Mixed with the shock was confusion over my own growing attraction to Paul, who was such easy company. He had called me every day. We'd had dinner a few more times. He was sweet and fun. He was how I wished Tom would be.

As soon as we arrived at the inn, Tom checked his emails. There was bad news to do with an upcoming trip, which I now learnt included Marie. Tom made a call. He was in a rage. I sat on the bed, on hold. A ping on my phone was a text from Paul.

'How're you doing?'

'Not sure,' I texted back.

Finally, Tom turned his attention to me. 'I need a drink,' he said. 'Dinner?'

While he showered, I checked with Ary that everything was ready for the surprise I'd planned. 'Don't worry,' she said. 'It will be done. Enjoy your meal.'

Tom was much calmer by the time we settled at a candlelit table in the garden of a nearby restaurant. I hoped the romantic atmosphere might bode well for us, but the hand that stroked my arm was my own.

Later, walking back through the throng of tables in the garden at the front of the inn, I caught Ardani's eye and she nodded. Putu gave me a thumbs-up. All the staff were in on the plan.

Tom had walked off ahead through the carved wooden gate that led to the villas around the pool. On the porch to ours, he stood aside so that I could unlock the sliding teak door. Inside, a lamp had been turned on, casting a golden glow. Tom sat down on the bed and reached for his iPad.

I walked into the bathroom and beheld the scene I had imagined: the deep bath had been filled two-thirds full. The water surface was covered with masses of colourful flowers – orange, pink, yellow, purple. Petals were strewn across the grey tile floor. Tea lights flickered softly at either end of the tub. The air was fragrant.

Although it had been my idea and I had asked the staff to create the scene while we were out, it still took my breath away.

'Tom,' I called.

Silence.

I went to the doorway. 'Come and have a look at this.'

'Hmm?' He didn't look up.

'Come and see this.'

'I want to write this email, Rob.'

I looked at him for a few moments, then turned away. In the bathroom, I stripped quickly. I didn't want him to find me hopping around awkwardly on one leg, trying to get out of my knickers. Wrapping myself in a towel, I sat down on the edge of the bath and dipped a hand into the water.

Shit, it's freezing!

'Rob?' He'd come to the doorway. 'Wow!'

'Isn't it gorgeous?'

'That would be a great photo with you in among the flowers.'

'But it's really cold!'

'No, it'll be great. I'll get my camera.'

Standing with one foot balanced on the bath-edge and the other on the sink, he took photographs of my breasts poking up through the blossoms and seemed not to notice the sound of my teeth chattering.

The next evening, we were among the audience waiting for a Legong dance performance to begin in the grounds of Ubud Palace. I'd been feeling confused by Marie's re-emergence as someone central in Tom's life. My palms were clammy even before I opened my mouth, but I couldn't hold back any longer.

'Tom, I'm upset that you didn't say earlier you'll be meeting Marie.'

'Why?'

'I didn't know she's been staying with you all this time. If I'd known, I might have thought this wasn't a good idea.'

'What do you mean?'

'Maybe if I'd known about it, I would have had second thoughts.'

He looked surprised.

'I always feel like I'm on unsure ground with you,' I said. 'I never know where I fit into the picture.'

'She's no longer my girlfriend.'

'Am *I* your girlfriend?'

It was time to know exactly how he felt about me. I'd given him space in my heart for three decades. He was going to have to claim it or move out.

'No, you're not my girlfriend.'

THE GAMELAN ORCHESTRA players assembled and sat cross-legged on the ground. They wore identical maroon lengths of cloth tied at the waist, loose white cotton tunic tops and maroon headpieces. Their feet were bare. Two dancers appeared in the carved stone doorway, their hands folded together in the position of prayer. When the musicians began to play, the discordance of the music sounded to my ears like my own jangled nerves and confusion.

After the performance, we ate in a casual local restaurant. When we left, Tom took the steep wooden steps two at a time and then walked off ahead in the direction of the inn without waiting for me. It was as if I didn't exist. It required all of my restraint not to turn away and just disappear into the night.

I had wanted him to come with me to the produce market at dawn, to see how the pale morning rays made the tables laden with fruits and vegetables appear like a Renaissance painting. 'It's so beautiful,' I said. 'But we need to be there early.'

'How early? I don't want to rush around all the time, Rob.'

'I know, but dawn is when it's really special.' I wanted to share with him an experience that I was sure he would enjoy.

'So, will you come with me early?'

By the time he was ready the next morning, the sublime moment had passed.

At lunch in a restaurant beside a vivid green rice field, we were having a discussion that wasn't going well. Tom was dismissive of my views. My frustration was fuelled by the slights and hurts I'd perceived over the past four days. When he interrupted me yet again, I smacked his arm.

'Tom, let me finish!'

He went rigid, then retreated inside his hard casing like a tortoise.

'I'm sorry,' I said. But it was too late; he had gone.

Had he ever said those two words to me?

The rest of the day was interminable. It was the same old, same old we'd been through too many times already. Like my drinking, there was no longer joy in it. We watched a movie together in virtual silence and shared the king-size bed without touching.

I had arranged with Gede to drive us into the interior of the island early the next day. When the alarm sounded, I pounced on it quickly. In the gloom, I looked across to where Tom lay, on the far side of the bed, his back to me. I slid across the expanse until my body lay against his and put my arm around him.

He bolted upright.

'What? Is it time to get up?'

'No, we have a few minutes.'

'Why did you wake me, then?' he spluttered.

His hair stood up from his scalp at all angles. His lips that I so wanted to kiss me, to smile at me, to laugh with me, to tell me that he loved me, were pulled into a hard line. I had no idea how to bridge the distance between us.

I had a sudden thought. 'Why don't you go on your own with Gede?'

'No.' He regarded me without emotion. 'I'll go and see —.'

I knew that he had a friend with a villa on the outskirts of town. 'Maybe it's best if you ask to stay with him. It's all too hard.'

He rolled his eyes. 'You do this every time, Rob! I don't know what your problem is, but you've got one ...'

I couldn't deny that this was the case.

'I'll wait for Gede out the front,' I said, finally. 'To pay him.'

Instead of returning to the room and watching Tom pack his things and disappear from my life yet again, I walked down to the market and took my usual seat on the bench in the basement.

'*Pisang goreng*?' asked the woman who tended the stall.

'No, just coffee today.'

I sat on the bench for a while, then went to a recovery group meeting. It was all I could think of to do next. Although I wished it could be different, it seemed that Tom and I would never be loving partners.

When I returned to the inn, Ary and Ardani were in the front garden decorating statues there with flowers and batik cloth in preparation for yet another festival.

'He left,' Ary said, touching my arm gently.

I nodded.

IN THE AFTERNOON, my phone rang. 'How're you doing?'

'Not so good.'

'What's happened?'

'He's gone.'

'Do you want to go for gelato?'

I sniffed and laughed weakly. 'Yes.'

In the past, I had used alcohol to plaster over the hurts I felt in my relationship with Tom. Paul was kind and attentive and *there*. I melted into him. For the next two weeks, I experienced what it was like to be wanted by a man who put his arms around me often and listened to what I had to say, who wanted to hear about my dreams, who was fun and playful, gentle and loving. He loved Bali and spoke Indonesian. I felt privileged to be with him, to see how the Balinese respected him for honouring their language and their traditions.

Paul invited me to start the new year with him, a Balinese–Hindu celebration based on the lunar calendar. We rode around town on his motorbike, picking up ingredients for a curry, then watched the parade to the soccer field of *ogoh-ogoh*, papier-mâché replicas of mythological beasts and demons. Later, we ate together on the verandah as the night closed in. The sounds of occasional motorbikes, pop music and voices drifted across the fields.

Paul put on some soft jazz, closed his eyes and started to dance. I watched him, admiring the way his body, clad only in a sarong, responded to the music. He held out his hand, and I rose and moved towards him. He reached for me and kissed me, then untied the knot that held my sarong in place. He knelt and slowly pulled down my orange knickers. I stepped out of them, and he tossed them aside. I untied his sarong and pulled it free of his body. And then we danced together, touching and moving apart, moving in our own arcs, feeling the music.

We had sex for hours that night. It was far too long a time for me. I craved sleep. I'd been up at five for a run. I'd worked on a challenging project for a client. My body and brain and chakras were knackered. Paul seemed to want to go on forever.

'Making love isn't about having an orgasm,' he chided me, when I tried to hurry him along a little.

'I'm really tired,' I whimpered. 'Please, just for tonight, could we make it about orgasms?'

The first day of the new year, *Nyepi*, is marked by silence: ghosts and spirits wander the island, and everyone remains indoors and quiet so as not to attract their attention. We read, played Scrabble, and tried not to speak other than in occasional low voices. Every now and then, Paul smoked a cigar. In bed that night, he wrapped his arms around me in the dark and sang an ancient mantra quietly against my ear.

He was the blessing from the universe hinted at by the Joker card I'd found in a dusty laneway. He appeared unexpectedly in my life, and helped to heal my hurt with his acceptance, affection and tender care. It wasn't love, for either of us, but it appealed to my sweet tooth. Paul reminded me of the transformative power of trusting in and flowing with the process of living, and of not always trying to shape an outcome. That I was thinking in such new-age terms indicated it was probably time for me to return to the real world.

I had plans in place in Europe, and Paul had other places to be, but we spent four days together in Malaysia before our paths disentangled. We had booked our plane tickets separately and were seated some rows apart. During the flight, I got up and walked towards the rear of the plane. Paul was seated on the aisle next to a middle-aged Western man. Without speaking or indicating that I knew Paul, I hesitated when I reached his row, caught his eye, held his glance, then bent down slowly and kissed him full on the mouth. Neither of us said a word before I continued on my way.

CHAPTER FORTY-EIGHT

Florence, like Ubud, New York and Kuching, worked well for me as a long-stay destination. Although I was busy with work, on most days I was able to visit a gallery or a museum, attend recovery meetings with people I knew from my previous visit, see a film, or just walk around, experiencing the city. Many of the streets in the area where I lived beside the Duomo were closed to vehicles. Locals sitting bolt upright on rickety bicycles crisscrossed the piazza, wending their way through small groups of tourists following a guide holding aloft a small flag, a brochure, a bright-coloured umbrella. Other visitors trundled wheeled suitcases across the cobblestones, making a distinctive clacking sound. Giotto's bell tower, just around the corner, sounded out the hours. 'Is that the time already?' Florentines had been muttering to themselves since the fourteenth century.

I'd hoped to run the city's popular Vivicitta Half Marathon but was unable to obtain the requisite *Sports Certificato Medico Agonistico*. Undaunted, I decided to run it as a bandit, without a number.

The course was two loops of a route through the historic centre and along both sides of the River Arno. As I was nearing the end of the first loop, my toe caught on a cobblestone and I was suddenly airborne. The warning from my doctor in Kuching rang in my ears: 'No falling!'

I lay still for a moment, then a hand grasped my elbow and helped me to my feet. Someone handed me my phone, which had skittered across the paving.

'*Grazie, grazie.*'

I made a quick assessment. There was a lot of abrasion on my right palm and forearm, and I'd skinned both knees. I was shaken up, but it appeared I'd been lucky. *I might leave it at that for today,* I thought. I hobbled off the course and through a side street back to Piazza Santa Croce, where the runners started their second loop.

Oh, what the hell ... I wasn't registered, so it didn't matter that I'd cut off a bit of the course. I started running again, keeping my eyes fixed firmly on the road just ahead and lifting my feet unnaturally high. It reminded me of the way I'd walked during the last months I'd lived in Hong Kong, back in 1993, when I was riddled with anxiety and unable to feel the ground properly.

Feeling chuffed with myself after I'd completed the second loop without incident, I decided to try to claim a finisher's medal. I joined a queue of runners and shuffled forward.

'*Numero?*' said the official, when I reached the head of the line. I had no number pinned to my chest that I could show, but I really wanted the medal.

'No *numero*. But I ran! I finished!'

He shooed me away: 'Must have *numero*!'

I can give in, or I can persist. I won't have another chance.

I joined another line, where I met the same response but refused to budge. 'Please, can I have a medal? I really earned it. I fell!' I shoved my blood-streaked, grazed palm in the official's face.

Recoiling, he thrust a hefty piece of grey metal at me.

'*Grazie mille!*'

IN LATE APRIL, I made a return visit to Venice. My small hotel on a tiny *calle* fronted on to a narrow canal. Before heading out for a walk, I spent a couple of hours working on a job for a client in Malaysia. From my room, I could hear the swish of gondolas gliding past just beneath the window, sometimes with an accordion-player singing 'Volare' or another tune guaranteed to earn them a big tip.

That evening I bought a single red rose from a flower vendor and dropped it into the canal from a bridge where gondoliers smoked cigarettes while touting for business. It swirled lazily in the current, before disappearing beneath the arch. Stepping to the other side, I watched it reappear on its way to the sea. I thought of Paul, and of Tom, and of my life flowing inevitably towards a future that was unknowable. I had always been adept at setting goals and making things happen; the challenge of the past year had been to bend with the winds that sometimes blew me off my anticipated course.

In the Doge's Palace, I lost my sense of direction and found myself peering out through the stone grilles from the Bridge of Sighs at the elusive pedestrian area along the waterfront. When I finally emerged into the daylight, two attractive young men were holding makeshift signs offering free hugs. *Perhaps they're doing it as a dare*, I thought, and smiled at them as I walked past.

After a few steps, I stopped in my tracks, turned around and went back for a hug from each of them.

CHAPTER FORTY-NINE

A stopover in Paris on my way to New York for the northern summer was further proof that I could still get my knickers in a twist if things didn't go my way.

I'd arranged to stay in the apartment of a French woman I'd sat next to on a plane from Singapore to Bali earlier in the year, but her tiny studio in Montmartre didn't do it for me. The internet signal was erratic, making it impossible to work; the sitting room was minuscule; the bed on a mezzanine shelf made me feel claustrophobic. I decided to bail and just leave cash for the one night I spent there.

Because I was unable to get online for more than a few seconds, I couldn't search for a suitable nearby hotel. Leaving the keys on the table, I pulled the self-locking door closed and then dragged my suitcase over cobblestones for some time, looking for a hotel. Finally, I found a dingy place on the seedy edge of Montmartre that had a vacancy.

'Three nights, *madame*. This is all we have.'

'But I need a room for a week,' I whined.

'All Paris is full for *le Tennis Open, madame*.'

The cramped garret with unreliable internet I'd just locked myself out of was starting to look a little more appealing.

'Do you have good internet?'

'*Oui, madame*.'

'I'll take it.'

After three days there, I located an overpriced boutique hotel in the Bastille area that could put me up for two of my remaining four nights before I was due to fly to Dublin. The internet was again problematic, cafés and local restaurants were closed whenever I went foraging for food, and I was running out of clean clothes.

'Is there somewhere nearby where I can have laundry done?' I asked at the front desk.

'We have a laundry service, *madame*.'

I'd checked the prices. 'I was hoping there might be somewhere nearby that wouldn't cost the equivalent of dinner at the Ritz ...'

'There is nowhere close, *madame*. But if you want to follow my complicated directions, I can suggest a laundry some distance from here that you will find shut each time you try it.'

It was the last straw. My room was expensive and I wasn't feeling the value. I still didn't have a bed for my last two nights. I was undernourished. And now I would have to spend a fortune to have a small bag of clothes washed.

Little in the past week had flowed smoothly or easily, but my poor handling of the difficulties had just made it worse. From the first night, I'd fallen into a black mood and I hadn't been able to climb out of it. If I'd sought out an English-speaking recovery meeting, I might have been reminded that it's usually not worth getting cranky over things I can't control. Instead, I decided to get the hell out of Dodge.

I'VE RARELY BEEN as frightened in a vehicle as I was in the taxi that took me to the airport for my evacuation flight to Ireland. The driver talked into a hand-held phone for the duration of the journey while changing lanes frequently and (to my mind) recklessly.

'You're a *terrible* driver!' I shouted, when we screeched to a standstill outside the departures terminal at Charles de Gaulle Airport. I threw 80 euros at her. 'I thought I was going to DIE!'

She got out of the cab, dumped my case on to the concourse and roared away.

'Your baggage is overweight, *madame*,' said *l'homme* at the airline counter.

Is this never going to end?

'You need to pay a large sum before I can issue your boarding pass.'

'Are you kidding me?'

'*Non, madame.* Pay at that counter, *s'il vous plaît.*' He held out a form, which I snatched from his hand.

I didn't feel like I wanted to drink, but I obviously had some work to do on the dummy-spit front.

A few hours later, I presented my passport to an immigration official at Dublin Airport. The flight had been smooth and uneventful.

'What's the purpose of your visit?'

'I hate Paris.'

He peered at me over the top of his glasses. 'I can't write that.'

'I'm here to see my hair stylist.'

An hour later, I was waiting patiently to check into my hotel near Temple Bar, my mind on the seafood chowder I would have at Foam after I'd made an appointment to see Carly for a trim and had dropped off my now-smelly bag of washing at a laundry I'd spotted around the corner. I noticed that a man and a woman of about my age were smiling at me.

'Sorry, did you say something?'

'We really like your style,' the man said.

'What?'

'We think you're very stylish.'

'You do?'

Were they swingers trying to pick me up for a threesome? I was unsure of whether to feel flattered or flummoxed. If our paths had crossed earlier in the day, in Paris, they might instead have thought me psychotic.

CHAPTER FIFTY

After four years of regular, extended visits, I had a life and familiar routines in New York and hit the ground running whenever I returned. 'Welcome home,' Eugene the doorman would say, and come out from behind the reception desk to give me a hug. 'How long are you staying?'

'Where've you been this time?' a friend from my morning recovery meeting would ask. 'Tierra del fucking Fuego?'

'We've missed you on our runs,' Maria would say. 'See you tomorrow!'

I fronted up in Central Park for races that celebrated Portugal, women, Israel, Gay Pride and people with disabilities. When a star from a Broadway musical sang the national anthem just before the starting pistol fired, I would place my hand on my heart without also putting my tongue in my cheek. America had been good to me. Once or twice that summer, I placed in my age group and earned team points for the Dusters.

When I wasn't running, or at recovery meetings or working for my clients at the kitchen table, I saw films and exhibitions and went to the theatre. One day, I walked the length of Broadway, from the top of the island to Battery Park at its foot. I loved how the character of the old Indian trail changed as I passed through predominantly Hispanic, Dominican and Black neighbourhoods, then through my own part of the city, the Jewish Upper West

Side, and on down to the New York most visitors knew – Midtown and the theatre district – before arriving at lower Manhattan and Wall Street. I left not just shoe leather and sweat on the hot pavements, but new memories and little pieces of my heart.

A rolling stone is said not to gather any moss. That's not my experience. Despite my nomadic lifestyle, I was gathering people who felt like kin. I was a solo traveller, not a loner.

In England on my way back to Europe, there were meet-ups with my walking friends Tony and Jo for a hike up Mt Snowden in Wales; and with Wendy, who had bought me a post-op glass of wine in Kathmandu in 2008. She and I scrambled along the cliff edge on Dorset's Jurassic Coast, and browned our bums in the sun on the shingles of a nudist beach, watching naked men posing like meerkats among the tussock grasses and cruising for hook-ups.

AFTER A MONTH in Budapest, which grabbed a big piece of my heart, I was back in New York in the late autumn with a touch of whiplash from all the Atlantic Ocean crossings and with a hair appointment to keep over on Lexington Avenue. My Russian stylist ran late with other clients and could only do my colour. 'Can you come back tomorrow for the cut?' she said.

I wasn't happy about it. A second visit would mean a second lot of tips for everyone who had touched a hair on my head or laid a finger on my coat. When the next day became a repeat of the first, I grizzled loudly.

By the time I was done and could leave, it was 30 minutes to curtain-up on Broadway, where I had a ticket to 'A Night with Janis Joplin'. My displeasure was apparent to all. I threw cash on the counter, snatched up my coat, raced out into the cold evening, tore down Lexington to the subway station, jumped on a crowded train to Midtown, then barrelled across the avenues to the theatre. I found my row, shuffled past people's knees to my seat, checked out the full house behind me while removing my coat, then turned and sat down just as the lights were lowered.

The actor channelling Janis was performing 'Piece of My Heart' when I scratched an itch on my shoulder. The fabric felt odd. My hand moved to my other shoulder, then to my chest, and then to my lap. I realised that I was still wearing the pale-blue nylon robe from the salon. I had been in such a temper about the amount of time and money the hair appointment had cost, and in such a rush to leave, I'd forgotten to remove the robe before throwing on my coat. It would have dangled far beneath the hem as I'd charged through the streets, and I had flashed it at everyone in the rows behind me when I'd arrived at my seat.

Oy vey. How could I not have seen the expanse of ugly pastel-blueness? I squirmed out of the robe, rolled it into a ball and pushed it into my bag.

Now I'll have to find a new hair stylist in Manhattan.

CHAPTER FIFTY-ONE

A man was looking at me and waving his arms in slow motion. His mouth was moving, but no sound reached my ears. Then everything went dark.

When I opened my eyes, I was lying on the roadway. I turned my head and saw my camera, which had flown out of my hand and was some metres away. Sounds rolled towards me, becoming more distinct. A hand came into view, followed by a face.

'Sorry! Sorry!'

Then another face, the one whose mouth I had seen opening and closing. 'Okay?'

'I don't know. What happened?'

'Not look!'

I'd arrived in Marrakech just an hour earlier from Spain and had gone for a quick walk before friends were due to arrive. Retracing my steps, I'd noticed a shop where I might be able to buy a mobile wi-fi device. I'd waited for a break in the stream of trucks, cars, scooters, bicycles and donkey carts coming from the right, but failed to look to the left and stepped into the path of a bicycle.

'Sorry!' the man said again. His face was creased with age and concern.

'It's my fault. Don't worry.'

He grasped me under my left arm and helped me to my

feet, then picked up my camera. When I tried to reach for it, I couldn't move my right arm. The signal from my brain wasn't reaching my hand. I cupped the elbow with my left hand and nodded towards the large door fronting the roadway that was the entrance to my small hotel. 'My *riad*.'

The young man who opened the door saw that I was distressed. Mustapha had wished me a pleasant walk just twenty minutes earlier.

'I've hurt my arm.'

'Sit here. I'll get you tea.'

I lowered myself into a chair by the door.

'Do you want to go to your room?' he said, when he returned with a glass of hot mint tea and a sugar bowl on a silver tray.

I shook my head. 'My friends will be here soon.'

I sipped at the tea and watched, dazed, while two young women laid tables in a small dining room off the courtyard.

'Maybe it's just dislocated?' Rita suggested, when she and Bruce arrived and found me huddled in the seat by the doorway. Artist friends from Albury, they lived in Marrakech for half the year. 'You do look pale, though.'

'I think I need an X-ray.'

'There's a good hospital near our place. I'll phone Abdou.'

It all suddenly became serious.

'I also need to contact my travel insurer.'

'Can't she go to a free public hospital?' the consultant asked Bruce when he got through to the insurance company on Skype.

'We're in bloody *Morocco*, mate. Not bloody *England*!'

At the hospital, a French-speaking doctor looked at my X-rays and nodded. '*L'humérus est fracturé.*'

My right arm – the arm that made possible my life as an editor without borders – was broken straight across, just beneath the shoulder. The humerus was unattached and floating. Surgery was needed to wire it back together. This was not good at all.

'How much will it cost?' I asked.

Bruce had got authorisation from my insurer, but on a pay-and-claim basis. I would have to cover all the costs of a hospital stay and surgery out of my own pocket and then claim back whatever I could. My finances were tight. Invoices were out with clients, but I had only enough cash to cover my accommodation and daily living costs for the month I was planning to stay in Morocco. Prepaid onward flights and accommodation had pushed my credit cards close to their limits. I couldn't afford this accident.

'Don't worry about that now,' Rita said, patting my hand. 'We'll work out something.'

In a tiny private room, a nurse helped me to change out of the clothes I'd been wearing since Madrid. Today was meant to be the start of an eight-week semi-holiday. I had cleared free time after finishing a huge job for a Sydney arts festival just two days before, in Seville, and was entered in road races in Morocco, Spain, Malta and Egypt. I lay awake in my hospital bed, a large pillow supporting my broken arm, and tried not to think.

During surgery the next morning, four delicate wire wands were inserted in my upper arm to stimulate fusion of the fractured ends of the bone. The arm was then immobilised and encased in a sleeve. I spent the rest of the day and another night in hospital on pain meds, floating in and out of the room.

'Don't give me anything addictive,' I'd mumbled to the nurse.

Rita and Bruce were leaving town for a week. I would be friendless in a city I was now unable to explore in the way I had planned. But I wasn't simply incapacitated; I felt vulnerable and fearful, too, just as I had done after being mugged in Chile.

'As soon as my client pays, I'll transfer the money to you,' I promised Rita, who paid my hospital bill so that I could be discharged. At the *riad*, my suitcase still lay unopened on the bed. For a second time, I returned to a guesthouse in a developing country after having had arm surgery under a general anaesthetic. This time, unlike in Kathmandu five years before, I didn't crave a glass of wine. Mint tea would do just fine.

Everyday activities such as showering were a challenge. While I sat on a stool, the two housekeepers scrubbed me, washed my hair, towelled me dry, and applied deodorant to my left armpit. There was no access to my right one. A couple of squirts of Chanel and I felt slightly human again.

I could only type one-fingered using my left hand. The *riad* wasn't cheap, but I was too afraid to venture out into the streets to look for anywhere more affordable. I couldn't feed myself easily. My sleep was broken, and I would need help with dressing and other daily tasks until I could move my arm again. One hand was one too few to manage luggage. All of my travel plans had effectively bitten the dust at the same moment my camera flew out of my grasp.

What should I do? I was dependent on others in an unfamiliar way, but without anyone to fall back on. There seemed only one sane course of action. I would fly straight to Malaysia. I would be at home in Kuching's Batik hotel; I was already well plugged into Sarawak's medical system; and I had family in Min and Sam, Emily, Jackie and Jo-Lynn. With them close by, I wouldn't have to manage on my own when I was feeling so helpless.

'Hi, Kelli,' I tapped out laboriously on my laptop to the consultant in Australia I used whenever the logistics of travel seemed too daunting. 'I need your help with some flight bookings, pls.'

The pain from the surgery soon lessened, but I had a weeping sore on the soft underside of my upper arm where the skin was pressed against my side.

'It's torture,' I said to Majdouline, the *riad* manager. 'I'm not supposed to move my arm for six weeks, but I'm going crazy after just a few days!'

'I'll take you to the doctor tomorrow. Don't worry. Everything will be okay.'

A knock at the open door was Mustapha with my dinner on a tray. He placed a low table beside the bed and removed the metal lid.

'Do you want me to help you?'

'Yes, please.'

He cut the lamb into small pieces, then fed me forkfuls that he circled in the air like an aeroplane before landing them in my open mouth.

'Like feeding my little boy,' he said, and we laughed.

The next day, the surgeon announced that everything was as it should be.

'But my arm is pressing against my skin here,' I whimpered. 'It's raw and weeping.'

'*Pffft. Ce n'est pas un problem.*'

'It *is* a problem. It hurts!'

'He says you need to come back in a few weeks to have the stitches taken out,' Majdouline said. 'But I've told him you're flying to Malaysia tomorrow.'

At the *riad*, she set me up with a sandwich lunch in a small lounge off the courtyard that had a couch and a large wall-mounted television. 'I hope one day you will come back to Morocco,' she said, and slipped *Casablanca* into the DVD player.

The next morning, Abdou picked me up at dawn to drive the

200 kilometres from Marrakech to Casablanca. At the airport check-in desk, I asked for a right-hand window seat all the way to Kuching. 'I've had an operation and don't want to sit next to someone and bang my arm.' I hoped that he might take pity and give me a complimentary upgrade.

'Do you have a doctor's letter saying you are fit to fly, *madame?*' he said instead.

'What? No, I don't. Do I need one?'

'Yes, *madame*. You cannot fly without such a letter.'

'I didn't know that! No one told me that!' I lurched into near hysteria. After everything that had happened – the pain, the disappointment at having to change all my plans, the challenges of trying to manage simple tasks with one arm out of action, the blow to my finances – it seemed too unfair that more problems should appear in my path.

I took a deep breath. 'I saw the doctor yesterday.' I stretched out the words. 'He knew I was flying today. He said nothing about a letter.'

'The airline cannot take the risk, *madame*.'

'Simple. I'll absolve you of any risk,' I said, speeding up again. 'I'll take all the risk.'

'*Non, madame*. You must have a doctor's letter or I cannot issue a boarding pass.'

I turned to Abdou. 'What am I going to do?'

He spoke with the official in Arabic, then switched back to English. 'We have to try to contact the doctor. Do you have his phone number?'

While I rooted around in my shoulder bag looking for the surgeon's name card, Abdou retrieved my suitcase from the check-in luggage belt. I found the phone number, which rang out twice when Abdou called. It was still early in the day.

I felt wobbly from this latest shock and needed to sit down, but I didn't want to move too far away. If I stayed within eyeshot of the check-in official and looked sufficiently miserable and pathetic, he might relent. I forced myself to breathe slowly and to try and stay in the moment.

Eventually, Abdou got someone on the phone.

'They will try to contact him,' he said, when the call ended. 'They will ask him to write a letter and they will fax it here to the airport. Now, we can only wait. It is in God's hands. *Inshallah.*'

Fresh in my mind was the image of Ingrid Bergman's character in *Casablanca*, whose future and that of her husband depended on their securing crucial letters of transit that would allow them to leave Morocco.

Eventually, an official appeared holding the faxed 'fit to fly' letter that would enable me to board my flight. With my boarding pass finally in hand, I requested a wheelchair. My arm was throbbing.

A medical attendant arrived with a chair, and I sank into it. Abdou tucked my carry-on case between my feet and then stood back.

'You will come again to Morocco. Next time will be better.'

CHAPTER FIFTY-TWO

'Hello, Auntie Robyn.'

When I heard young Sean's greeting at Kuching Airport, I realised I'd been half holding my breath for the past twenty-four hours. He had talked his way into the baggage claim area to help me with my luggage. Outside in the arrivals area, I could see Min waving at me and talking on the phone – possibly to Samantha to say I'd made it. I was home.

The journey from Morocco to Sarawak had been interminable. I hadn't slept during the three back-to-back flights from Casablanca to Dubai, to Kuala Lumpur, and then to Kuching. I'd read my book or closed my eyes and recited the Serenity Prayer over and over. I had tried not to think about where I was, what had happened to put me there, and what lay ahead. Slowly, the seconds had turned to minutes, the minutes to hours, and today became yesterday.

Sam was on the mainland, visiting her folks and Sara, who was doing her national service. Min gave me their bedroom, and I spent the weekend there, beginning the long and frustrating process of putting together my travel insurance paperwork to claim for emergency treatment, changed flights, lost hotel prepayments and other costs.

It seemed that my sobriety needed to be tested periodically by a calamitous event that would push me to my limits. Each time I had to deal with my insurer on the phone, my stress level soared.

'If you post that on Facebook, Sean,' I threatened when the teenager photographed me mid-dummy spit, 'you are *dead.*'

WE DROVE TO a hair salon where I could have my hair washed and dried, and then to the Sarawak Club for Malaysian comfort food – *char kuey teow* noodles. After lunch, I pecked out emails on my laptop with one finger while Min swam laps of the pool. A broken arm was a major pain in the bum, but it would have been so much worse had I not already stopped drinking. I wouldn't have been able to get my daily dose without my addiction being very visible. How much more self-respect would I have been prepared to trade off? I could be grateful that only my plans had been shattered, and not my life.

When Sam returned from Kuala Lumpur, she helped me move into the Batik, showered me, dried my back, unpacked my suitcase, and left me a fish pie I could eat one-handed. Two days later, she drove me to the hospital where, the year before, a doctor had warned me of the risks of falling. I needed to schedule removal of the stitches.

'These wires aren't strong enough,' the orthopaedic surgeon said, looking at my X-ray. 'You need a plate to hold your arm together while it begins to heal. It will give you more movement, too.'

'Well, *that* would be a relief!'

We discussed costs, dates and the need for follow-up physiotherapy.

'I'll have to talk to my bloody travel insurer before I can confirm.'

As I expected, they again put me through hoops.

'This is optional surgery,' they said. 'We're not a health insurer. If you want to have another operation, you should go back to Australia and have it done there under the free health system.'

Eventually, they agreed to contribute the equivalent of a budget flight from Malaysia to Australia. I would have to cover the rest of the expense of surgery and physiotherapy myself.

The surgeon replaced the wires with a massive metal plate that extended from my shoulder almost to my elbow. Finally, I could raise my arm and relieve the torment of having skin pressed on skin. My recovery could now begin.

Running was out of the question, but I could still take some exercise. The following Sunday morning, I walked to the river-front where Eng Hooi regularly coached a group of high school athletes. Normally, Min and I would join in the circuit runs and drills after our long run. One time, a teenage boy had appeared suddenly at my elbow during a circuit and made a show of sprinting past me.

'I told him you're his grandmother's age,' Eng Hooi said later at breakfast. '"Do you want your grannie to beat you?" I'd said. That got him moving!'

The kids were already running loops along the paved promenade when I arrived, nursing my arm. Next to the railing was a body.

'What …?'

'We've called the police,' Belinda said. 'They're taking a long time.'

'What happened?'

'We don't know. He was here when we arrived. He's naked. Eng Hooi covered him. The police said he's probably just drunk.'

There but for the grace of something …

I sat down beside Belinda and stared over at the shape lying on the ground. 'Maybe he's dead?'

Just then, Sam pulled up. 'What's going on?'

She went across to the prone figure, squatted down beside him, and lifted the cloth to get a look at his face. I could see her mouth moving. She shook his shoulder and he moved; then slowly, with her help, he sat up. He pointed to a row of shophouses behind us. Sam helped him to his feet and walked him across the road. When a door opened, he disappeared inside.

'It was drugs, I think,' she said, joining us again. 'He lives there. He doesn't remember what happened, but he's okay.'

I was in tears. The situation had paralysed me, but Sam hadn't hesitated to get involved and to offer help. I'd known her and Min for only three years, but I knew that if I were ever in any doubt about what was the right thing to do, I should just do whatever I thought Sam would do. She did it instinctively; I had to think things through a bit first.

After the surgical staples were removed from my arm, I started working with a physiotherapist. Sam would pick me up and drive me out to the clinic in the suburbs, where I practised walking my right hand up a wall or turning a wheel with my palm. I think she was as relieved as I was when I made good progress and no longer needed her help with showering.

At Chinese New Year, because I was single, my married friends gave me traditional lucky red envelopes containing a small sum of money; as an 'auntie', I gave similar envelopes to their children. It was another Year of the Horse: time to get back in the saddle and pick up the reins again.

Now that I'd regained use of my right arm, I was fit for work. A publisher contacted me about editing a huge textbook on everything that could go wrong with the human body. They had been referred to me, there was the possibility of future work and the content would be interesting. The fee would lift my finances out of their current blood-red state into a shade of grey. The timing was perfect. 'I'll do it,' I said.

Soon after, a Malaysian Airlines plane went missing on a routine flight from Kuala Lumpur to Beijing. Sam and I heard the news on the car radio one day after a physio appointment. Across the river, I could see the large banner strung along the foreshore that proclaimed 2014 as 'Visit Malaysia Year'. It was a tragedy for everyone involved. I could think of a number of friends who might easily have been on that plane, but I was also mourning for my adopted country.

AFTER SPENDING SOME months back in Bali and Australia, I was in Kuching again in August to run a half marathon. My return to running had been tentative. Although I felt reasonably fit again, I finished the race lying flat on my back on the roadway with leg cramps. Two young medics stood over me, holding a foot each and trying to untwist my toes.

At the airport later that day, I spoke with one of the Kenyans who had run the marathon event that was held concurrently with the half. Based in Kuala Lumpur, she was paid appearance money to compete in races around the region. She told me a bit of her story, and I found her inspiring – not just because of her natural ability, but because of her determination to become good enough to compete as a professional at the elite level.

'I'd like to do one more half marathon at close to my personal best time,' I said, plucking an ambitious goal out of the air. My best time over the distance was in my first-ever half when I was forty-four.

'If you focused your training, you could reach your goal, and maybe even do a lot better.'

I knew that the half-marathon world record for a female runner of my age, sixty-two, was a minute per kilometre faster than I'd ever run the distance. I just wanted to revisit *my* best effort, not anyone else's. But I couldn't expect even that result unless I was prepared to do the training required. By the time I was buckling my seatbelt, I'd signed her on as my coach.

A couple of weeks later, I received an email with my first month's training program. On six days a week, I was to run at 6 am, 11 am and 6 pm; Sundays were a day of rest, meaning only two training sessions plus a visit to church. Looking ahead, in the lead-up to some as-yet-to-be-decided event, I would spend two weeks training with my coach in Kenya, in the hill country where the elite runners trained.

It was a flattering picture, but it wasn't based on any reality. I would have to motivate myself to run not three or four times a week – all that was required for basic fitness – but three times a day. When would I have time to work? I'd spend hours taking showers and doing laundry. I wasn't a churchgoer, unless there was a gospel choir ...

On day one of the program, I did the first two runs, then skipped the evening one because there was a film downtown that I wanted to see. On day two, I missed all three runs.

I handed in my notice to the coach. 'This isn't going to work. I have a full-time job. I have a full-time life ...' My career as an elite-athlete-in-training had lasted around six hours.

It was a reminder to keep my head out of the clouds and my feet on the ground. Running was my preferred exercise for staying reasonably fit, and I'd been fortunate not to suck at it or to suffer from running-related injuries, but it wasn't something

I needed to take too seriously. I ran mostly because it was so much fun to run with friends, and with people who sometimes became friends through running together. Over the years, my training companions all over the world had helped me to change direction so that I could finally live the life I wanted.

CHAPTER FIFTY-THREE

In mid-November, Bella arrived in New York from Toronto. I hadn't seen her since just after I'd quit drinking three years before. She was still struggling with it and looked as pale as a ghost. 'I'm putting one condition on our holiday,' she said. 'I need to drink how I need to drink. Don't make me feel bad about it.' She sounded flat, sad, resigned.

We went by Amtrak train down to North and South Carolina, then on to Georgia. The Pharrell Williams song 'Happy' was playing everywhere and seemed to me like a manifestation of my own state of wellbeing.

Bella was so fragile, the slightest of southern breezes might have picked her up and deposited her high among the Spanish moss on one of Savannah's oak trees. Her interest in anything outside of her own painful skin was fleeting and muted. Her mood wasn't dark, but dull. She drank what she needed to drink to maintain the medicated state that helped her to avoid experiencing her life.

I was fascinated by the true-crime book *Midnight in the Garden of Good and Evil* and wanted to visit some of the places where events recounted in the story had occurred. Bella tagged along on these excursions, but with little enthusiasm or interest.

On the Sunday morning, I convinced her to come to a local Baptist church for the gospel singing.

'You've seen *The Blues Brothers* film, haven't you? It's like that.' During the service, I was led up to the front with a few other visitors. The band was funky and the members of the congregation were rocking, calling out enthusiastic responses to the minister's praises. Beside me, a man danced wildly, flinging his arms and legs in every direction. I swayed on my feet, feeling stiff and awkward. In my old life, I'd lose my inhibitions after a few whiskies. Sober, I was still too self-conscious for free-form dancing. I thought of the runner I'd rendezvoused with eighteen years before in New Zealand, who had been invited to dance a Maori *haka* and of whose lack of style I'd been so critical. Karma sometimes takes a while.

At around four o'clock the next morning, I was awoken by the sound of footsteps outside my door. My room was at the end of a corridor, around the corner from the elevator. There was no need for anyone to pass by my door.

The floorboards creaked softly as the footsteps traced a path back and forth for an hour or more. My hands clutched the bedcovers to my chin. My ears were alert to every sound. My breathing was shallow, my scalp itchy. I was spooked. I needed to go to the loo, but I was too scared to leave the bed.

Finally, I dozed off. When I opened my eyes, I could see light behind the curtains. The sound of creaking floorboards had been replaced by reassuring morning noises: the bell of the lift door opening, voices, muted traffic. I sprinted to the bathroom and then took a quick shower.

On my way to the breakfast room, I stopped at the front desk. 'Um, do you have a ghost here?'

'Did you have a visit from Charlie?'

'Well, *something* was outside my room ...'

'What room are you in?'

'Uh-huh,' he said, when I told him the number. 'That's Charlie's floor.'

'Oh, god … What's the story?'

'He was working here as a builder in the 1850s. He fell to his death from your floor. Did he come into your room?'

'What? No! I would have had a heart attack!'

'He likes the girls. One guest said he tickled her feet.'

Aiyaah.

BELLA WAS LEAVING the following morning. I was heading further south, to St Augustine in Florida, for Thanksgiving with friends from Australia. That night, Bella and I talked again about what she could do. She vacillated between going to a rehab facility and retreating into despair and hopelessness.

'Darling, it's frightening seeing you like this. Please ask for help. It's possible to get better, to not have to drink.'

'I know, I know …'

'You don't have to feel this way.'

She nodded again. Tears welled in her eyes. She seemed hollowed-out.

I lay awake thinking about her, and about how things had changed for me since I'd stopped drinking. I no longer experienced everything through a veil of fear and anxiety. I was optimistic for myself, excited about the possibilities that each day held. I didn't awake in the mornings with a hangover, physical nausea, shame, guilt or regret. I was strong physically, emotionally and mentally. Although I didn't pray and was deeply superficial in my spirituality, it seemed there were forces in my life that looked out for me and steered me in the direction I needed to take. I thanked them every day.

My old friend saw ending her life as a possible viable solution to her problems.

When Bella's taxi arrived to take her to the airport the following morning, I hugged her goodbye, careful not to crush her, and wondered if I would see her again.

CHAPTER FIFTY-FOUR

'Come for dinner and meet our new friend, Miklos,' Julie said. Jules and I had become friends in Budapest the previous year, when I'd spent all of September and a week in December there. She was irreverent, cheeky and forgiving, and I'd found lots of space for her in my heart.

Budapest, which straddled the Danube – as well as Central Europe's tumultuous past and tentative future – in spectacular fashion, immediately felt like home. I'd even found there a new hygienist who accommodated my dental anxiety.

On this third visit, just before Christmas 2014, the city seemed like it could work for me as a possible home base in Europe, the way Kuching was in Asia and New York in North America. I was also starting to accumulate more boots, bowls and books than my suitcase could hold. I applied for a permit to make Hungary my country of residence. After all the paperwork was in order and submitted, and immigration officials had grilled me as to my reasons for wanting to live in their country, I let it go. The wheels would turn in their own good time. If it happened, it happened.

At Julie and David's apartment near Budapest's main synagogue, I met the tall young man with short, spiky black hair they had recently befriended. In his arms was a tiny grey-and-brown Yorkshire terrier. Miklos kissed me first on one cheek and then on the other.

'*Szia*. Hi. Call me Miki. And this is Joki, the world's most fantastic dog.'

EARLY IN THE new year, my application for a Hungarian residence permit was approved. I'd hoped for two years but was given five. The gods had been generous.

On Facebook I saw that a new group, the Budapest Zombie Runners, was organising a Saturday afternoon run around Margaret Island. I signed on. The meet-up was a fun half hour of social running with a group of people I wouldn't have met otherwise. Sina (from Germany) and Tiago (from Portugal) were medical students; Riyadh, a software engineer, was from Libya. Vanessa was from the US; someone else was from Kazakhstan. But I was really looking for a training partner to run with a few mornings a week – a local equivalent of Di and Frannie in Australia, Min in Kuching, Maria and the 5.30 am gang in New York.

'WANTED: Reliable running partner for early runs on weekday mornings,' I posted the next day on the Zombies' Facebook page and a few other Budapest community pages.

When my request drew a blank, I changed tack: 'AVAILABLE: Reliable running partner Monday to Friday, 7 am, Margaret Island. 5K at chatting pace.'

The next morning, I turned up ready to run, not knowing if I would be alone or have company.

'Hello.'

'Ah, great! *Riyadh*, right?'

'Yeah. Or Rio. I saw your post.'

We ran a circuit of the island at a pace that was comfortable for me and not too slow for him, talking the whole way. Aged in his late twenties, he was interesting and interested, quick witted and funny, good at the give-and-take of conversation, an easy person to like.

Walking back across the bridge to Pest side for a coffee afterwards, I asked if he wanted to meet again. Maybe he wouldn't feel it was worth his while to run with someone his mother's age.

'*Igen*. Yes,' he said. 'I want to get very fit.'

'Yay!'

Later in the week, I had a text message from Miki: 'Rudas baths on Sunday?'

'*Igen*! I'll even shave my legs.'

'You don't have to.'

What a gentleman …

That weekend, he and I were in the spa's Ottoman-era octagonal-shaped pool. Sunlight penetrated the dome above our heads as rays of white light. The voices of other bathers were muffled by the burble of running water.

'Shall we go to Istanbul for a few days when you come back from the States?' Miki asked.

'*Igen!*'

CHAPTER FIFTY-FIVE

As usual on a Tuesday whenever I was in New York, I joined the 5.30 am group at Engineers' Gate to run around Central Park. Our pace was slow enough to chat. Afterwards, back at our starting point, I peeled off to head home across the park. The others all lived on the Upper East Side.

'*Ciao*! Thanks for the run!'

After stopping at a drinking fountain beside the bridle path, I walked up on to the track that skirted the reservoir. Runners passed me by, but I was content to walk now. My stride was relaxed, my arms swinging freely. I held my head high, smelling the warm air. The towers of the El Dorado apartment building were visible above the tree line.

On a white ironwork bridge on the west side of the reservoir, I stopped to retie a loose shoelace. Crouched down, my head bowed, I whispered *thank you* to the forces that had been at work in my life. I felt at home wherever I was in the world and grateful for the people whose journeys had connected with mine. It was nearly four years since I last felt the need to numb myself with alcohol. In that time, I'd learnt to trust the path I was making. I didn't get things right all the time. I still had dummy spits when my patience was stretched to the limit. But I felt comfortable now with who I was, with all my flaws. I would keep trying to change the things I could and to accept the things I couldn't.

Somewhere in the world I had mislaid my 'superpower' orange knickers – maybe in Kuching or Hong Kong, in Florence or Reykjavik. Perhaps I forgot to retrieve them after my lover in Bali tossed them aside one moonlit night in his villa beside a rice field. It didn't matter. I had my own power back. The days of fear and anxiety were in the past. I was no longer afraid of what others might see should I let down my guard. I felt at home in my skin now, free to be me and to let what was on the inside show on the outside.

As I passed the tennis club, I felt the warmth of the sun on my arms, where a veneer of perspiration glistened on the hairs. I looked across to the buildings that lined Central Park West. The apartment that was my home in New York was just a few blocks away.

A snail was making slow progress across the path, forging its way to no particular destination; the journey was everything.

A slight breeze carried birdsong, the sound of distant, muted traffic, and the *whoosh* of a passing group of cyclists in training on West Drive. A squirrel darted across the grass and up the trunk of a tree that was lush with summer growth.

Ahead, two golden retrievers were playing on the grass, watched over by a man of about my age. I stopped to watch them, too. The dogs' eyes were shining, their mouths stretched in wide grins, their fat tongues lolling. Sunshine gleamed off their ginger coats as they ducked and turned, springing into the air, always in motion, exulting in being alive.

'I saw them here yesterday,' I said to the stranger. 'They're gorgeous dogs.'

He smiled at me.

'You're gorgeous, too.'

AFTERWORD

In writing my story, I've learnt a lot about myself, and about the relationship that researchers have found to exist between adverse or traumatic childhood experiences and susceptibility to addiction. In his book *In the Realm of Hungry Ghosts*, Dr Gabor Maté, an expert on addiction, trauma and child development, writes: 'Trauma is not what happens to you. Trauma is what happens inside of you, as a result of what happened to you.' And: 'Addictions … are emotional anesthetics [that] ease psychological discomfort … A hurt is at the center of *all* addictive behaviors.'

At one end of the spectrum of childhood adversity or trauma is abuse so horrendous, it's traumatic even to imagine it, let alone experience it. At the other end are the physical, psychological, and emotional bumps and scrapes that everyone experiences, and that make us resilient and equip us to live in the real world. I got off lightly, apart from harsh physical discipline by my father that caused me to feel fear, pain and resentment, and an incident involving an unknown person that I could endure only by numbing all my feelings. Around those negative experiences was a general sense, from a very young age, that I was on my own in some essential way. I experienced insufficient attachment and nurturing from my parents, not through neglect or design, but because they were young, overburdened and stressed. My mother and father had themselves experienced adversity and been insufficiently nurtured as children. So, in addition to specific negative experiences, I lacked certain important positive ones as a child.

'Stressed parents have difficulty offering their children a specific quality required for the development of the brain's self-regulation circuits: the quality of attunement,' Gabor Maté writes. '*Attunement* is, literally, being "in tune" with someone else's emotional states. It's not a question of parental love but of the parent's ability to be present emotionally in such a way that the infant or child feels understood, accepted, and mirrored. Attunement is the real language of love, the conduit by which a preverbal child can realize that she *is* loved.'

The place where I might have felt more nurtured than I did became a void, which raised for me two basic questions: *Who was I?* and *Was I loved?* That empty space sought to be filled by *something*. (We know that nature abhors a vacuum.) I tried to soothe myself with food, sex, cigarettes, recreational drugs, alcohol, but the answers to these questions always proved elusive.

Along with using substances and behaviours to try to fill that empty space, I turned to them to numb feelings that were too uncomfortable to experience unfiltered. So, I emerged from childhood with the two classic preconditions for addictive behaviours: a void that I sought to fill, and emotional pain that I sought to numb.

I also, of course, had many positive experiences as a child. Nevertheless, I learnt early to be my own primary carer; but, inexperienced and damaged as I was, I wasn't always the best person to care for me. Not knowing who I was meant to be, I felt insecure around being seen, which made it difficult to be intimate in later relationships.

My addictive substance of choice became alcohol, specifically white wine. Wine is legal, socially sanctioned and readily available. I could be seen to drink a glass of wine and yet have my dependence on it remain mostly invisible. I was under the radar, the way many grey area drinkers are. 'Grey area drinking' is now understood to be drinking that doesn't qualify as a severe alcohol use disorder but is problematic enough for the drinker to worry about it. 'Is my drinking normal?' they frequently ask themselves. 'Do normal people drink the way I feel the need to?'

After more than forty years of drinking, the last two decades of which I spent trying to manage my growing dependence, I admitted defeat. The personal cost of the momentary relief alcohol provided was too great. I was no longer prepared to trade my dignity, self-respect, peace of mind, happiness, and physical, mental and spiritual wellbeing for a bottomless bottle of wine.

How, then, was I to break my addiction?

First, I had to fully and finally accept that I had tried and failed to drink in a way that didn't cause me harm. I could then begin to reprogram myself. I turned to Alcoholics Anonymous, which helped me to break long-established habits and routines around drinking and provided opportunities to develop relationships with people who knew how I felt and had found a way to change their lives for the better. AA had come out of America's Bible Belt in the 1930s, and I had to overcome my resistance to its Christian associations and language in order to get the message that I need never drink again. I clung to the tradition that *AA meetings are open to anyone with a desire to stop drinking*. I didn't have to identify myself as an alcoholic to attend meetings, and I didn't have to use AA-speak. I could take what worked for me and leave the rest.

Connection with and attachment to others who understood why I had used alcohol the way I did inspired me to find other ways to meet my unmet emotional needs. I slowly became used to feeling and acknowledging whatever emotions came up, and I broke big things down into manageable chunks, just as I did when running a marathon or hiking at altitude or over a long distance. Slowly, I became more confident that I could handle whatever might happen between when I awoke in the morning and when I lay down to sleep at night. My senses sharpened and I experienced sights and sounds and smells more acutely. As my confidence grew, the gatekeeper that had protected me since childhood from the unpredictable, sometimes hostile world around me was able to relax its vigilance. I was finally starting to change on the inside.

Today, there are many alternatives and supplements to the AA model. Someone who is concerned about their drinking need only google search words like *alcohol recovery, grey (or gray) area drinking, alcohol free, sober, sober life* or *sober curious* to find communities that can provide understanding, empathy, support and inspiration. Public awareness of the benefits of limiting one's alcohol intake is growing through initiatives such as Hello Sunday Morning, One Year No Beer (OYNB), Sober in the Country, Dry January, Dry July, and more. For many people, being 'alcohol free' can be a lifestyle choice that doesn't carry the stigma that may still attach to being 'sober'.

I have lived an alcohol-free life since 29 August 2011. In order not to drink, I have had to find ways to nourish and nurture my body, mind and spirit, instead of harming them. I believe that we must each find our own path to a place of self-acceptance from where we can choose the life we want to live. I can (mostly) live comfortably with myself now and be fully present in my relationships.

This book took six years to write. Only during the last year did I become aware of the true nature of my experience of addiction and of how it related to family dynamics in my childhood. That learning is an ongoing process of reading, listening, talking and feeling, so that I can understand, accept and forgive myself as much as anyone else. I know that I was loved as a child; I also know that sometimes that love was shown in ways that caused me to emerge from childhood slightly bent out of shape emotionally and spiritually.

I can still be impatient and intolerant. I'm working on trying to change those parts of me. As for the rest, I'm grateful to the universe for having looked after me, for having put incredible people in my path during the past sixty or more years, and for giving me the imagination, stamina and resilience to get over myself and create an amazing life.

ACKNOWLEDGEMENTS

This memoir was much harder to write than I'd expected. There were a number of false starts after I began writing it in 2015. At times, I doubted that I could complete it. But I scheduled some winter months over 2018–19 in an apartment beside the Parthenon in Athens to fill in all the missing bits of the timeline and emerged with a first full draft. From then on, it was a process of constant revision and fine tuning, facing my fears and doubts, saying less, saying more, opening my heart and trusting that my story is worth telling. I couldn't have done it without help.

To my publisher, Jon MacDonald, and everyone at Brio Books, *grazie mille* for your enthusiastic championing of *Skinful*. Thank you to: Bernadette Foley of Broadcast Books for production, editorial and other support; Dee Dee Choy for the wonderful cover image; Christa Moffitt for the cover and internal design; Polly Yu for typesetting (and three decades of friendship and support); publicists Nicole Webb (in Australia and New Zealand) and Deirdre Roberts (in Ireland and the UK) for help with bringing *Skinful* to the notice of readers; Helen Newman of Nomad Films for the video, and Steve Sandberg for the music; and Kindred Design for the website. I love the work you all do!

I would also like to thank the following people for helping me to find the right shape for my story. Christina Yother's comments on two late drafts brought the book's themes out of the shadows and into the light. Christina, I am so grateful. Susy Bryceson's editorial comments on two early drafts pointed the way forward. *Köszönöm*, dear Susy! Tamara Davidson provided useful insights in the final stretch. I want to say a special thank you to Rio Al-Ghaber. On every one of our runs in Budapest between 2016 and early 2020, he asked how the book was going. Here it is, mate!

This memoir ends in mid-2015, halfway through my decade spent travelling the world as a nomadic freelance editor. I would love to name all the incredible people I became close to during that time, as well as the friends who enriched my life in the years before and those who have made Australia feel like home again since my return. However, I've been reminded that the purpose of these acknowledgements is to thank those people who helped me with this book, not with my life. To that purpose, I wish to thank the following people who read parts or all of the manuscript and gave me useful feedback: Kathryn Ali, Bill Bachman, Tami Bacskay, Annette Baker, Lisa Distelheim Barron, Lynne Blundell, Yvonne Boag, Mary Coe, Peggi Cooney, Chris and Merelyn Costello, Dianne Cullum, Sally Denshire, Jennifer Eagleton, Cathy Hilborn Feng, Patrick Gallagher, Sarah Gaze, Chiu Yin Hempel, Susan Johnson, Laura Kennelly, Maria Kessler, Judit Kiss, Loose Lips Book Group, Trish Loughran, Carole McCulloch, Darryl McGill, Julie Molnár, Allan Morton, Mary Murphy, Chris Newson, Peter and Amanda Oates, Dora Ohrenstein, Debra Oswald, Paul Pankhurst, Bruce Pennay, Orsolya Polyacsko, Nicholas Pounder, Roslyn Russell, Nicola Sapsford, Jenny Seymour, Dotti Simmons, Roula Stratou, Martyn Sullivan, Barb and Bill Thompson, Wendy Watts, Nic Wallis-Smith and Nick Wallwork.